THE UNCLAIMED

THE
UNCLAIMED

..

ABANDONMENT AND HOPE
IN THE CITY OF ANGELS

..

PAMELA PRICKETT
STEFAN TIMMERMANS

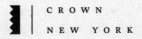

CROWN
NEW YORK

Published in the United States by Crown,
an imprint of the Crown Publishing Group, a division of
Penguin Random House LLC, New York.

CROWN and the Crown colophon are registered
trademarks of Penguin Random House LLC.

"On Passing a Graveyard" from *To Bless the Space Between Us:
A Book of Blessings* by John O'Donohue, copyright © 2008 by
John O'Donohue. Used by permission of Doubleday,
an imprint of the Knopf Doubleday Publishing Group, a division of
Penguin Random House LLC. All rights reserved.
Audio rights are administered and used with permission from
the estate and the publisher, Sounds True, Inc.

LIBRARY OF CONGRESS CATALOGING-IN-PUBLICATION DATA
Names: Prickett, Pamela J., author. |
Timmermans, Stefan, 1968– author.
Title: The unclaimed / Pamela Prickett and Stefan Timmermans.
Description: First edition. | New York: Crown, [2024] |
Includes bibliographical references and index.
Identifiers: LCCN 2023048688 (print) | LCCN 2023048689 (ebook) |
ISBN 9780593239056 (hardcover) | ISBN 9780593239063 (ebook)
Subjects: LCSH: Unclaimed dead. |
Death—Social aspects—United States.
Classification: LCC HQ1073.5.U6 P75 2024 (print) |
LCC HQ1073.5.U6 (ebook) | DDC 363.7/5—dc23/eng/20231213
LC record available at https://lccn.loc.gov/2023048688
LC ebook record available at https://lccn.loc.gov/2023048689

Printed in the United States of America on acid-free paper

crownpublishing.com

2 4 6 8 9 7 5 3 1

FIRST EDITION

Book design by Barbara M. Bachman

For Sariya, Merel, and Jasper

IN THE HOPE THAT
THEY WILL CLAIM US

May perpetual light shine upon

    The faces of all who rest here.

May the lives they lived

    Unfold further in spirit.

May all their past travails

    Find ease in the kindness of clay.

—JOHN O'DONOHUE,
"ON PASSING A GRAVEYARD"

CONTENTS

..

AUTHORS' NOTE

· ·

THIS IS A WORK OF NARRATIVE NONFICTION. DIALOGUE AND events were witnessed firsthand or reconstructed based on interviews, archives, and published accounts.

The unclaimed are all too soon forgotten. Out of respect for their lives, we use the names they went by; to mask their identities would mean complicity in a double erasure. The names of their relatives, friends, neighbors, as well as the workers charged with tending their bodies and the volunteers who show up to mourn, are also unchanged, unless indicated in the notes to protect their privacy.

THE UNCLAIMED

Sometimes I feel like I don't have a partner

Sometimes I feel like my only friend

Is the city I live in, the City of Angels

Lonely as I am, together we cry

—RED HOT CHILI PEPPERS,
"UNDER THE BRIDGE"

PROLOGUE

..

ASHES

CLOUDS OF THICK SMOKE ROSE FROM THE CITY'S RIDGES into a dusky blue sky. It was early December 2017 and the hills north of Los Angeles were burning. Nine months of apocalyptic dryness fueled by strong Santa Ana winds had primed the region for destruction. More than 230,000 residents fled as fires threatened thousands of acres of parched paradise and the homes, schools, and businesses nestled in them. Miles downwind, a blanket of thin white ash had settled on the windshields inching along Interstate 5—"the Five" as locals call it. Even with the windows shut tight, drivers breathed in the unexpectedly sweet smell of smoldering sage, chaparral, and pine.

In Boyle Heights, a largely Mexican American working-class neighborhood east of downtown, life carried on. Mothers pushed strollers down broken sidewalks lined with brightly colored iron-barred bungalows, taquerias, and auto body shops. Cars drove past sun-bleached murals, their colors muted by shadows cast from the tangles of power lines overhead. Street vendors sold fruit amid the occasional rooster crow. And, in the heart of the neighborhood, at the corner of Lorena and First Streets, behind the brick wall and iron gate of a county complex few Angelenos knew existed, two Black men, dressed in full-length white hazmat suits and surgical masks, moved through a chalky plume of dark gray ash. But the particles that billowed around them weren't from the wildfires. They came from cremated bodies.

The taller of the two men, Craig Garnette, grabbed a brown plastic box the size of a small cigar humidor from the bed of a white pickup truck. Many of the boxes had been warped from pressure and time, and their lids had started to pop. Craig leaned over an eight-foot-deep open grave and emptied the box, tapping the sides of the container to be sure every bit of cremains fell out and then tossing it onto the ground beside him. Puffs of ash had settled on his eyebrows and nose bridge, making him appear older than he was.

The other man, Albert Gaskin, nearly a foot shorter and decades more senior, picked up the empty boxes and carried them to a nearby cargo van, where he threw them into the hold. Then he returned to the pit and helped Craig dump ashes. Six sets of ashes had no names, and others—the cremains of infants—had been stored in small envelopes tied carefully with string. Albert and Craig moved quickly. They were under strict orders to finish by the end of the business day. Over five hours, the men poured 1,461 boxes and envelopes into the grave—a year's worth of ashes.

Every box, every envelope, every cloud of gray ash, was once a person with a story. Someone who'd lived and died in Los Angeles County. Someone who'd had no family to claim their body. The ashes of these nearly 1,500 people cremated by the county would join the remains of 100,000 other people already buried in the scrawny patch of land that made up the potter's field of Los Angeles. Fewer than four acres, the public cemetery serves as the forever resting place of these abandoned souls. Their remains, reduced to their organic essence, commingled and disappeared into the soil.

Albert took a break from transferring the emptied boxes. He looked past the pit in the ground to the mountains surrounding the Los Angeles basin, their sharp contours blurred by distant smoke. After nearly fifty years working at the cemetery, the reality of a mass grave, hidden among the everyday rhythms of neighborhood life, still troubled him.

He did what he could as the appointed caretaker for the county cemetery. He and Craig emptied ashes into a grave once a year; the rest of the time, they spent their long days cremating abandoned bodies and placing the cremains in the brown plastic boxes for storage. The county's policy was to store ashes for three years, just in case a loved one showed up to retrieve them. Albert had been known to hold ashes longer; he understood what it took to scrape together the roughly $400 claim fee. But retrievals were rare. Where Albert grew up, in Louisiana bayou country, if you had to sell a cow to bury your mama you would. Here in L.A., he felt people were fine to leave their mamas to be cremated and dumped in a common grave by strangers. In fact, Albert felt, people seemed to care less and less.

Albert thought lives should be remembered and death should be witnessed. It was the least a community could do. But county bureaucrats wanted to dispose of the abandoned dead as cheaply and quickly as possible, and Albert's boss preferred to keep the burial out of the public eye. Behind the scenes of the county's Office of Decedent Affairs, a fight was brewing. It might come down to who retired first. Albert wasn't going to be able to work forever. His plan had always been to return home to Louisiana.

He took a deep breath. Smoke hung in the air, a reminder of the precarious balance between life and death. But there was no time to ponder the fires, or the fate of the dead. He stretched his back and shoulders and stood up. The ashes were calling.

. .

DEATH HAS NEVER BEEN A SIMPLY BIOLOGICAL EVENT. EARLY anthropologists observed that, even as our bodies undergo a physiological process when we die—the decay of flesh and bones—our death also sparks a social process, in which we ease out of this world and settle safely into the memories of the living. Across cultures and time, this re-situating—of body and person—has occurred through funeral rites, burial, memorialization, and personal grief. It is essential to who we are: As the Italian historian Giambattista Vico reminds us, "*humanitas* in Latin comes first and properly from *humando,* burying." In this way, burying the dead, the German philosopher Hans-Georg Gadamer wrote, "is perhaps the fundamental phenomenon of becoming human."

Yet not all of us receive a decent burial. The poor have always been more likely than the wealthy to end up in unmarked graves and in so-called potter's fields—the useless, pockmarked tracts of land dug up for clay since biblical times by pot makers. Because the extractions left large holes in the red clay, those barren fields became the place of choice for burying the indigent dead. Today's potter's fields continue to be located in undesirable city plots or on the far reaches of existing cemeteries, outside the view of visitors. They are where we inter "the most worthless"—as determined by those who consider themselves worth more.

Until the late nineteenth century, Los Angeles had no need for a potter's field. The region was a landscape of sweeping vistas, small ranches, adobe dwellings, and citrus trees, with the dead buried in plots next to churches. But when the Mexican war ended and the gold rush began in 1848, and California joined the Union in 1850, the population exploded. Settlers and migrants from across the country and around the world arrived in search of gold and sun. A once quiet pueblo town turned into a lawless western outpost. Los Angeles, in the words of journalist D. J. Waldie, "drank, whored, brawled, lynched, and murdered" itself into infamy. The completion of the Southern Pacific's transcontinental railroad brought still more growth and a new desire for respectability. A town of fewer than 6,000 in 1870 burst into a city with more than 100,000 inhabitants by 1900. Suddenly, leaving last night's vigilante murder victim in an unmarked grave seemed uncivilized, and the city faced new questions about how to handle its indigent dead.

In 1877, Los Angeles established a potter's field in the neighborhood of Boyle Heights, then called Paredón Blanco, part of a land deal with a private cemetery developer. The city received nine acres to use as a public graveyard; the developer secured a zoning permit to turn the other sixty-nine acres into the first private cemetery in Los Angeles, Evergreen Cemetery.

The potter's field ledgers began to fill in 1896, around the time Los Angeles became more industrialized and scores of people were left behind in a widening gap between the haves and have-nots. The first person recorded for public burial was Gour Fong, whose skin color was listed as "yellow." Fong was thirty-five years old when he died from a knife wound on December 28, 1895. An undertaker interred him five days later and charged the city $15 (about $541.72 in today's dollars). That was more than twice what the same undertaker charged the city to handle the body of a twenty-one-year-old white woman two weeks later. In the nineteenth century, Chinese Americans were prevented from marrying, banned from most shops, and subjected to racial violence. When they died, they were consigned to a corner in the potter's field. "They were treated like animals," said Irvin Lai, a member of the Chinese Historical Society of Southern California.

Across the country, many poor Americans deprived themselves of life's small necessities to pay into burial insurance funds and avoid the stigma of an unadorned pauper's grave. Freshly landed immigrants joined burial societies, pooling funds in the hope of sending their body to their homelands or, if interment in the "right soil" was out of reach, to at least be buried in a real cemetery with a proper funeral. The late-nineteenth-century Italian Club Cemetery in Tampa was modeled after a lavish Italian burying ground. And by 1938, New York City alone had more than three thousand Jewish burial societies.

In the shadow of Evergreen's ornate granite and sandstone mausoleums, L.A.'s anonymous, barren potter's field served as a moral warning to the intemperate and the fallen. Many poor Americans perceived a "correlation between the quality of one's grave and one's soul." They were punished in death, guilty by virtue of their destitution. In Upton Sinclair's *The Jungle*, a mother loses her senses when she realizes that her child's corpse might be turned over to the city to be buried in a pauper's grave. "If it had come to this," the narrator says, "they might as well give up at once, and be buried all of them together!"

The expectation that relatives should bury their dead was codified in American law in 1856 after New York City widened Beekman Street in downtown Manhattan. The expansion disturbed the graves of close to one hundred people in a churchyard, and the city offered $28,000 as compensation. But who should receive the money: the church or the relatives? The Surrogate's Court recognized that families have a common law "natural and fundamental" right to possess human remains and protect those remains after interment. This right of sepulcher gave the next of kin the power to control human remains before disposition, select the place of burial, and change it at will. Many states followed, and over time, the right of sepulcher turned into a legal responsibility and only the most destitute ended up in paupers' graves.

Public graveyards sprang up across the United States in the mid- to late nineteenth century, their lots filling with the rising ranks of have-nots. The most famous was Hart Island, east of Manhattan, where burials began shortly after the Civil War and more than one million of New York City's indigent dead have been buried since, their plain box coffins stacked in trenches. Others would include Blue Plains in Washington, D.C., where the unwanted dead include executed Nazi saboteurs; Cook County cemetery in Chicago; Holt Cemetery in New Orleans; and Snake Hill Cemetery in Secaucus, New Jersey. Every city and town has had to find a place to put the abandoned dead to rest, and all have struggled to keep costs down.

In 1922, with 11,809 densely packed bodies buried in the Boyle Heights potter's field, Los Angeles County installed its own crematorium—long before cremation became accepted as an alternative to burial in the United States. Turning bodies into ash was cheaper and took up less real estate. In 1962, the potter's field shrank to make room for more wealthy bodies next door: Evergreen had become the most desirable final resting place for the real estate tycoons, oil barons, and circus performers of Hollywood's Golden

Age. The county sold 5.1 acres back to Evergreen, keeping a small strip of 3.9 acres for the burial of cremated remains.

While the residents of Evergreen Cemetery tended to have their names chiseled in granite and marble for posterity, most of the tens of thousands of individuals deposited in the neighboring Boyle Heights potter's field would have been lost to history, if the county had not recorded their cremations. Even then, only a few details—their name, date of birth, sex, supposed race, and date of death—survived. They remained the secret dead, invisible in life and forgotten in death.

That's what makes the story of Aurora Mardiganian striking: She represented a shift in who ends up at the potter's field.

Craig and Albert cremated Aurora's body on March 5, 1994. Aurora had been a member of Armenia's minority Christian community when, at seventeen, she witnessed the brutal murder of her parents and all but one of her siblings during the 1915 Armenian genocide. Aurora fled hundreds of miles—from Armenia to Russia to Norway—before arriving at Ellis Island in New York. A reporter and novelist heard about Aurora's story and turned it into a book titled *Ravished Armenia*. The book sold widely and was serialized in two Hearst newspapers with a combined print circulation of two million. The novelist tricked Aurora, who was illiterate, into signing a contract to star in a silent movie of her life. While on tour to promote it, she suffered a breakdown.

By 1920, Aurora had retreated from public life. She married, changed her name to Hovanian, and gave birth to a son, Martin. Around her seventy-seventh birthday, she moved from New York to the Los Angeles suburb of Van Nuys to be closer to him. But Martin's wife was jealous of Aurora and refused to let him see his mother. Aurora spent her final years living alone, tormented by nightmares about Turkish killers, and eventually died in a nursing home at age ninety-three. She was one of the last known survivors of the Armenian genocide. Even though she lived among the largest Armenian diaspora in the United States and her story had helped to raise $117 million (equivalent to about $2 billion in 2023) for the Armenian community, no one, not even her son who lived a couple of miles away and had money, claimed her body.

Aurora's story heralded a new kind of resident of the nation's potter's fields. Indigent souls still end up in common graves across the United States, but now more and more Americans—people of means, people with jobs and homes and families—are ending up like Aurora. The term of choice for those sent to the potter's field is no longer *indigent* but *unclaimed,* reflective of relatives' inability or unwillingness to take care of their dead. Whether they intend to or not, these relatives are rewriting the rules on what family members owe one another.

THE STORY OF THE UNCLAIMED IS, urgently, a story for today. In the first decades of the twenty-first century, an estimated 2 to 4 percent of the 2.8 million people who died every year in the United States went unclaimed—up to 114,000 Americans. This is roughly how many Americans die annually from diabetes. And that number is increasing. In Los Angeles County, the most populous county in the United States, the unclaimed used to make up 1.2 percent of adult deaths. That number inched up to 3 percent by the turn of the century—and it has continued to rise. The increase means that hundreds more residents every year end up in the Boyle Heights mass grave. In Maryland, one of the few states to keep track of unclaimed deaths over time, the percentage of people going unclaimed, adults and infants, has more than doubled in twenty years, from 2.1 percent of total deaths in 2000 to 4.5 percent in 2021.

COVID-19 made things worse. Medical examiners and coroners estimate that the number of people going unclaimed rose nationwide during the pandemic, resulting in as many as 148,000 unclaimed deaths each year. An investigation in Arizona's Maricopa County, the fourth-largest county in the United States, revealed a 30 percent spike. Reports streamed in from across the country, underscoring the problem. The Chicago medical examiner's office cremated twice as many unclaimed bodies in a three-month period in 2020 as in the entire previous year. Montcalm County in Michigan saw a 620 percent increase in unclaimed bodies in 2020. In Fulton County, Georgia, officials oversaw burials for 456 unclaimed bodies in 2021, 150 more than in previous years. In Hinds County, Mississippi, the coroner commandeered a refrigerator truck to store unclaimed bodies after the number ballooned.

There is no federal agency to track or oversee the unclaimed, just a patchwork of ad hoc local practices. In smaller cities and towns, burials for the unclaimed happen, if they happen at all, randomly. Ashes can languish for years in the desk drawer or office closet of a local county sheriff or wind up abandoned in private funeral homes.

The unclaimed mostly go uncounted and unseen. Megan Smolenyak is a genealogist and founder of Unclaimed Persons, a web-based group of more than four hundred genealogists who volunteer their sleuthing skills to resource-strapped forensic communities across the country. They locate kin when government employees cannot. Smolenyak describes the rising numbers of unclaimed as its own "quiet epidemic."

THIS BOOK GREW OUT of our efforts to unravel the mystery of the unclaimed: Who are they? And why do they end up where they do? We follow four individuals who died between 2012 and 2019—some destitute and some with means, some with close relatives, some without—as they wend their way through L.A. County's death bureaucracy. To piece together the story, we observed the work of county employees who care for the unclaimed: those who field phone calls from concerned neighbors, those who go into homes and hospitals to retrieve bodies, those who call families to try to compel them to claim, and those who divvy up the dead's assets.

As we immersed ourselves in this world, the book morphed into a quest to better understand what we owe one another in death and in life. The unclaimed raise pressing existential questions: If you die and no one mourns you, did your life have meaning? If a common grave can now be the final destination for anyone, rich or poor, what does that say about us? What does it say about America? The answers we found were daunting and, at times, disheartening. The unclaimed bring today's fractured families into sharp focus.

And yet, we found hope. Los Angeles, a city mocked around the world for being fickle and vain, points the way. Far from the glitter of Hollywood and ostentation of Rodeo Drive, nestled in quiet pockets of the county, some Angelenos have devoted their lives to making sure that the unclaimed are not forgotten. These citizens who have taken it upon themselves to care for the dead receive no money and few accolades. But they feel a moral responsibility to step in where traditional families have failed—creating new kinds of kinship, rebuilding local communities, and caring for the most overlooked, even in death.

. .

AFTER DEPOSITING THE ASHES IN THE COMMON GRAVE, Craig and Albert returned to the crematorium and stripped off their white disposable protective coveralls. Albert absentmindedly pulled at his gray beard while he scanned the paperwork that would dictate the rhythm of the following day. The Office of Decedent Affairs had a permanent backlog, and the morgue was filled with bodies awaiting cremation. Their ashes would be placed in the brown plastic boxes he and Craig had just emptied. He read through the list of names. How had their lives unraveled to the point where they ended up being abandoned? Why had no one shown up to claim their remains? What was their story?

PART ONE

..

ALIVE

One lives in the hope of becoming a memory.

—ANTONIO PORCHIA, *VOCES*

1.

NEW DIRECTIONS

..

Bobby Ray Hanna paced backstage. He was fifty-one years old but looked younger, his brown skin smooth and unlined. His hair and mustache were freshly trimmed, accentuating the roundness in his cheeks. As he tried to walk off his nerves, Bobby made sure not to wrinkle his collarless black button-down and matching slacks. His ex-wife, Clara Hanna, teased that he was worse than a girl when it came to his obsession with clothes. And shoes: If Bobby had money in his pocket, he couldn't resist buying a pair. He had taken care to have his dress shoes mirror-shined for that night's special performance. It was June 2010, and the once homeless air force veteran was about to sing live on national television, for the NBC show *America's Got Talent*. He was there with the New Directions Veterans Choir, comprised of veterans who had either gone through the full-service treatment center or, like Bobby, were currently there.

Bobby had been dreaming of catching a musical break since he was a little boy sitting next to Michael Jackson in elementary school back in Gary, Indiana. The two boys, born only seven months apart, competed for solos in school recitals. Michael won every time. Bobby knew he was nowhere near the level of talent of the future King of Pop, but he was convinced he could have made a successful career in music if his life had taken a few different turns. Now he would sing in front of millions of viewers, hoping for a shot at $1 million with his group.

It was Bobby's tenacity that had gotten him into the choir. He hadn't been in the New Directions treatment program long when he heard that the group would compete on television. He had little time to master the song the choir would sing on the show, "Ol' Man River," from the 1927 musical *Show Boat*. Bobby would be a tenor if he made the cut, but the choir's founder, George Hill, didn't think Bobby could learn the complicated song in time. Bobby wasn't a trained singer, and his self-taught guitar skills were useless in an a cappella group.

He would not let go. This was the closest he had been to becoming a professional musician since his days in the air force in the 1980s, when he worked a side gig deejaying on river cruises in London.

George understood Bobby's need to sing. There were days in his twelve years living on the streets that George didn't care if he lived or died, but then he would start singing. He would belt out tunes for hours in the tunnels of MacArthur Park near downtown Los Angeles, until he felt better. George told Bobby that if he aced the song, he could join the reality competition. Sure enough, Bobby learned the lyrics and harmonies, earning his spot as a member of the ten-person, nearly all-Black group.

BOBBY SNUCK OFF FROM the group backstage to make a call to Clara. The British-Indian expat was sitting in her West Los Angeles apartment, the same one that the former couple had shared in the last years of their marriage. They had met when Bobby was stationed in England, near a McDonald's where then-eighteen-year-old Clara worked. Bobby came in nearly every day for lunch, dressed in his uniform, trying to impress her. She knew her Catholic parents would not approve of her dating an airman, who they thought would break her heart. Two years passed before she said yes to a date. Soon after, the young Englishwoman found herself cruising the Thames, partying alongside her American boyfriend.

The adventure ended when Bobby was discharged and returned home to Gary, Indiana. They kept in touch by phone and, in 1990, Bobby convinced Clara to meet him in Redlands, California, east of Los Angeles, for a fresh start. Clara didn't love Redlands—it was more for families with young children than a thrill-seeking couple—but she was happy to be with Bobby. They married, and at first things were stable. But as the years passed Clara realized that Bobby's carefree and confident London attitude had been dampened by the years in Gary. He started staying out late, spending entire nights away from Clara. The couple split and reunited several times. Then came Bobby's involvement with drugs and run-ins with law enforcement. He was arrested for fighting and spent fifteen days in jail. A felony charge for possession of a controlled substance with intent to sell soon followed. Bobby was sentenced to two years in a state prison. For years, Clara had told herself, "It's going to get better." But seeing Bobby on the inside, she knew she was done. She had divorce papers served to Bobby. He called her from a prison pay phone, angry and desperate. He wasn't Catholic, but he knew how important Clara's faith was to her. Bobby taunted her, "Catholics aren't supposed to divorce."

"No," Clara replied, "but on the other hand, nowhere in the Bible does God say I have to be unhappy."

Following his release, Bobby flitted from party to party, until one by one his friends kicked him out. In 2009, seven years after the divorce, he was down to a single duffel bag and nothing else. He camped out on Sepulveda Boulevard, near the I-10 and 405, at one of the busiest interchanges in the country. After two restless nights, he called Clara and asked if she would pick him up.

Clara struggled to enforce boundaries with Bobby. He was her first love. She drove to the freeway underpass, and Bobby climbed in. She handed him a Tupperware box with leftover rice and beef. As he wolfed down the food, Clara said she would take him to a motel two miles south, where she paid for one night and left Bobby to think about what he should do next. The walls were thin enough to hear when someone turned on an air conditioner in the next room. But the louder noise was the voice of self-doubt inside Bobby's head. He knew about a rehab facility for veterans, and he also knew the program required therapy. Bobby did not like to talk about himself. It was one of the reasons his marriage had failed.

When Clara returned the next day and pressed for a plan, Bobby hesitated. He mentioned New Directions, explaining it was run by a nonprofit and located on the grounds of the VA. Clara wanted Bobby to check in right away. They went back and forth, until Clara announced, "We're going. I'm dropping you off because you need help." This was Clara's moment of tough love. She drove Bobby to the facility, in West L.A., and wished him luck. Then she drove back to her apartment.

When he called from backstage at *America's Got Talent* the following year, Bobby tried to persuade her to come down to the live taping. Clara thought about how long the line to get into the theater would be and how hot it was outside. She said, "I know you're disappointed, but I can't." She promised to watch the performance on TV.

"Oh, it's all right."

Bobby had given her the line he always did when he felt hurt. He had a habit of downplaying his pain to save face. It was part of the reason he'd started to use drugs, to escape. He did everything he could to distance himself from failure.

FOR THE MONTH OF JUNE 2010, the *America's Got Talent* reality show set up in the Orpheum Theatre, a historic playhouse in downtown Los Angeles with an iconic Beaux Arts façade that opened in 1926. After vaudeville had faded away, the theater became host to top musical acts, featuring Black American performers like Ella Fitzgerald, Duke Ellington, and Aretha Franklin. Now, like many venues in Los Angeles, the playhouse had to tap into the city's growing reality show industry to stay relevant. On the night Bobby performed, the theater's nearly two thousand seats were full. Fast-moving cameras panned between the screaming fans and stage. The New Directions Veterans Choir was one of twenty-seven acts competing that evening to go to the next round in Las Vegas.

Comedian and television presenter Nick Cannon met the group backstage and, with an infectious smile, pumped up the ten members before they went onstage for a live audience. "This is the moment," he said.

"This is the moment," George Hill returned with a radiant smile, his voice calm.

"You guys ready?"

The eight men and two women answered in unison, "We ready." Bobby bounced in anticipation, his face stoic but his body jittery.

Before every performance, one of the members would pray them in, and tonight it had been Bobby's turn. He asked God to bless the performance and to let their voices be as one.

The choir would need to answer the questions of the celebrity judges before their act. Piers Morgan, a grumpy Brit, took the lead. "Who're you guys?"

In the polished style that George had practiced at performances and fundraisers, the former marine said firmly, "We are New Directions Choir. We are comprised of formerly homeless sailors, soldiers, airmen, and marines."

"And you said you were all homeless?" Morgan asked.

"We were all homeless." George was usually a jokester onstage, but tonight he was all business. "In my particular case I was homeless for twelve years, living in MacArthur Park and Skid Row."

Morgan continued, "Tell me, what do you hope to achieve by appearing on *America's Got Talent?*"

"We want to let people know, all of the other veterans and especially the active-duty armed forces know, that it's okay for a warrior to seek help."

"Okay, well, best of luck." Unlike the crowd, Morgan didn't seem moved.

The auditorium quieted, a long six seconds of silence amplifying Bobby's nerves. George Hill blew into a pitch pipe, and the group began the first lyric, *Let me go away*. It was then that the members of the choir heard themselves sing through a professional sound system for the first time. They also heard the audience react. As the choir sang about how the unsparing Mississippi River kept on flowing while workers on its riverbanks had no rest, Bobby, George, and their fellow choir members felt they were on a magical journey, taking the crowd with them. The three celebrity judges, including Morgan, stood to join the audience in ovation. Bobby bounced with excitement: They had nailed it. This was his rags-to-riches moment.

The applause in the Orpheum died down and the choir waited for the judges to speak. Bobby held his mic at his side. Though for a moment he looked ready to answer questions, he had a tendency to shrink as soon as he was done singing. Today was no different. He took a step back, fading behind the other choir members.

The judges took turns praising the performance, with Piers Morgan last. He asked what the performance meant to the choir. George Hill said it was proof that people can change. "There was a period of time that you might not would've wanted to see us coming, but the fact is now this shows what change can do."

"Well, look," Morgan said, "I think I speak for everybody here when I just say that was one of the most powerful, emotional, and inspiring things we have ever seen on *America's Got Talent*. So, thank you." The judges voted unanimously to send the New Directions Veterans Choir to the next round. Many in the audience took to their feet again.

Bobby's smile widened. God had done just what Bobby had asked Him to do. He hoped that Clara had been watching.

AGING IN PLACE

· ·

INSIDE HER DUPLEX ON FREEMAN AVENUE, EIGHTY-NINE-year-old Lena Brown reached for a can of baked beans, bending just enough to lift the can out of a cardboard box on the floor. Someone—Lena thought a neighbor—had been leaving food outside her front door. Whoever it was knew Lena well enough to leave only soft foods, like soups, beans, and oatmeal.

Lena struggled to get a tight enough grip to work the can opener, using her arthritic fingers to pry open the can just a bit and then dumping the sweetened brown beans in an old electric coffeepot. She flipped the machine's burner on and waited for her dinner to heat up. Her stove was unusable. The gas had long been switched off because of unpaid bills. It wasn't for lack of money. She had savings and monthly income from Social Security, and the house was paid off. The problem was her eyesight. She strained to read bills and notices from the city. She was also forgetting things, hardly unusual for a woman born in 1913, but it made it hard to stay on top of her finances. Her checks expired before she remembered to take them to the bank. She had kept an envelope with cash in her refrigerator but then accidentally threw it out. Soon the fridge stopped working. She still stored milk in it out of habit and it spoiled quickly. She had no plumbing in the bathroom, and there had been no heat in the place for years. She kept warm by piling coats on top of her petite body. Her hot water heater didn't work, either, and the plumbers she hired had taken her money without fixing the problem. Only the electricity continued to stay on. Not that it mattered much. Most of her light fixtures were broken or missing. Lena spent entire days alone in the dark.

She stirred the battered coffeepot. Her clothes, which once hugged her slim frame, hung loosely now. She wore threadbare robes and muumuus, even during the sweltering Southern California summer, and tied them together with a piece of string. Her white hair was unkempt, wiry wisps that flew in different directions. She paid someone thirty dollars to cut her hair every now and then but didn't bother keeping it up between visits. She rarely bathed, afraid of climbing in and out of the bathtub. A fall could be the end of her if she had no way to alert others. Besides, even if she was found in time, she would likely lose her independence. That was her biggest fear.

Lena pushed aside a stack of public nuisance notices from the city of Hawthorne, an annexed suburban city nestled in southern Los Angeles where her detached duplex was located. Like many homes built in a booming Southern California in the 1940s, the stucco duplex was thrown up hastily and needed steady repairs to fight off aging. It was more than Lena could handle. Over the years, she left broken windows unfixed, grass untended, and piles of trash out front. By 2002, anyone passing by could see the duplex had lost the battle against the erosion of sun and time.

Lena grabbed a fork from the sink and had taken only a couple of bites when she heard meowing outside. She reached for an old mop to steady herself—some of the boards of her living room had warped and buckled from water spilling over from the kitchen. She carefully shuffled over to the back door of the rear unit. She opened the door and walked around the side yard toward the front unit, holding on to her makeshift cane. She threw some food scraps to a clowder of feral cats that lived in her yard. She liked them; they kept the rodents at bay. Two neighbor boys passed through the alley along the southern edge of her property. One whispered "*La bruja*," Spanish for witch.

From where she stood, Lena heard a knock on the door of the empty front unit. She ignored it, staying to the side of the duplex and out of view of the street. She couldn't remember when she'd last had visitors. She waited and hoped the person would go away. Then, a second set of quick knocks. She had nieces and nephews living in the area, but it had been ages since they'd visited. She knew one neighbor who lived a couple of blocks over. Maybe she wanted to talk?

A third set of knocks. Lena peeked around the side of the house. A young woman in business attire was at the door. She noticed Lena standing in the overgrown grass. If the stranger was taken aback by Lena's bedraggled appearance, she quickly recovered, launching into a short version of her spiel: She was a realtor and real estate investor. She asked whether Lena was the homeowner. Lena didn't respond. Undeterred, the woman said that she had good news. She would be willing to fix up the home and then buy it from her for $20,000. Lena could stay in one unit or move into a nursing home. The realtor handed Lena a card with her contact info. Lena's phone didn't work, but she didn't tell the woman.

Lena stood motionless and mute. Unsure what to make of the old woman before her, the realtor told Lena to think it over. She was happy to come back next week.

The realtor was about to turn away when Lena shrieked, "Go to hell!" Then, for emphasis, yelled, "Get out!"

Lena returned to the back unit, her heart pounding in her chest. Her appetite was gone. She'd leave the beans in the coffeepot and reheat them tomorrow.

LENA HAD MOVED INTO the Hawthorne property after she married Benjamin Franklin "Frank" Brown, Jr., an upholsterer in the aircraft industry, in 1944. Frank's father, Judge Benjamin Brown, had built the double units on a plot of undeveloped land, allowing his son and Lena to live in the front while Brown Sr. and Frank's mother, Flavia, lived in the back. What would later become endless city blocks were barley fields hedged by large eucalyptus trees when the couple first moved in. Judge Brown died in 1949, and Lena cared for her mother-in-law until she, too, passed. When Lena's husband died in 1966, at the age of only fifty-seven, the house's title was transferred to her. For a while she lived in one unit and rented out the other. It was her insurance against outliving everyone else— a prospect that had seemed likely even long ago, given her husband's penchant for alcohol.

Lena managed well enough for the first decades, befriending the Piersons, a family that lived nearby and held Jehovah's Witnesses gatherings in their home. Lena, who never had children of her own, took to spoiling the family's nine-year-old daughter, Donna, with packaged sweets like Hostess Twinkies and Cupcakes. The Piersons invited Lena to join them on outings to public gardens and dinners at a local Spires chain diner. Donna remembered that Lena always carried a purse when they went out, closely clutching it to her side. Even when she posed with the Piersons for photographs, Lena kept the purse under her arm, never letting it go.

As the decades wore on, the Piersons saw Lena less. She became more reclusive, spending her days alone and inside. By the time she reached her seventies, she struggled to understand what was happening. Tenants took advantage of her. They preyed on her frailty, skipping rent and letting the apartment fall into disrepair. In the rough years of gang violence in 1990s South Los Angeles, a young woman had squatted in her front unit and trashed the place.

Each year since her husband's death, Lena retreated further inward. By 2002, she lived a life devoid of human interaction, which made her anxious. Little by little, her circle had shrunk. As Lena saw it, the realtor confirmed her fear that people were out to get her and wanted to take her house. Alone, no lock on her front door, the old woman had taken to sleeping with a hammer next to her pillow.

SEVERAL MONTHS LATER, LENA stepped out of the back unit and shuffled two blocks. She wore slippers with gaping holes. At a well-kept white bungalow, she opened the black metal gate, walked through a well-tended colorful garden with abstract concrete statues, and rang Lynda Pierson's doorbell.

Lynda was taken aback when she saw how small, dirty, and disheveled Lena looked. If it wasn't for her distinctive shrill, squeaky voice, Lynda would not have recognized her old friend. Lena said that she had run out of food and couldn't make it to the grocery store, assuming it was Lynda who had left her the food she had been eating these last months. But it turned out not to be Lynda.

Lynda asked Lena about her family. Lena insisted that they were not interested in her. One of her nieces, Marlene Avila, lived less than a mile away and occasionally walked by, but they didn't get along and had stopped talking. Lynda promised to stop by Lena's house later.

Lynda went to the store and bought drinking water and some of Lena's favorite foods. She put them in an ice chest in her car and drove to the Freeman Avenue duplex. Lynda gasped when she entered the back unit. It was the first time in decades that she had been inside Lena's house, which she had remembered as neat, if not clean. Even in the darkened rooms Lynda could see and smell the filth. She placed the ice chest down and promised Lena she would bring more food tomorrow.

Lynda had a soft spot for all abandoned beings: She nurtured stray dogs and cats, revived houseplants, and even tried to keep hurt bugs alive. For years, the family looked after a disabled bird that Lynda had found; they took it camping, with Lynda setting up a hanging fruit basket as a makeshift bed. She wanted to help with Lena's house, but her rescue projects to that point had been limited to small things. This would be a massive endeavor. She asked Lena if it would be okay to bring a friend over who knew about real estate and elderly issues.

With Lena's permission, Lynda called another neighbor, Teena Colebrook, who owned a triplex in Hawthorne, living in one unit and renting out the other two. Teena had come a long way since her childhood, when she lived in a shack in England with no running water or indoor toilet. Her mum had to boil water to put in a tin tub to bathe Teena and her siblings. Teena moved to the United States and earned a degree at Cal Poly, where she became a thirteen-time NCAA Division II All-American in track and field, and now had a growing real estate portfolio. She felt fortunate and was determined to give back. She had chosen to focus on helping elderly neighbors. Most of the older folks Teena helped just needed assistance with their gardening or stringing up their outdoor Christmas lights. Lena's case would be far more complicated.

When Teena visited Lena, the older woman reminisced about her past, saying how she missed getting dressed up to go to church with the Piersons. Though it was hard to tell from looking at her now, Lena had always loved clothes. Working as a laundress when she was in her twenties had exposed her to the finest garments, and she missed running her fingers along the seams of a well-tailored dress.

The women got along well, but Lena was still suspicious. "Why do you want to deal with an old lady like me?" she asked.

"Because you're a human being," said Teena. She thought back to the shack she grew up in and couldn't believe that forty years later, here in the United States of America, someone suffered in similarly deplorable conditions. "That's not the way people should live."

Over the coming months, Teena accompanied Lena to the bank and helped her withdraw money to buy new shoes. She set up a surgery appointment to remove two orange-size lumps in Lena's abdomen. Lena reluctantly consented to the procedure on the condition that she wouldn't be subjected to blood transfusions, which as a Jehovah's Witness she believed was against God's will. The hospital cleaned Lena up, and she started to look less disheveled. Even her sense of humor returned. When a home health aide that Teena had hired asked whether Lena was interested in purchasing adult diapers, Lena gave a firm no. "I don't want Depends because then I'd have to depend on the Depends."

Once Lena's physical health was under control, Teena broached the more difficult topic. She admired how the old lady had fought to stay in her home on her own terms, but something had to be done or she would lose it. Leafing through the pile of city nuisance notices citing disrepair and deterioration and letters in red bold font threatening a lien on the house for unpaid property taxes, Teena presented her new friend with two choices. "The city is either going to come in," Teena said, "or I can try to find someone who I know will fix the place up and let you live there for the rest of your life rent free."

Lena knew it was possible that the city would condemn her house, leaving her homeless. She wanted the familiarity of home and the feeling of independence, even if there were risks to living alone, especially if her mobility or mental state declined. The alternative—moving into a long-term care facility—was also a risk. Far from the people who knew her, she could become isolated, shaving years off her life.

Lena was adamant. "I want to die in my home."

"Are you sure?" Teena asked.

"Yes, I am."

Teena turned to a friend named Philip Kirkland, who was in real estate and construction. Kirkland offered to purchase both of Lena's units, renovate them, and let Lena live in the front for a life lease. She wouldn't have to pay rent. In exchange for the deed transfer, Kirkland would pay Lena $80,000 in cash. He also agreed to pay all utilities and her back taxes, repair the boiler and furnace, and reconnect the phone service.

Lena was grateful for Kirkland's offer. Being able to stay in her own house was all she really cared about.

Kirkland fixed up the front unit even before the sale went through. One month later, in February 2003, Kirkland videotaped Lena signing the real estate forms while she said that she agreed to this transaction. He knew how it might look to outsiders that he was buying an old woman's house. Lena told Teena how delighted she was with the chance to stay in her house.

Soon after the sale, Kirkland started finding handwritten notes at his door from a Rudy Estrella and his wife, Lynda. The notes demanded details about the sale of the home and what repairs were being made. Rudy, Lena's nephew, was acting also on behalf of his sister, Marjorie Ramos, and his cousin, Marlene Avila. When Kirkland brought the note to Lena's attention, she stiffened. She recognized the names of Marjorie and Marlene—she'd seen them occasionally over the years—but she struggled to remember what Rudy looked like.

Her family's sudden reappearance put her on edge. What did they want?

Unbeknownst to Lena, Marlene, the niece who lived less than a mile away, hadn't been as absent from Lena's life as she thought. It was Marlene, not Lynda, who had been leaving food on Lena's doorstep. Marlene, a Jehovah's Witness pioneer, tried to do what she could to help her mother's younger sister, albeit discreetly. She had always had a tense relationship with her aunt, and their similarly strong-willed personalities frequently led to conflict. Marlene thought it wiser to stay in the shadows. But when she caught wind of the deal with Kirkland, she knew she couldn't keep quiet. Marlene figured that Lena must have been confused and now was the victim of a profiteer. Eighty thousand dollars was rich people's money for someone who grew up in the 1920s, but the average house price in 2002 in Hawthorne was $240,000 and had gone up 14 percent since the previous year. Surely a duplex would be worth even more.

Marlene alerted her cousins that Lena had sold the property for below market value. They hesitated to get involved. Marjorie was close to Marlene, but not her aunt. Marjorie recalled how she used to chauffeur her mother, Anna, from East Los Angeles to Lena's property in Hawthorne. The sisters would catch up and then Marjorie would drive her mother back home. But that was in the early seventies, and in the three decades since, Marjorie had seen very little of her aunt. She doubted that her brother, Rudy, had laid eyes on Lena since they were small children. Marlene was persuasive, though. "Go see her," she urged her cousins. "I think she needs to talk to somebody."

When Rudy and Marjorie visited Lena after the sale, Lena was visibly upset. She turned to her niece and said, "Oh, Marjorie, I thought you were a nice person." Lena reported back to Teena Colebrook that her family was interested only in the property and didn't care for her.

Rudy was undeterred by Lena's reaction. Backed by his cousins, he hired a lawyer and filed a complaint against Teena for elder abuse, claiming she fleeced his aunt. He resented that she had encouraged Lena to stay in a hospital to recuperate from the abdominal surgery, thinking the expense unnecessary. To Teena, the issue was simple. Lena had the money and the insurance.

Rudy also sued Philip Kirkland. In the suit, Rudy alleged the house was worth $433,000 and that Kirkland had swindled Lena by paying less than 20 percent of the property's value and "erroneously" taking possession of the house. Rudy argued that Lena was deaf and blind, and that Kirkland had taken advantage of her. He demanded that the court rescind the title transfer.

The allegations of abuse set the county system's elder protection gears into motion. On September 3, 2003, Leona Shapiro was appointed by the Los Angeles Superior Court to act as Lena's attorney. Shapiro was on the county's probate volunteer panel, a group of attorneys who register with the court to assist in probate cases for reduced fees. Shapiro's job was to advocate on behalf of the vulnerable as a neutral party. Her involvement in the legal panel originated from her own negative experience with her mother's caregiver. One evening, Shapiro had stopped by her elderly mother's house unannounced and discovered that the aide her mother had hired was nowhere to be found. Shapiro sat with her sleeping mother until the aide returned, after midnight, and promptly fired her. Later, Shapiro discovered that the aide had given her mother a sleeping pill before going out. She vowed then to stand up for older adults who could no longer advocate for themselves.

Shapiro drove from her home office in Beverly Hills to the duplex on Freeman Avenue on October 23, 2003, and spent approximately three hours observing Lena. Even in that short time it was clear to Shapiro that the older woman needed help. Lena said she had Social Security and some income from oil leases. She also knew she had an account at Bank of America and a "special CD or something" with money somewhere. But the details were fuzzy, and she couldn't locate account numbers.

Lena suffered no confusion in one area. She absolutely did not want Rudy, or any other relative, to become her conservator. She told Shapiro that she liked how Teena had taken care of her and wanted the woman to stay in her life—a prospect that was becoming increasingly improbable. The case of elder abuse was quickly dismissed when Teena produced receipts for everything she had bought for Lena, but even with her legal vindication, Teena had little say in what would happen to Lena. Rudy held more power as a family member. He insisted to Shapiro that he should take care of his aunt. When Shapiro, trying to honor Lena's wishes, proposed a nurse with real estate experience as a third-party conservator, Rudy protested.

The family's next step was to present their case to probate court. They arrived at Stanley Mosk Courthouse in downtown Los Angeles for the hearing. Lena sat in the front of the courtroom, Rudy and Marjorie at her side. The setup was symbolic: Aunt Lena was their responsibility. Teena Colebrook and Lynda Pierson, the two women that Lena had come to trust most, sat in the back among the wood auditorium seats for witnesses and observers.

The family presented a united front of devotion to the elderly Lena and accused Lena's friends of maltreatment. Teena heard the family tell the judge that Rudy was her favorite nephew. She scoffed at the absurdity of the claim. She felt her muscles tense and her blood pressure rise. She wanted to speak, but she was intimidated by the unfamiliar court proceedings. The judge listened to the county and family present their arguments.

A few days after the hearing, Lena confronted Teena. "Why weren't you there?"

"I was there," Teena assured her. "I was right behind you."

But Lena seemed unconvinced. "I was waiting for you." The disappointment in her voice would stay with Teena for years.

COURTS ARE HESITANT TO bring in third parties as conservators when relatives are willing to provide care. Lena's case would be no different. On April 7, 2004, despite Lena's wishes, Rudy was appointed conservator.

One win under his belt, Rudy continued with his lawsuit against Philip Kirkland. He charged that Kirkland, as Lena's "friend and business advisor," had "made false representations" when he presented the sale as "fair and reasonable and in her best interests," actions that caused "damage in the amount of $353,000." The probate court seemed less persuadable on this matter. It was difficult to argue that Kirkland had misrepresented the sale or forced Lena in any way when he had a videorecording of her signing the contract and another of her discussing her relatives with Teena. She had appropriately participated in the discussion and was mentally alert. Under legal advice, Rudy agreed to go to mediation, where he settled the case with Kirkland for a onetime payment of $8,500, to be put into Lena's account. Kirkland had already agreed to let Lena live rent-free in the front unit until she died or left at her own will. As promised, he would also pay her phone bill, real estate taxes, and utilities. In return, the property would remain in his name.

Over the next several years, Rudy and his wife brought Lena weekly groceries and other essentials. Her Social Security took care of most of these charges, leaving her savings for larger expenses. When the house proceeds were added to her existing savings, Lena's accounts were flush. Knowing that his aunt had close to $150,000 in the bank, Rudy had no qualms about buying a new TV from Best Buy for $807 or ordering DirecTV at $40 per month, providing Lena with something to do during the days.

On a routine follow-up visit, Lena admitted to Shapiro that Rudy was doing a decent job as conservator, but she remained skeptical about her family's involvement. And she pushed back if one of her nieces or nephews tried to exert too much control: When Marjorie bought a new pair of shoes from Sears to improve Lena's heel support, Lena cut holes in them the following week. She said it was to ease the pressure on her bunions, although Marjorie wondered if Lena wasn't just trying to goad her. Another time, Rudy purchased a small couch, but Lena didn't like the cushion covers. She took them off, which baffled Rudy. To her family, Lena was stubborn, plain and simple.

Rudy told Shapiro that, although he did not initially know Lena well, taking care of her was a way of honoring his mother, Anna. He felt that he was doing the right thing by stepping in. His sister, Marjorie, agreed. She said later, "If you can't depend on your family, who can you depend on?"

3.

MY WAY

. .

OR THE FIRST FOUR YEARS OF HIS LIFE, DAVID GRAFTON
Spencer refused to talk. Spoke not a word. It was the mid-1940s,
and David's father, Orrie Grafton Spencer, Jr., worked as an assistant
supervisor in a factory producing Western hats—a business that
catered to ranchers and oil speculators in Southern California, and
budding actors who wanted to look the part. David's mother, Juanita, was a homemaker, caring for David and his older sister, Judith.
Both parents were eager for David to say something, especially
Juanita. She wanted the family to rise in the social ranks, and a
feebleminded son wasn't going to aid her ambition. She took David
to a doctor who checked for signs of what was then known as mental retardation. The doctor quizzed Juanita on how she mothered
David because, according to the beliefs of the time, an overbearing
mother could stunt a child's emotional growth. None of the usual
tests suggested anything pathological. The doctor looked skepti-
cally at David.

"Kid, how come it is you don't talk?"

The little boy quickly composed his first sentence.

"I ain't got nothing to say."

WHEN HE WAS TEN, David developed asthma, and his parents
sent him to live with his grandfather near Death Valley. Los Ange-

les in the 1940s and '50s had turned into a smog bowl. Millions of cars emitted pollutants that then became trapped in the L.A. basin. The smog also produced a bleach smell that irritated the eyes and lungs. Death Valley National Monument, established by presidential proclamation in 1933, was relatively unspoiled.

Squeezed by the formidable Panamint Range to the west and the slopes of the Funeral Mountains to the east, the valley was one of the earth's hottest places in the summer, but it was pleasant in winter. Largely unsupervised, David enjoyed the cool nights and clear days exploring desert flora and fauna. The desert was rich with animals but most, with the exception of the wild burros that had become the pack animal of choice during the area's mining days, were nocturnal and shy. When David wasn't outside, he passed the hours reading encyclopedias and memorizing facts. His favorite subject, besides animals, was the Shoshone Nation population that lived nearby at Furnace Creek Ranch. Later, David would reflect on his time in Death Valley as the best in his life.

His grandfather died in 1954, putting an end to David's desert adventures. Back in his parents' home in conservative Orange County, David joined his high school baseball team and marching band, the kind of all-American activities that a budding socialite would want for her son. But David wrestled with convention and authority and, by his own account, became a juvenile delinquent. In his senior year, David enlisted in the navy. He would later tell people that he got into trouble with the law and a judge gave him a choice to shape up or ship out.

With a family that was anything but typical—a maternal grandmother who changed her full name with each of her four marriages, an aunt incarcerated for performing an illegal abortion, a great-aunt who died by suicide after drinking Lysol, divorce up and down the family tree—David likely felt destined for a life bigger than the sleepy suburbs of Orange County. He started telling people stories to ease his way in the world. The stories *felt* true, especially if listeners connected the dots. And David thought he was justified in his embellishments: His grandfather lived near Native American res-

ervations, so David would say that his grandfather *was* "Indian."
His mother had been born in Sweetwater, Texas, a hub for cattle
production, so David would tell people that his mother was a Co-
manche orphan who had been raised by Texas ranchers after she
was found wandering along the side of the road. As if that story
wasn't bizarre enough, David also intimated to friends that he had
been trained as an assassin. When he enlisted in the navy, his training had likely included riflery, and David indeed became an excel-
lent marksman. But he went further and said he had been involved
in a top-secret government project, in which he learned to parachute out of a plane and shoot and kill a target, before being pulled
out and sent to a secure location to "decompress."

What is more believable is that sometime after the navy, in the
early to mid-1960s, David moved to Las Vegas. The city was a play-
ground for adults, catering to every sin imaginable, and David dove
into a Hunter S. Thompson–esque life there. He drank heavily and
dabbled in psychedelic drugs. To support himself, David told
friends, he worked as a card mechanic, fixing tables for the casinos
to stop gamblers' winning streaks. Most gambling in Vegas in the
late 1960s was run by the mafia, and David was vague about exactly
whom he worked for or what he did. Adding to the air of mystery,
he slept with a gun. At least one friend he met in Vegas thought
David was "a little paranoid."

In Vegas, David was exposed to L. Ron Hubbard's controversial
writings on Dianetics and Scientology. Hubbard had built a growing fan base, many of whom were male loners who seemed eager to
embrace a different reality from the one they lived. Hubbard wrote,
"No one has any right to force data on you and command you to
believe it or else. If it is not true for you, it isn't true."

David had arrived in Vegas during the city's golden era, when
the Rat Pack still reigned. By the late 1960s, the city was becoming
a corporate spectacle, and David was anything but corporate. He
also knew that years of heavy drinking and running cons had taken
their toll on him. He leaned into his Scientology studies, taking
classes at a local center. Teachers found him an engaged student. He

experimented with spiritual cleanses and audits, in which a fellow Scientologist took him through past lives to rid him of negative influences. But coming clean wasn't enough. At twenty-seven, David longed for a more ethical life.

Hubbard defined ethics as a series of eight stages, or "dynamics." The first dynamic was the self; the eighth was infinity or God. In between was sex and family, the group (that is, Scientology), mankind, all living creatures, the matter we live in, and the spiritual. Believers' ability to successfully move from one level to the next demonstrated not only their devotion to Scientology but also their ability to survive. David was stuck on the second dynamic. He needed to start a family.

David grabbed a sheet of paper. He made a list of all the women he knew and, next to their names, their pros and cons. The list wasn't that long. The navy had hardly been an ideal place to meet women, leaving him with two sources for prospective wives: ladies he worked with in the casinos and ones he had met through Scientology. The latter were the safer bet.

David looked at the list. Susan Fitch had been in one of David's Scientology classes at the organization's center in Las Vegas. She was reliable, well-read, funny in an understated way, and came from a good family. David circled her name. She was the lucky winner. He packed everything he owned and moved to Sparks, the Reno suburb where Susan had taken over a private Scientology center. David ignored the fact that Susan had a live-in boyfriend.

Once in Sparks, David mapped out his plan, finding ways to deepen his connection to Susan. He gave up smoking because he knew Susan would never approve. He also made himself available to her, showing up at the center and taking time to listen to her talk about her daily struggles. When she was angry or upset or having difficulty with something, she found herself calling David. In their long conversations, David confirmed some of the stories Susan had heard about him, including his secretive involvement with Scientology founder Hubbard. David had served on one of Hubbard's ships, he said, and recounted adventures in the Mediterranean. Susan was skeptical, but she knew David had been well liked by the teachers at the Scientology center in Vegas. So, instead of doubt, she gave him a challenge: Prove you can do what you say you can.

David took her to one of the casinos in nearby Reno where he worked. He stood at an empty blackjack table and combined two sets of cards into a single deck. He formed a perfect rainbow with the cards, tiers of white, red, and black falling from his hands. Then, with three fingers on the edge of the long side of the tall deck and his index finger on the right outer corner, he moved his hands across the table to deal. As he did, he slipped a card from the bottom to the house's hand. Even an eye primed for the trick would have missed the sleight. David hit blackjack.

After the card trick, Susan was curious to see what else David could do. He told her to pick an empty roulette table and put down some money. "Act like you're a customer," he said. Susan placed a few bills on a felted number. David spun the wheel. The white ball landed on Susan's chosen number. After a few more spins, Susan watched her money increase. She had to admit that the growing pile felt good. As they continued playing, Susan became lost in conversation with David and kept choosing different numbers.

Underneath her soft voice and plain appearance, Susan was a woman who hungered for adventure. From David's stories, she felt the thrill of being on the ship with Hubbard or parachuting out of a plane to make a kill. Plus, he *looked* the part of a gangster, with dark eyebrows, a black turtleneck, and gold chains.

When she next paid attention to the wheel, she saw her money had dwindled. David had lulled her into complacency. Instead of playing a number, she doubled down on red. David smiled. The ball landed on black. She again doubled down on red. Black again. She bet everything she had left on red. David looked at her with a glint in his eyes. Black again. She lost it all. David laughed. He explained that this was how the casinos had people hooked. She asked to see the device David used to control the wheel, but he told her there was no device. He was just that good. He could put a spin on anything.

AFTER LIVING IN SPARKS for a while (weeks or maybe months, no one recalls), David decided to take things to the next level. He rang Susan and said he had a question.

"How'd you like to get married?"

David heard a laugh on the other end. Susan reminded him that she had a boyfriend. Besides, she and David had never even dated. Where was this coming from?

David insisted that he wanted to marry her. Susan thought he was crazy and ended the call.

Then she turned to her boyfriend, who was sitting next to her in the living room. "That was David. He just asked me to marry him."

"Why don't you?"

His reaction shook Susan. She realized their relationship of three years was not going in the direction she had hoped. At thirty, she didn't have time to spare if she wanted something more. A few minutes later, Susan rang David back and said, "Let's get married." It was the most impulsive decision she had ever made.

Not long after, on November 1, 1969, David Grafton Spencer married Susan Kay Fitch at the Sparks Scientology Center. Susan was eager to avoid the kitschier traditions of a 1960s American wedding. There was no smashing cake in each other's faces, and their first dance was far from showy, though they both wore wide grins, Susan's head tilted back as David whispered in her ear. Susan wore a cream-colored sweater with black trim, and the groom wore a light-colored blazer over his signature look: a dark turtleneck with a gold chain. His brown hairline had receded at the temples and his eyes were so deep set that they appeared lined in kohl. He looked older than his thirty-year-old bride, despite being three years younger.

The bride's parents, who lived in nearby Reno, attended the ceremony. Susan's father was a retired colonel in the U.S. Army Dental

Corps and a former periodontics consultant to the surgeon general. Her mother was an active member of several Nevada social clubs. David lied to cover up his trail of family estrangement. He told his new wife that his own parents were dead and he had no other family. Neither was true—he had parents and two siblings back in California, plus aunts, uncles, cousins, and his grandmother with four first names. Susan would remain blissfully unaware of the truth for years. She was happy to become a Spencer, happy with the new alliteration in her name.

The newlyweds settled into married life, with David turning out to be an ideal roommate. He cleaned up after himself. He was amenable to most of Susan's suggestions. And he never yelled, no matter how frustrated he was. His wife thought that was important, since she could be forgetful in a way that had irritated earlier partners. Once, she left her purse under her chair at a restaurant with a wad of David's casino earnings in it. He didn't get upset, didn't raise his voice. Just calmly suggested they go back and get it. Susan thought, *God, we're very compatible.*

But she wasn't seeking compatibility—she wanted passion. Once she understood this, she couldn't let go of it. She started to see David more as a friend than a lover. True, he was a fascinating conversationalist, eloquent and filled with factoids about engineering, technology, and history, but Susan pined for more. She would go to work and when she came home, David would leave for a graveyard shift in the casinos. Even when they went out and did things together, like skiing, David was always a step behind her. Her husband was kind and easygoing but not the adventurer she had imagined.

Only a few months had passed when David sensed that Susan was having doubts about her impulsive decision. Finally, she told him that she wished there was more passion between them. David wasn't sure what to do. They got along well. They didn't fight. He did the dishes. What else did she want? Susan wouldn't say, and David had no plan. For him, getting married had been the plan.

To show Susan he was committed to making their union work,

he agreed to counseling. He sat patiently as Susan bemoaned their marriage to the counselor. "What are we doing here?" she asked in a session. "There is no future." David didn't want to break up, but he wasn't the type to argue. When Susan said she couldn't imagine living the rest of her life in a passionless marriage, David accepted her decision and signed the divorce papers. He moved out of their apartment, taking his clothes, books, and guns.

They stayed friends. David lived close by and helped her when she needed it. But he understood after the divorce that he was not cut out for marriage, and he had no desire for children. In fact, he was hell-bent on not spreading his genes, believing that his eccentric family's DNA was tainted. Over time, he slipped into a contented solitude. There was no need to impress others. He could live on his own terms and do it his way, as Frank Sinatra sang. In many ways, being divorced gave David a chance to do what Hubbard had always urged: find his own truth.

4.

VAN LIFE

. .

INEZ "MIDGE" GONZALES STRUGGLED TO BREATHE. SHE FELT a crushing pain in her chest and worried she would faint. Fearing death, the sixty-one-year-old climbed out of her Dodge passenger van and hurried toward the double glass doors at the back of the Westchester Church of the Nazarene. Midge lived in her van in the church's parking lot, under the flight path for Los Angeles International Airport. For weeks, she had been feeling warm, and she blamed it on the weather. She pulled her dark brown and gray hair into a ponytail to cool the back of her neck. A tomboy who preferred baggy clothes to cover her heavy five-foot frame, she had started opting for T-shirts instead of her usual sweatshirts. The church was close to the ocean but had no trees, and Midge moved the van to a shaded intersection when the high noon sun bore down.

She didn't realize it was her health, not the weather, that was making her suffocatingly hot. The pain in her chest changed her thinking. She ran as quickly as she could, down a short hallway to the office of the church secretary.

At the sound of footsteps, Nora Spring looked up from her desk. A few months earlier, Nora had allowed Midge to reside in the parsonage, a three-bedroom ranch-style home seven blocks south of the church, while the congregation was between pastors. When it was time for the floors in the house to be redone, Nora had to ask Midge to leave. Nora made it clear it wasn't anything Midge had done but the incoming pastor was allergic to cats, and Midge had two, Mouse and Lucy. Midge still took offense, ignoring Nora as punishment.

Were it another homeless person, the Church of the Nazarene would have asked Midge to leave. The church was kitty-corner from a park where a growing number of unhoused people lived in tents. They often knocked on the powder-blue church's doors for help, lucky to get a dollar or some food. The small congregation, which by 2007 was down to fewer than a hundred members, could not take care of every need. They made an exception for Midge because she had attended the church since the late 1990s, before she lost her home. When she first joined, she worked as a caregiver for an older bedridden woman in neighboring Inglewood. The woman died in 2006 and Midge lost not only her income but the room she'd stayed in. With two previous evictions on her record, she was forced to live in her van with her cats. She planned to stay only a few nights. But being poor never gets easier in America. A few nights turned into a few years.

After their fight, Nora was content to ignore Midge back. But when she entered the office, Nora quickly noticed that Midge's olive-bronze skin was unusually pale. Before Nora could ask what was wrong, Midge said, "I need to go to the hospital. I can't breathe."

Nora sensed Midge's fear. She knew the Christian thing in that moment was to put aside any irritation and help.

"Let me go get my keys," she said.

Nora, who lived next door and often walked to the church barefoot, hurried out of the office, past the fellowship hall, and out the back door to her apartment on the other side of the alley. She grabbed a pair of shoes and her car keys and drove Midge to the nearest emergency room. Midge clutched her chest for much of the five-mile ride, sure the pain and dizziness signaled her end.

When they made it to the hospital, the triage nurse told them to wait. Hours passed with the two women huddled together in the waiting room. Nora grew impatient. Like Midge, she was overweight, but she had several inches more in height and wielded her physical presence when she wanted to protect someone she cared about. Usually it was her two sons; today it was Midge.

"This lady's having a hard time," she told the nurses, her voice firm.

"Ma'am, you have to wait your turn—"

Nora stood taller. "She's gonna pass out here because she can't breathe." When a nurse finally wheeled Midge into a room, Nora insisted on staying. "I want to hear what the doctor says." Midge had no problem with Nora's mama-bear behavior. Midge's earliest memories were of longing for family, and she was relieved to have someone by her side.

Midge and Nora waited while the physician ordered an EKG and a blood panel, followed by an echocardiogram. He came back with the results: Midge had congestive heart failure. There was fluid in her heart and lungs, making it more difficult for her to breathe. She also had diabetes.

Midge protested, "I don't have diabetes."

"But your blood sugar is really high."

Midge ignored him. She was focused on the pain in her chest and demanded, "Why can't I breathe?"

The physician directed a nurse to insert a urinary catheter to drain trapped fluids. Once the catheter was in, Midge, color finally back to her cheeks, smiled at Nora.

"Midge, you're glistening."

"Yeah," Midge replied with obvious relief. "I just peed." She erupted in laughter, and Nora joined. They laughed harder than the joke warranted, grateful for any release from the tension of the ER. The women spent the rest of the afternoon resting while Midge received her first dialysis treatment. It would be a year before the water around her heart was fully drained, and still more time for the diabetes diagnosis to feel real to Midge.

NORA WORRIED ABOUT MIDGE returning to her van. She didn't think that Midge should be sharing the small space with the cats and their litter box. But while Nora worried about practicalities, Midge saw their reconciliation as divine intervention. She told Nora that God had given them a time-out, so that when Midge needed help, she was free to ask. She felt she'd been given an opportunity for a true friendship, and she made a conscious effort to repair the relationship.

Soon after her hospital stay, Midge made a habit of showing up at the back door of Nora's apartment every day around the same time. She knew that Nora was looking for paid work and spent the first hours after her boys went to school scouring online job postings. By ten A.M., Nora was ready for a break, and Midge entered. Rather than ringing the doorbell, Midge yelled, "Knock, knock!" and opened the door before Nora could respond. Even after Nora and her husband gave Midge a key to their apartment so she could enter as she pleased, Midge stuck to her routine of saying "Knock, knock" loud enough for the upstairs neighbor to hear.

"Whatcha doing?" Midge always asked once she was inside the living room. It was her signature phrase and Nora's cue to close the browser on her computer. Some days Midge brought her laundry to wash in the apartment, or toiletries so she could take a shower. Other days, it was food. Nora, who was far from wealthy but had enough to cover her basic needs, thought it was crazy that a homeless woman spent her money on food for others with full pantries. Then Nora would remind herself that Midge found joy in giving and trained herself to graciously accept.

While Nora would sink into the deep cushions of the couch to watch TV, Midge would sit in her favorite chair next to the cage with Nora's gray-headed green and orange Senegal parrot, Sparky. Midge usually preferred fast food, but sometimes brought a healthier option to share with Sparky. One day it was a pomegranate, Midge's favorite fruit and a seasonal treat in L.A.'s early autumn. Midge adored giving treats to animals, maybe even more than to humans. "One for you," she told the bird as she placed one of the pomegranate seeds in front of him on the swing. "One for me." She popped a handful of seeds in her mouth.

Nora and Midge settled into a daily routine of watching TV. Midge liked house-flipping shows, pretending she was part of the crew doing the work. She had worked as a carpenter before she was a caretaker, but her declining health made the prospect of using her hands for future work unrealistic. Though Midge told people she had her diabetes under control, she had developed a number of health problems since her ER visit that made it harder for her to move. When a house on the television screen had a raised entry, Midge complained to Nora, "I don't like stairs going up to the house. I can't walk those." She had been diagnosed with neuropathy and fibromyalgia, and she had bad knees.

Seeing her friend snack in front of the TV, Nora worried. Midge was on regular dialysis for her diabetes and waved away any talk about diet. She insisted that she didn't need to make changes because she had already given up alcohol. Midge had been an alcoholic for more than twenty years. She was thirty-one years old when she decided to stop drinking and go to Alcoholics Anonymous. Midge's devotion to staying sober was the reason she had gravitated to the Westchester Church of the Nazarene. Her AA meetings had been held at the church and she appreciated that the congregation did not serve wine at communion.

When Nora's boys returned from school, Midge often tried to help them with their homework. She didn't have children, but she believed herself an expert in raising them. When she was in her early forties, she enrolled at nearby Loyola Marymount University and majored in psychology. "Many a fight we had when she tried to use psychology on me," Nora recalled. At other times she benefited from Midge's counsel. When Nora's parents died unexpectedly, Midge was able to console her. *God puts people into your life,* Nora thought.

Her sons—Thomas, who was in middle school, and Justin, who was in elementary school—thought of Midge as an aunt. They rolled their eyes at her attempts to be strict, as kids do, but generally followed her instructions. They knew if they did, they would get to help with the animals she fostered. Midge once placed a days-old kitten in the front pocket of ten-year-old Justin's overalls, teaching him how to feed it with a syringe. Other times she asked him to help her walk a puppy she was pet-sitting, the pain in her hands too intense to keep a firm grip on the leash. The boy grew to have a deep, lifelong love of animals thanks to her.

Most nights, Midge ate dinner with the Springs. It fomented the feeling she was like family. When night rolled around, Midge would return to her van to sleep beside Mouse and Lucy.

FOR THE NEXT FEW years, Midge survived by relying on the families at church. For the most part, they were happy to help. Midge had a rebel spirit that made members in the conservative congregation laugh. Once, she grabbed a child's tricycle and rode it through the fellowship hall, giggling with joy as she cycled around the room. She earned a reputation as the resident pet whisperer after successfully pet-sitting for several members. And she was generous, some thought to a fault. Midge's friends bought groceries because they knew that if they gave her money, she would probably feed her cats before she would take care of herself. She was also known to give away her clothes, including the sweatshirt on her back, to other homeless people who wandered into the church cold. Nora was reminded of the biblical story in Luke about the Widow's Two Mites. The widow's small donation (the eponymous copper coins) to the temple treasury counted more than all the contributions of the rich, because she had given away all she owned. Midge's willingness to give when she had nothing encouraged others in the congregation to be more generous.

For Midge, what mattered most was that she felt loved. She didn't have a home, but she had her church family. Holidays were finally a source of fun rather than dread. Her favorite was Thanksgiving, when she could eat her way from house to house. She started the day early and spent as much time as possible with each family, playing board games and solving jigsaw puzzles. She saved Nora's house for last—and she returned first thing the next morning for the family's traditional Fry-day. Nora's husband, Howard, deep-fried their Thanksgiving turkey and kept the oil hot. On Fry-day, they would take turns picking out new items to throw in the vat. "You can do that?" Midge once asked bright-eyed. Over the years, they deep-fried Oreos, ice cream, pickles, okra, potatoes, and parsnips. They learned the hard way to freeze a Snickers bar before tossing it in.

When she wasn't with Nora and Howard, Midge celebrated holidays with Emery and Elaine Pankratz. Midge had a dedicated setting at their table. She would serve herself from the family-style dishes, keeping one of the serving spoons for herself. Someone inevitably teased her, "Is that so you can shovel it in faster?" Midge didn't take offense. Her ability to laugh at herself was one of the traits that had endeared her to dozens of families at the church. But she wasn't an angel. She called people out when she thought their politics conflicted with their Christianity. Elaine, a registered Republican, had different views from Midge, and it had led to some tense moments. If a test of feeling like family is that you don't always get along, then Midge was part of the clan. The Pankratzes agreed to not talk politics when Midge came over.

Like the Pankratzes, Lynne and Mike Patti were more conservative than Midge. They believed in personal responsibility and giving to those who seemed deserving of aid. Midge was a different kind of homeless person in the Pattis' eyes because she didn't ask for anything. Lynne might have said as much on occasion, which surely irritated Midge. She spoke up when she thought Lynne was acting more like a savior than a friend.

Lynne and Midge had known each other since 2002. Two years later, Lynne married Mike, and the couple changed churches. But Midge stayed in their lives. She house-sat when they went east to visit Mike's family or took a vacation. She also stayed with the couple for short periods when she needed to recover from a health procedure—an increasingly frequent occurrence. After one surgery in 2009, she was staying in Lynne's guest room when the friends got into a fight—probably over something trivial—and Midge announced that she was leaving. "You can run away from us," Lynne responded. "I will always stand on the front step and wait for you to come back."

PASTORS CYCLED IN AND out, but Midge stayed in her van in the parking lot and Nora remained as church secretary. Together, the friends ran Vacation Bible School for young children, and Midge later became the church's missionary president and oversaw the Wednesday Youth First program. As her involvement in the church grew, Midge developed a sense of ownership of the Westchester Church. By 2013, she had moved a lounge chair into one of the offices and, without asking permission, started sleeping there, while her cats stayed in the van. Midge wasn't the orderly type, and any space she occupied tended to become overrun with papers, blankets, and stuffed animals. People in the congregation pretended not to notice.

Except for the church's latest pastor, John Huddle. He was an evangelist who felt called upon by the Lord to help the homeless. In addition to pastoring, he worked for World Vision, a global Christian missionary organization with a number of housing and water projects in Africa. Huddle combined the two roles every Friday when he put on a barbecue for unhoused residents of the park near the church. Midge joined him, missing only once, when she was too sick. Huddle saw Midge's health problems as incompatible with her living situation. She had gone from receiving dialysis once a week to three times a week, and she was at risk of having her foot amputated. She also needed a new kidney. But she would have to secure housing to get on a transplant list.

Huddle stepped in. He obtained a federal housing voucher and even found a place that would accept it, but Midge turned down the apartment when she heard she would have to give up one of her cats. The unit also lacked space to park her van. Midge felt that she had no choice but to keep living on the church lot.

That wasn't going to work for Huddle. He understood how reticent Midge was about abandoning the van. He would have to take a dramatic step if he wanted to force change, and he wouldn't ask her first.

Huddle drove to the Westchester home of Mike and Lynne Patti, who had recently returned to the Nazarene church. (Mike hadn't planned to go back but, on a whim, he stopped by one day, and Midge answered the door. He saw it as an omen.) Mike's career as a music composer for films and theme parks had made the couple one of the most successful in the congregation. Huddle hoped to tap into their charitable impulse and devotion to Midge.

Mike Patti opened the door and found Huddle wearing his signature charismatic smile. The pastor wasted no time. "We have to do something about Midge."

PART TWO

. .

FORGOTTEN

Our dead are never dead to us until

we have forgotten them.

—GEORGE ELIOT, *ADAM BEDE*

5.

GONE

· ·

AFTER SEVEN YEARS OF LIVING IN HER VAN, MIDGE WAS about to have a home of her own. Pastor Huddle had convinced the Pattis to convert half of their garage into an apartment for Midge; the other half would remain Mike's music studio.

Though it was Lynne who first befriended Midge, Mike felt more strongly that they had to help her. "She cannot live in a van," he told his wife. Midge had become a surrogate grandmother to their children, and Mike saw how their oldest, Emma, adored her. Mike was also quite fond of Midge. He saw her as someone who lived without anything the outside world would value, yet had a deep, almost divine wisdom. When they talked, he felt as if Jesus was speaking through her.

His wife wasn't convinced. Midge had stayed with them a few months earlier, in August 2013, and Lynne had found it difficult. "Somebody else needs to take this burden on," she said. But when Huddle prodded her, saying that of course she should feel overwhelmed, Lynne took his words as a challenge. *God doesn't meet you in complacency,* she thought. *He meets you when you put yourself out there.* As she conferred with her husband, she drew on scripture to help her navigate what to do. Jesus asked his followers to look out for the orphans and widows. Lynne decided that now they were being called.

Mike told his wife, then pregnant with their third child, that there would be strict boundaries. "We cannot take her to dialysis. You can't be doing that with the kids and homeschooling."

Lynne agreed, "She's got to figure it out."

With that decided, the next step was to convince Midge. As much as she craved permanent housing, she didn't want to give up her van. After repeated conversations, Midge promised to leave the church parking lot and move into the garage apartment under the condition that she could bring her cats, Mouse and Lucy. Lynne wasn't thrilled. The cats were feral and often rejected their litter box. But she gave in when Mike told her he felt guilty about how much money he was earning as a composer.

In October, Lynne helped Midge go through her belongings at the church, including what she'd stored in the office. They threw away hundreds of pens and papers. They separated the books that Midge would keep from the books that she would give away. When Midge began to pack a collection of stuffed animals that had been ruined by water damage, Lynne said, "Midgey, this isn't healthy. These have mold in them, and you can't breathe that in." Then, like a firm mother, she said, "I don't want you to bring that to your new place."

Meanwhile, Nora mobilized members of the church to remodel the Pattis' garage. By December, Midge had a small kitchen, living area, bedroom, and bathroom. A small hallway was left without a ceiling, to allow the garage door to close—a design flaw the Pattis would come to regret when the cats discovered it as an escape hatch. While the church financed the construction, Mike and Lynne paid to have the unit furnished. They installed Ikea furniture and hooked up an Apple TV box to a flat-screen, linking it to their account.

Once she moved in, Midge insisted on paying rent. The Pattis told her they didn't need anything, but Midge said it would give her a sense of pride. They agreed on twenty dollars every month, drawn from Midge's Social Security benefits. It didn't take long for Midge to feel at home, filling the apartment with stuffed animals, books, and cat toys.

Safely inside her own place, Midge took to watching the first Harry Potter movie on repeat. She played and replayed the scene of Dudley's birthday. Midge detested the way the Dursleys treated Harry, sticking him in a broom closet under the stairs while they lavished attention on their biological son. It hit close to home.

She spoke occasionally to her friends about her childhood. She said that she had spent the first years of her life in a Catholic orphanage, praying that someone would adopt her. Her adoption hadn't gone as she had hoped, though she didn't share many details. She said only that she had lived with a foster family and that her brother, the family's biological son, had received all the presents on holidays, while she would go to bed hungry.

"Oh my gosh, I can't even imagine," Lynne told her. "Midgey, what do you do with that? Where do you put that?"

"Oh, it's all gone now," Midge said. "You guys, you took me in, and it's done now. It's gone."

WHILE MIDGE WAITED FOR a kidney transplant, she settled into a new routine: dialysis, rest, church, more rest. She preferred to treat her diabetes naturally. No one ever saw her monitor her blood sugar or adjust her food intake. Midge claimed to sense when her body wanted her to hold off sugar and needed insulin. But she also gave herself forbidden treats, like a freshly baked brownie or Coca-Cola. Her body paid her back. Her leg muscles weakened, damaged nerves caused numbness in her feet, and she had trouble carrying her weight. She had to rely on a wheelchair more often.

She started to drop hints about items on her bucket list. Going to Disneyland was at the top. Nora and Howard conveniently had season passes and went several times per year. Nora would share stories about the rides they had gone on, the Disney characters they'd encountered in the park, and the food they'd eaten. Midge ached to join them. That's what families did together and what she had missed when she was growing up. At last, Nora told her they would buy her a single-day ticket.

On a late spring day in 2014, Nora wheeled Midge under the awning of Disneyland's entrance. People stood in the queues around them, eager to press through the park's turnstiles. The crowds of children were giddy from excitement. Midge took all the energy in from her wheelchair.

"Oh look, they have cotton candy." Midge's brown eyes widened. "Can I get some cotton candy?"

Nora thought about Midge's blood sugar and decided to redirect her friend. "There's an ice cream place. You want to get some ice cream?"

"Okay."

After they entered the park, Howard asked what ride she wanted to go on first.

"I don't know," Midge said. "Which rides do you go on?"

Howard and Nora had agreed this would be their friend's day. Howard said, "We're here for *you*, Midge."

At Peter Pan's Flight, Nora and Howard helped Midge out of her wheelchair and into a flying pirate galleon. They rode over the star-filled skies of London, through Wendy's bedroom, and into Neverland. Midge bounced as she sang along to the words of "You Can Fly! You Can Fly! You Can Fly!" Most of the passengers in the other carriages were under five, but that only made Midge more excited.

Midge was keen to go on the Buzz Lightyear Astro Blasters ride in Tomorrowland. One of Nora and Howard's sons had worked this Disneyland ride and held the local shooting record among the staff. Midge announced that she was going to beat his score.

When Buzz Lightyear encouraged the riders to go to the battle stations and be armed, signing off with "To Infinity and Beyond," Midge asked, "How do you do the game?"

"You just pull this trigger," Nora explained.

Midge was worried. "I can't pull with my hand."

Nora reassured her, "Do it the best you can." Midge had to use two hands to pull the trigger during the ride, which didn't allow her to move the Star Cruiser's joystick into position for some of the targets. When she looked at her picture with her score in the kiosk at the end of the ride, she was disappointed.

"I didn't get a very good score."

"But," Nora asked, "did you have fun?"

Midge brightened. "Yeah."

The high that day in Anaheim was 71 degrees, but it felt much warmer to Midge, and she was easily worn out. Her dialysis compounded her chronic fatigue and fibromyalgia. Nora and Howard rolled her into the Big Thunder Ranch for lunch and a rest. They found a red-and-white-checkered table close to the stage where actors sang classic American country and folklore songs. For $24.99 per person, they dug into all-you-can-eat metal buckets of barbecue ribs and chicken, and large red melamine bowls of baked beans and coleslaw. Before the waitress could return to take the half-empty buckets after their last round, Midge pulled out a gallon-size Ziploc bag from her fanny pack. Howard and Nora looked at each other and laughed. Midge filled the bag with leftover meat, then licked BBQ sauce off her fingers and smiled wide, an outer ring of sauce circling her lips.

More than food, the day at Disneyland fed Midge's appetite for family. She started wanting more days like that. Now that she lived behind Lynne, Mike, and the kids, she hoped they would embrace her more closely as kin.

Her body had other plans. Over the next year, Midge's health rapidly deteriorated. By late 2015, she had grown irritable from chronic pain and exhaustion. Lynne kept her distance when Midge turned gruff, which only deepened Midge's sense of rejection. She was still going to church with the Pattis but worried she was becoming invisible to them. They were busy with their three kids and had a fourth on the way. Mike was working too many long hours in his studio to address the growing tension between his wife and Midge.

Midge chafed at the restrictions that Lynne had set around their shared living. Midge wasn't allowed to go inside the Pattis' without permission, and the children were not to enter Midge's apartment. Lynne worried that the kids would step on one of the needles Midge used to inject her insulin. Lynne had also become annoyed with Midge's cats, who preferred to climb up and relieve themselves in the opening between the ceiling and the door rather than use their litter box in the hallway.

The true Christian sentiment, Midge asserted, would have been to welcome her into the house and treat her as someone they cared for and loved. Instead, she felt that they merely tolerated her as a charity case. She lashed out at Lynne one day in late January 2016.

"You think you can throw me in the garage, and this is good enough!" With bite, she added, "I'm not an animal. You can't just feed me. I need connection."

Lynne thought Midge was being unfair, not recognizing the sacrifices she and Mike had made. She reminded Midge of all they had done for her, and then retreated to cool off. When they fought, Lynne found herself thinking, *We are not family. She's not our kids' grandma.*

Days passed. On Tuesday, February 2, 2016, Midge went to her regular dialysis appointment. She was too tired the next day to go out and whiled away the hours inside her garage apartment, playing computer games on an iPad that the Pattis had given her. Her favorites were CityVille and FarmVille 2. She posted her results on Facebook. When night rolled around, she was agitated and couldn't sleep. At three A.M. on Thursday morning, she responded to the Facebook prompt, "What's on your mind?"

> What's on my mind? Where are my friends? Is it enough to store me in an unfinished garage? But where are my friends? Do they have too much to do? They should be ringing my phone or tapping at my door. Great joy. Love one another as I have loved you. It may seem impossible to do,

but if you will try to trust and believe, great are the joys that you will receive. Amen.

Those would be Midge's last words.

. .

THE NEW DIRECTIONS VETERANS CHOIR'S SUCCESS ON *America's Got Talent* gave Bobby Hanna a much-needed boost. The choir didn't make it past the Vegas round of the reality show, but they were in demand. They performed locally in 2010 and later hired a booking agent to help them travel the country, raising awareness for veterans through performances at community centers, nursing homes, and professional sporting events. It didn't matter who they were singing for—the elderly or a national television audience— Bobby gave everything he had to the music. He prodded his chorus mates to practice and get their timing, steps, and notes perfect. He also wanted everyone to look sharp. It was the former military officer in him: If a shoe could take a shine, it damn well better be shiny.

Bobby applied a similar sense of determination to improving himself. New Directions for Veterans embraced a hard-core "tough love" approach, challenging the men to shape up as they had done when they joined the military. In return for a comprehensive palette of services—clinical therapy, housing support, VA case management, education, job training and placement, as well as parenting and money management classes—New Directions residents had to agree to the program's nonnegotiable rules. They had to check in and out when leaving the building, and they couldn't invite visitors without prior approval. Food was allowed only in the cafeteria or in a designated outdoor dining space. These rules weren't easy, especially for men who had become accustomed to what they called the "freedom" that came with living on the streets. Many dropped out. But those who made it through the program came away with housing, jobs, computer skills, savings accounts, and the support of mentors and peers.

New Directions considered Bobby a success story. He took business administration classes to help in his employment search. He learned to balance a checkbook. He also became sober, proudly putting his name on a sobriety plaque posted in the front lobby. And Bobby had thrived in therapy: The counselors at New Directions prodded him to take responsibility for his past and to stop blaming others for life's missed turns. The probing questions during group therapy sessions brought up childhood memories of abandonment that Bobby had not shared with anyone, including Clara. He recalled accompanying his mother to a medical appointment. His mother, who was struggling with addiction, had left Bobby in the waiting room. He had screamed for her, but she had never come back. Bobby had then moved in with a foster family, which came with its own set of traumas.

The therapy hadn't been easy, and in his first months a counselor had asked Clara to visit Bobby as a show of support. Clara stopped by on Sundays after church. She also picked him up once to go to a Stanley Clarke concert, remembering that he had told her stories of the jazz musician visiting Bobby's childhood home in Gary, Indiana, and jamming with his foster father. She hoped it would bring him out of his funk. Eventually—and with the confidence that music gave him—Bobby started to keep a journal. He also started to reach out to people back home in Gary. Clara knew Bobby had turned a corner when he told her, "I realize that it's me. I need to first fix whatever the problem is with me, before I can move on." Clara wished that Bobby had entered New Directions earlier, because the therapy might have saved their marriage.

For his part, Bobby became determined to win Clara back. He was so focused on proving to his ex-wife how much he had changed that he missed some of the clues she had been dropping that she, too, had become a different person. No one at work or church even knew that she had once been married. Clara cared for Bobby but did not want to risk the new life she had built, a life filled with travel and weekend walks with close friends. When Bobby broached the idea of getting back together, Clara tried to soften the rejection by explaining that if she reunited with him, it would be for the wrong reasons. Bobby was heartbroken, but he played it cool. "Oh, it's all right" was all he said.

Bobby graduated from New Directions in 2011. A housing navigator helped him find an apartment on La Brea, and he had a work-study job in the VA that might one day lead to full employment. A case manager also helped him get retroactive disability pay from the VA, which Bobby used to buy a brand-new black Chevy Camaro in cash. He had a home, his dream car, the choir, and his veteran friends.

Once he was on his own, Clara sensed her relationship with Bobby was changing. He curbed their phone calls, limiting himself to her birthday and occasional check-ins. She figured he had moved on, and she was content to watch his progress from the sidelines. Truth be told, she was relieved. He never forgot about her, though. Occasionally, he would call her out of the blue and say, "Hey, Slim," using the nickname he had given her during their marriage, "How are you doing?"

EVEN AS BOBBY'S MENTAL health started to improve, his physical health declined.

Before he entered New Directions, Bobby had hurt his foot playing basketball at a neighborhood court in San Bernardino. He had come down hard after a layup and something snapped. When the pain didn't go away, he went to a doctor at the VA, who told him he would need surgery. After the procedure, the pain worsened. Bobby became convinced the doctor had botched the operation.

Like a lot of people tormented with chronic pain, Bobby learned to live with it. Before New Directions, he self-medicated with weed. After he got clean, he tried meditation. But between 2012 and 2016 the pain intensified. He could no longer run or play sports, and he struggled to keep his weight down, which made dressing up a frustration. Even walking had become a challenge.

Although George Hill had started the New Directions Veterans Choir, it was the group's baritone, Carleton Griffin, who took it upon himself to make sure the members arrived on time and were appropriately attired. For the first several years after *America's Got Talent*, Carleton never had to worry about whether Bobby would show up ready to sing and looking his best. Though he didn't own much, Bobby had always made the most of what he had. Bright-colored suits with wide shoulders, sports coats, patterned ties with matching handkerchiefs, the occasional fedora, and always his cobalt-blue-and-silver Masonic ring. Bobby never went onstage without it. The ring paired well with his signature blue ostrich cowboy boots. The base around his foot was a deep royal blue, while a pale blue encased his calves. George Hill teased Bobby for the flashy boots, but everyone enjoyed Bobby's flair. Carleton said it gave the choir something to laugh about on the road.

As his health declined, Bobby took shortcuts to ease the pain. He showed up to gigs barefoot, waiting until the last possible second to put on his boots. He would go onstage and belt out the music with pride—like he did at the 2016 Rose Bowl Parade—but as soon as he was offstage again, he grimaced. Carleton and some of the other members tried to persuade Bobby to stop wearing the boots or dress shoes of any sort. They didn't want him to be uncomfortable. *What was the point?* Carleton asked. Bobby hit back, "You got yours. I got mine. I know I'm not supposed to have them on, but they feel good anyway." Eventually they learned not to bring up the boots.

Then Bobby started to arrive late. His lack of punctuality became an issue with the other members. They knew he would show up, but it was always at the last minute, making things tense backstage. Eventually, Carleton and George caught on that Bobby was too proud to admit that he couldn't move as easily anymore. They tricked Bobby with the call time, telling him it was thirty minutes earlier than it really was; then half an hour turned into an hour.

Carleton had become a counselor for the VA after his graduation from New Directions, and his professional training told him that Bobby was in trouble. He pressured Bobby to talk. But Bobby slid back into his old ways, keeping his struggles to himself.

"No, I don't need anything," he told his choir friend. "I'm going to get through this. I'm going to push until I can't push no more." Other than those few words to Carleton, Bobby did everything he could to hide his condition. He kept it from everyone who cared about him, including Clara.

For a while, Bobby's strategy worked. He got himself to gigs and took care of himself, but then his body slowly shut down. He was living in near-constant agony. Even simple tasks like getting dressed or hauling groceries were difficult, and he could no longer work or pay his bills. He slipped into depression. Clara heard he had been evicted from the apartment on La Brea, but she couldn't get Bobby to tell her what had happened. He mentioned finding a lawyer who was going to help him fight the eviction. Clara wasn't sure what grounds Bobby had to sue. The apartment looked to be in fine working order the last time she visited. It was Bobby who needed repair.

Bobby's health deteriorated to the point that he could no longer travel with the choir or perform, but he was too proud to admit this to the other members or their booking agent. He also didn't share that he had lost his apartment. The booking agent wondered if Bobby had relapsed, but he didn't pry.

Carleton knew Bobby's exit from the choir was health related, but he figured it was the foot pain. He didn't know that Bobby had been diagnosed with chronic degenerative arthritis, as well as a bleeding ulcer, or that Bobby needed both hips replaced and would have to use a walker for the rest of his life. It was only when Bobby took to Facebook in an uncharacteristic public plea for financial help that people in his life, including Clara, learned he had lung cancer as well. The VA doctors had discovered cancerous lumps in Bobby's throat and lungs. The posts were atypical for Bobby, and no one seemed to know what to say to him. A few friends commented that they thought his account had been hacked. Clara was troubled, thinking Bobby had gone off the deep end (he'd also started posting conspiracy theories). She decided not to say anything that might set him off.

When Bobby received no donations on his Facebook fundraiser, he posted dejectedly, "I have no choice but to let the cancer take its course."

BOBBY WAS FIFTY-NINE YEARS old when he reentered the New Directions residential facility in 2018. The sobriety plaque he had added his name to in 2009 remained in the front lobby. He grabbed a marker and updated the years of sobriety to ten. It was a reminder that Bobby had found his place there once before, and he would again, surrounded by people who knew and supported him. Living at New Directions, Bobby would also be closer to the VA doctors who were treating his cancer.

But his second stay was harder than he expected because of his mobility issues. Bobby spent more time in bed than in the common areas. When he had the energy to make it downstairs, he played a piano or strummed one of his favorite guitars in the rec room. Otherwise, he kept to himself. When Carleton saw Bobby hobble slowly across the sprawling VA campus toward the hospital, taking pauses to lean on his walker and catch his breath, the former choir mate knew not to ask too many questions.

Bobby wanted to be known and remembered as a gifted musician. He approached the program's manager and said he wanted to leave, to live out his days by himself. The manager respected Bobby's need to guard his dignity. A housing coordinator found Bobby a vet-subsidized studio in a low-income building in El Monte, east of L.A. and closer to where he had first settled when he moved from Gary.

Before he moved to El Monte, Bobby invited Clara to join him for a pre–Fourth of July celebration in the New Directions cafeteria. It was late June 2019, nine years to the month since he had sung on national television. Clara was hesitant; she thought it was crazy how much she had supported Bobby in the seventeen years since their divorce. But something in his voice struck her and she agreed to make a quick visit.

When Clara entered the New Directions building, she stopped in disbelief at the sight of her ex-husband. She hadn't seen Bobby in a year. At that time, Bobby had gained a considerable amount of weight, which he'd hid in baggy T-shirts and pants. Now his face was sunken in, and his clothes hung loosely on his frame. He had a breathing tube attached to him and an oxygen tank that he dragged across the linoleum floor. Clara realized that Bobby was much sicker than he had let on.

She didn't rush the visit. She stayed for lunch, sitting in the cafeteria and eating hot dogs. They made small talk with the people sitting nearby. After some time, when they were alone, Bobby said he had some things he needed to discuss with her.

"Slim," Bobby said. "I was jealous of you."

"Why, Bobby?"

"Because you had really good friends."

Clara sensed her ex was lonely. She wondered where Bobby's kin back in Gary had been during the past year, but she kept the question to herself.

Bobby continued, "You know, Slim, I think I've had a pretty good life. My only regret is that I did you wrong." He apologized for the way he had treated her during their marriage, repeating how sorry he was and how he wished he could have been better to her. Then he dropped a bombshell.

"I'd really like to remarry you."

Clara didn't know what to say. She wanted to be honest, wanted to tell him that she didn't love him the way she once did. But she couldn't hurt Bobby when he looked that frail. She gave him a half truth, something to dissuade him from asking again. She told him that her family would not be happy if she remarried him.

This time, he didn't say "It's all right." He shook off Clara's rejection and stayed focused on making amends.

He promised to help her get a new car. They had bought her blue Toyota Celica together on Palm Sunday in 1995. She remembered because she had worked hard to buy a stick shift, her first car in Los Angeles. Neither had any credit, and Clara's boss had to cosign. When Clara and Bobby entered the Celica for the first time, they cranked up the music and went for a spin, the wind blowing through Clara's hair and reminding her of their days on the Thames party boats. Now the car's tires were worn, and Bobby was worried they were unsafe.

"I want to see you in something better."

"I really appreciate that," Clara said. "But *you* got to get better."

"Don't worry about me. I'll be fine. I still want to do something for you."

Clara felt closer to Bobby in that moment than she had in years, acutely aware that even at this point, as sick as he was, he was thinking about her. When it was time to say goodbye, the two stopped and looked at each other. Bobby finally broke the silence.

"Slim, I'll see you on the other side."

· ·

LENA BROWN WAS MISSING. AN INVESTIGATOR WITH THE probate's office tried to reach her in April 2008 at the duplex on Freeman Avenue, but there was no answer. The investigator called Rudy Estrella, Lena's nephew, multiple times, leaving urgent messages. He never called back. On April 22, the investigator alerted Leona Shapiro, the Beverly Hills attorney who had served as a neutral legal authority during Lena's conservatorship hearings. It wasn't the first time she had been called about Lena's case since Rudy was declared conservator. Two years earlier, a different probate investigator had contacted Shapiro, saying they were "concerned about the state of repair of the home, and the fact that there was an inoperable telephone." Rudy had stopped answering calls then, too.

Shapiro kept reaching out to Rudy and also called his attorney.

He hadn't heard from his client, either. Finally, Rudy picked up. Rudy told Shapiro that his aunt had been moved to a nursing home two months earlier, following hernia surgery. Lena had reluctantly agreed to the operation on the condition that she would be able to stay in her home. She handled the surgery well but afterward the surgeon told Rudy that living alone was no longer viable. She was tough for ninety-five but she couldn't lift anything herself, and she would either need round-the-clock nursing care or she would have to live with relatives who could provide help.

Rudy had known that this day would come and wasn't totally unprepared. He drove a FedEx delivery van, and he'd been inside a lot of nursing homes. He understood that they varied widely. In some, the overpowering smell of chemical disinfectant could barely mask the dank reek of urine, while in others, nurses interacted with the residents in wheelchairs and had daily activities written in bright colors on whiteboards. He decided on one in the latter category, knowing that his aunt's account was flush. She would be able to pay the $2,400 monthly fee.

Compared to other nursing homes he'd seen, Le Bleu Chateau in Burbank stood out for its bucolic setting and amenities. The facility was clean (not a given in elderly care) with views of the foothills of the Angeles National Forest. It offered special assistance for people with memory impairment, including sing-alongs and math challenges, which Rudy hoped would keep the aging Lena busy and entertained. But when he informed his aunt that she wouldn't be returning to Hawthorne, she was devastated. She couldn't process his description of the mountains or bingo. All she heard was that she would no longer be able to live on her own, in the place where she'd spent most of her adult life. She had always suspected that her family would someday take her out of her home.

Rudy promised he would visit regularly and at first, he did. He and his wife went to Le Bleu Chateau several times, with his sister, Marjorie, joining them on at least one occasion. Marjorie was impressed with the facility and thought it was the kind of place she might like to be in when she was too old to care for herself. The visits weren't frequent or long, but they provided Lena with a link to the outside world.

Then, in 2008, Rudy's wife died from ongoing health complications, and less than one year later, his twenty-eight-year-old son passed away from a drug overdose. Rudy was too overwhelmed to do anything. He stopped taking calls, and he ignored the piles of letters in his mailbox. It wasn't long before he dropped out of Lena's life, telling Shapiro that he "no longer had the strength" to be conservator. His wife had been closest to Lena, and when she died, the bond was broken. Visiting his aunt had become a painful reminder of his own losses.

Only a probate judge could legally release Rudy from his role as conservator. Rudy would have to petition the court to resign or be removed for failure to perform his duties. A court hearing was set for the following year. In preparation, Leona Shapiro would visit Lena at Le Bleu Chateau and evaluate her for the court.

Shapiro arrived at the nursing home in September 2009, six years after her first encounter with Lena. The once feisty and fiercely independent woman was both sullen and shrunken. She had lost weight again. Her light olive skin had turned a pale shade of yellow. Her hair had thinned, probably from a combination of aging and inadequate nutrition. She appeared to lack dentures—or, more likely, refused to wear them—making her mouth slack. Most disconcertingly for Shapiro, Lena would not engage with the people around her. She sat in a wheelchair in the front room and stared at the television. Nor did she participate in any of the games or eat with the other residents. Lena seemed to have withdrawn from life. There were no pictures on her bed stand, nothing that made her cold, institutional room, with its beige walls and furniture, feel like home. The only recognizable feature was the brown leather purse that she wore over her shoulder and pressed to her body. The nursing aide who had accompanied Shapiro joked that the purse was Lena's security blanket.

Teena Colebrook would have made the trek to Burbank, had she known where Lena was. But after the court hearing to determine conservatorship in 2003, the family had made it clear that Teena was no longer welcome in Lena's life. Teena felt she had let a friend down in the worst way. Lynda was also cut out. But unlike Teena, who had turned inward and blamed herself, Lynda had directed her frustration at Lena's family. She told Teena, "No good deed goes unpunished."

Lena's heart still beat, but in many ways she was no longer alive. Once her family stopped visiting her, she became, in effect, "socially dead." Uprooted from her neighborhood, she had lost her few remaining social ties, a sense of history, and what Shapiro described as "any chance of resuming some kind of dialogue with society." Lena's declining health and disappeared friendships had led to a new set of losses that had immobilized and isolated her. Her lack of engagement with others at Le Bleu Chateau further signaled diminished personhood. The nursing home staff and residents, anticipating her imminent death, treated her as if she were already gone.

At the facility, Shapiro reviewed Lena's medical records. A doctor had diagnosed the now ninety-six-year-old with dementia and hypertension. She was incontinent and disoriented, confined to a wheelchair. She could still dress and groom herself but needed help with other activities. The woman who once joked that she wouldn't depend on Depends now wore adult diapers because she refused to notify a nurse when she needed to use the bathroom.

Shapiro had never known Lena to be "friendly," and she'd had enough experience with older adults to understand that dementia would make her harder to deal with. Shapiro tried a gentle approach: "I don't know if you remember me, Lena, but we have met before."

Lena did not respond right away. She sat motionless. She eventually said she was "okay" but didn't want to talk, and she preferred to be alone.

Then she looked at Shapiro and said quietly but firmly, "Get out."

Shapiro brought her findings to the court in 2009, making the case that Lena's conservatorship should be transferred to the Los Angeles Office of the Public Guardian. That office was tasked with managing the finances and care of physically and mentally vulnerable people who didn't have family to help. It was a "conservator of last resort," intended to protect the county's fragile older residents. Whether it fulfilled that mandate was unclear. A couple of years earlier, a *Los Angeles Times* investigation had revealed extensive problems at the agency, including heavy caseloads, missed court deadlines, and inflated fees (for instance, the office charged $18 to pay a $5.79 phone bill). Most alarming was not how many cases they were handling but how many they turned away. Over a six-year period, the public guardian received four thousand referrals; it rejected 84 percent of them. Incapacitated and disabled indigent seniors who had their cases rejected by the public guardian were on their own. In this way Lena was blessed. Because she was already at Le Bleu Chateau with round-the-clock care (making the public guardian's job easy) and because Shapiro was practiced at petitioning the court, Lena's transfer of conservatorship was approved. At this point, it was the best Lena could hope for.

FOUR YEARS AFTER THE probate investigator reported Lena missing and Leona Shapiro discovered her in a near-catatonic state inside the Le Bleu Chateau facility, the ninety-eight-year-old lay near death, her eyes closed and mouth open. Nurses were keeping her comfortable, moistening Lena's lips and encouraging her (but not forcing her) to eat.

On July 7, 2012, a nurse entered Lena's room and checked for a pulse. When she didn't find one, she notified the institution's physician, who would attest to the death and fill out the necessary paperwork. The nurse closed the door and pulled off the blankets, tossing them to the floor. Then she rolled a plain white sheet around Lena and knotted it, first at her feet and then at her head, so that Lena's small frame looked mummified. She would stay that way until the county could reach her relatives.

. .

DAVID GRAFTON SPENCER AND HIS WIFE, SUSAN, HAD BEEN divorced for several years when Susan heard a knock on the door of her townhome in Zephyr Cove, near Lake Tahoe. She opened it to find a uniformed sheriff's deputy. The deputy said he needed to see David about his mother, who was ill and requested that her son return to Los Angeles. Susan's town house was David's last known address. (The two had stayed close friends after the divorce, even rooming together for a short time. David had helped with the mortgage on Susan's dream townhome. She had asked David to leave when her boyfriend at the time discovered David's guns in her house and couldn't comprehend why she stayed close with her ex.) Susan told the deputy she remembered David saying that his mother was dead.

Afterward, Susan confronted David. He admitted that both his parents were alive. He refused to say exactly why they were es-tranged. He simply said that he hated his mother, and they didn't get along. David also confessed that he had two siblings, an older sister and younger brother, but he wanted nothing to do with them. Again, he offered no explanation. Susan was upset. She had caught David in a blatant lie—a major lie. She started to question how well she knew her ex. Then she reconsidered. Scientology founder L. Ron Hubbard had declared people who were openly opposed to the movement to be Suppressive Persons, or SPs. Disconnecting from SPs, including family members, was a prerequisite for spiritual growth. Susan was willing to give David the benefit of the doubt. If he said his mother was evil, Susan believed it.

Despite David's feelings about his mother, he agreed to live with her in L.A. But it was not a harmonious reunion, and he didn't stay with her long. After he moved out, David spoke of his mother in the past tense (she didn't die until 2003). Susan never again heard him mention his father.

BY THE MID-1990S, DAVID SPENCER was back in Los Angeles and living a life of solitude. His post-divorce years had been a journey of self-acceptance—a discovery of what life could be like not bogged down by what others thought. He leaned into Hubbard's teachings, focusing first on himself. He had moved on from the casinos and found a job working as a security guard at the NASA Jet Propulsion Laboratory in La Cañada Flintridge, outside Los Angeles. Even his relationship with Scientology changed. After David Miscavige took over as leader of the Church of Scientology, David became disillusioned with the organization. For a while he practiced with an independent scientologist who operated separately from the organization, and then cut himself loose to study Hubbard's original writings on his own.

A bachelor with frugal tastes, David had saved a modest amount of money and figured that he could retire early if he kept his expenses down. His biggest monthly cost would be rent. He found a two-bedroom in Monrovia, a sleepy suburb in the foothills of the San Gabriel Mountains. The Royal Park Apartments on Royal Oaks Drive were built in 1967 to house doctors at the nearby City of Hope cancer hospital. City of Hope had formed in 1913 as a tuberculosis sanatorium, developing into a leading cancer and, later, HIV/AIDS treatment center. But even as the City of Hope hospital evolved, the apartments on Royal Oaks Drive fell into disrepair. Doctors moved out, and drug dealers and sex workers moved in. Some residents installed special lights outside their doors, using different colors to indicate whether they were selling drugs or sex. Eventually, a new owner took over and cleaned up the vice, but left the dated appliances and Formica counters. David could get a good deal. At $1,075 per month, the modest apartment offered David an affordable place to live with plenty of extra space for his cats. He didn't mind that his ground-floor corner unit was run-down. He preferred old things. When something stopped working, he would fix it or live without. That's what he'd done when his prized Jeep died. Why spend the money on a new truck when his bicycle could get him wherever he wanted to go? He also was keen to avoid newer cars because they came with computer chips that would track his every move.

David's unit offered easy access to the main entrance off Royal Oaks Drive, where he could walk five minutes—ten if his back hurt—and be on the Duarte Recreation Trail, a flat paved three-mile path winding along the base of a hill. The hiking trail put David closer to nature and within view of a range of dry desert mountains that reminded him of the most cherished part of his childhood. Horses, dogs, deer, hummingbirds, even the occasional pet llama made appearances on the trail. David liked to walk early, before the sun became too intense.

At the end of his walks, David occasionally stopped by the leasing office to visit Diana Lynn. Diana had managed the property since 2004 and took a special interest in longer-term residents like David. By 2017, he was well into his seventies. His hairline had receded, and the remaining gray strands sprang out in two-inch waves. His ears had always been too large for his head but now they appeared cartoonlike against the half mane, their round shape contrasting with his pointed nose. But it was David's intellect more than his looks that stood out to Diana. He used words that felt anachronistic to Diana, words like *curmudgeon*, which might have described David. He didn't just drop the word into a conversation. David would make a lesson out of it: telling her when the word was first put into use, when it changed meaning, and when it disappeared from the lexicon. Diana liked smart men, and she thought David might have been a charmer, had he been fifty years younger.

Diana had planned to be a social worker before she entered apartment management, and she understood that older people required patience. She noticed that most people weren't willing to wait for David to get to his point when he told a story. Even she tended to zone out when he started talking about the animals he'd seen on his walk. He had a way of going from nature to literature to computing to spirituality and back again. In his mind, it was all connected. And he tended to repeat stories, like the one about his trick for surviving a chance encounter with a black bear. "Look at him straight," he would tell her. Do not scream or yell, he'd say, because that would frighten the bear and make him more likely to attack you. Diana was happy to indulge David's need to talk. (Given her preference for air-conditioning over the great outdoors, she was unlikely to ever encounter a bear.)

Diana believed she knew David pretty well, or as well as you could know a loner. He wasn't bitter like some of the older folks she'd met. Some people fight aging, pretending they can ward off mortality by changing their appearance or flashing the latest iPhone, but David wasn't a fighter. He seemed to have accepted his fate. Diana also had the impression that he had no family left. He had spoken to her of a grandfather but no one else. In fact, David didn't seem to talk to anyone besides her, Jesus (the building's super), and Susan. And since he was coming by the office less and less as his body slowed down with age, Diana suspected that David went days—maybe longer—without talking to anyone.

David didn't necessarily feel lonely, but his social network was small. And having few ties, especially as a man, put him at higher risk of dying prematurely. Researchers have found that social connections are essential to health; they matter more for longevity than even our genes. About a quarter of Americans aged sixty-five and older are considered socially isolated and therefore at higher risk of a range of diseases such as heart disease and dementia. Older adults—who lose family and friends as they age and have few opportunities to replenish their ranks—are more likely to end up living and dying alone. David was among them; his space in the world had been collapsing for years. First his number of friends dwindled, then his body shrank, followed by the radius he was able to travel. David had never been a tall man but with aging came the contraction of bones. He went from riding an adult bike five miles a day to riding a child's bike that better fit his smaller frame. Eventually he walked the bike to and from the store, using it mostly to transport groceries or cat litter. Inside the apartment, David steadied himself with a thick carved wooden walking stick, one of a collection he kept on hand.

When Diana worked late, Jesus would come into the office and make her a cup of tea, and the two would talk. Jesus lived next door to David and drove the older man to the store when he needed something too heavy or bulky to carry in his bike basket. Diana and Jesus wondered together who David may have been as a younger man. They knew he spent hours toiling on old computers and enjoyed talking with Jesus about how the first CPUs worked. David would rattle off facts about their size and computing power. Diana had the sense he'd been into the machines early on but, because he now seemed out of touch with technology, she figured he was probably self-taught and didn't have the money to keep up with the next generation of devices.

One thing David was not coy about was death. He talked often with Diana and Susan about his ideal death and what he would experience in the afterlife.

Once, while he was visiting Diana, he casually mentioned that when it was his time, he would make a final trek into the mountains. He would walk until he couldn't go any farther. He would find a spot to rest, and then just melt into the earth. He wanted his body to be left there to become part of an eternal cycle of composition and decomposition. He was nothing more than a leaf falling from one of California's coastal live oaks in autumn. His body would be recycled in the dark soil and dispersed in the breeze while his mind would go elsewhere.

He told Susan a different but equally specific story. During one of their occasional phone conversations, he said that his death would follow the Scientology script. David believed that every human was an immortal being who resided only temporarily in a physical body. When he died, David was convinced that his spiritual self would roam free. The idea sprang out of Hubbard's writings about the thetan, an eternal soul who bore a striking resemblance to a superhero. The goal of religion, according to Hubbard, was to exist spiritually in a way that was independent of the body. Once liberated from a body, the thetan could prosper and "rise to greater heights."

Part of Hubbard's marketing cleverness was that a person didn't need superhuman physical strength or the ability to fly to become free. They only needed to learn to conquer their mind. Hubbard tapped into human experiences that science had yet to explain and offered logical, if implausible, ways of understanding them. It was more philosophy than theology, with roots in Hubbard's earlier science fiction writings, and it appealed to a generation of men like David who saw themselves as self-taught intellectuals searching for spiritual enlightenment. According to journalist Lawrence Wright, Hubbard suggested that Scientology could "awaken individuals to the joyful truth of their immortal state" and "rescue humanity from its inevitable doom."

David was most intrigued by what Hubbard had taught about exteriorization, a process of intentionally leaving one's body to explore other universes. Hubbard argued that many, if not most, humans had so-called out-of-body experiences, and that Scientology could teach people how to harness this power to liberate their inner thetan. In *The Creation of Human Ability*, Hubbard wrote that with guidance, the thetan could be instructed to explore all elements of the universe through a "Grand Tour" that would take him inside of black stars and down plumes on the sun—all while the body stayed on earth.

David practiced. He would sit in a chair and think of himself in the right corner of the room. Then he imagined himself in the left corner of the room. Hubbard wrote that in about half of cases, a person could exteriorize himself with a simple command: "Be three feet back of your head." The exercise was one way for David to imagine what his afterlife would be like, when his thetan would be released from its earthbound vessel.

If others in Scientology dreamed of their thetan selves living in extraterrestrial grandeur, David's vision was much simpler. When he left his mortal body, he imagined floating in a canoe with his cats. He believed he would be in his own universe, one that he'd created, paddling through endless placid waters alongside his feline friends. He would create his own cosmos and live alone in it, by choice.

On the morning of May 23, 2017, Diana asked Jesus to inspect David's water heater. The super knocked. There was no answer, but he could hear the cats meowing loudly inside. Jesus realized he hadn't seen David in days, since taking the older man to the grocery store to buy cat litter. He called Diana and asked for permission to enter, which she gave. Jesus was supposed to say "Management here" after he opened the door, but the overpowering smell hit him before he could say anything. He moved to the bedroom and quickly noticed David's naked body on the carpeted floor, behind a small table with a thirteen-inch television and stack of DVDs. The old man's eyes stared into an abyss, ants crawling over the open sockets.

Jesus had no way of knowing if David was in his private universe canoeing with his cats. But he would have a hard time sleeping that night, alone in his apartment next door, knowing that David had been dead for God knew how many days.

6.

INVESTIGATION

..

KRISTINA MCGUIRE STEERED AN UNMARKED WHITE SEDAN out of the parking lot of the Los Angeles County Medical Examiner–Coroner's complex, on the western edge of the LAC+USC medical center, just north of Boyle Heights. Kristina, a death scene investigator, worked out of the Forensic Science Center, a flat stucco building tucked behind a more impressive brick structure, the former administration building of the old Los Angeles General Hospital. The brick building had earned the strange designation as a "California Bucket List" destination on a *Los Angeles Times* travel guide because of its gift shop selling monogrammed mugs, caps, beach towels with body outlines, and, in the weeks before Halloween, body bags. The medical examiner's complex was close to three key arteries through the city, and Kristina headed east on I-10.

She had only the most basic information, typed on a single sheet of paper on her metal clipboard: "Decedent lived in an apartment on Royal Oaks Drive in Monrovia, CA. White, male, born 1/22/1942." Kristina knew from her supervisor that the case was unlikely to involve foul play. Instead, she was headed to what investigators call a "trash run"—when an elderly person, often a hoarder or a recluse, is found in a neglected dwelling, after decomposition has set in and a foul smell has alerted a neighbor. Jesus's discovery of David's body set the wheels of L.A.'s bureaucracy in motion.

There were three distinct county agencies that handled the bodies and estates of the dead, as well as notifying next of kin, and often their work overlapped. Kristina's employer, the Los Angeles County Medical Examiner–Coroner, was responsible for investigating suspicious deaths—anything violent or unexpected. They were also called in when there was no doctor to sign a death certificate, likely because a person was not an active participant in the healthcare system. This was the case with David. By state law, in these situations, a deputy medical examiner would determine the cause of death and issue the death certificate. In 2019, 64,517 deaths were reported in the county; the medical examiner's office was called in to investigate 27 percent (17,940) of them. Most of these did not actually fall under the office's jurisdiction or were handled without an on-site investigation. But in a quarter of the cases (more than 4,000), investigators like Kristina were dispatched to the scene of death. They completed a preliminary physical examination of the deceased, collected evidence and personal property, took photographs, and conducted interviews with neighbors and relatives. Their job was to gather clues that could help determine who the deceased was and how they died (information later shared with a pathologist). Investigators were also expected to notify next of kin.

The second agency involved in handling deaths in Los Angeles was the Office of Decedent Affairs. Like the medical examiner's office, the Office of Decedent Affairs was under the bureaucratic umbrella of the Los Angeles County Department of Health Services. Families often confused the two agencies, but they had different mandates. Whereas the medical examiner's office dealt with suspicious or indeterminate deaths, the Office of Decedent Affairs handled more run-of-the-mill deaths—those that occurred in nursing and convalescent homes, hospitals, and residences. This office also oversaw the county crematorium and cemetery in Boyle Heights.

The public administrator's office, the third agency, operated under the purview of the County of Los Angeles Treasurer and Tax Collector. The office had opened during the California gold rush to intervene when miners died so that others couldn't steal their gold and tools, shortchanging their heirs. In the time since, the public administrator had become the protector of people's property when they died without known descendants or a will, or when a neutral party needed to mediate between relatives feuding over an estate. Their work involved liaising with the medical examiner and the Office of Decedent Affairs, as well as a number of other county agencies. Often, the public administrator's office conducted its own scene investigations, similar to the medical examiner's, but with a focus on finding information about assets and next of kin rather than determining cause of death. The overlap often caused confusion—most Angelenos tended to lump everything under the medical examiner, assuming, probably from television shows, that "the coroner" was in charge of all deaths.

Kristina had first dreamed of becoming a coroner investigator when she was ten and watched the 1976 TV miniseries *Helter Skelter* about the Manson murders. In an early scene, a detective accompanied Roman Polanski's business manager through a blood-soaked house to identify the victims. When the manager saw the butchered body of Sharon Tate, he ran outside and threw up in some rosebushes. Kristina turned to her mom and said, "I want to see what he saw." She was fascinated by what people were capable of doing to each other—and themselves.

When she reached high school, Kristina decided to test herself. She spent a couple of days shadowing forensics staff in Kern County, north of Los Angeles. Autopsies fascinated her. She would have become a pathologist but was too daunted by organic chemistry to go into medicine.

Kristina double-parked beside an unmanned police car outside the two-story Royal Park Apartments complex. She exited the vehicle and slipped on her black L.A. County Coroner jacket, then retrieved a brown leather bag containing the gear she would need to inspect David's body: a digital camera, rubber gloves, measuring tape, notebook, pens. She took a sip of water from an oversized cup and placed it back in the car's cupholder. Like a lot of investigators, the idea of eating or drinking at death scenes made her stomach churn.

Kristina was, as she put it, "built like a linebacker," and as she made her way toward the courtyard, her thick-soled black boots crunched against the concrete. She left the shoes at the office in the evenings, to avoid contamination at home. Her clothes were as practical as her shoes. Everything was machine-washable and durable: black slacks with a high polyester count and cotton tops with the occasional burst of hot pink. Her dark hair was pulled tightly into a bun, another pragmatic choice that also revealed a small, jeweled neck piercing.

Two uniformed officers from the Monrovia Police Department stood outside David's apartment. Kristina followed them inside, stepping over the Snoopy-themed welcome mat and stopping to look around the stuffy living room. The windows had been closed since David died, and the sour smell of decomposition had already permeated the carpet. If the odor affected Kristina, she didn't show it. She was aware that the male police officers were watching her every move, and she refused to be intimidated. Her bosses were men, most of her colleagues were men, and the police officers she dealt with were almost always men. She used humor to diffuse the tension and show she was game. When police officers told her dead bodies freaked them out, Kristina mocked them: "You stick your hands up someone's butt looking for drugs. When I go into people they don't talk back!"

Kristina skirted two child-size bicycles disassembled on the carpeted floor next to wrenches, ratchets, bolts, and other tools. Plastic containers of cat litter were stacked throughout the apartment. Pasadena Humane, a local animal shelter, had already picked up David's cats.

Kristina moved to the kitchen and cleared part of the counter to record and bag any items she would take with her. She slipped on two pairs of rubber gloves and walked down the short hallway to the bedroom on the right, where David was naked on the floor with his legs slightly splayed. He looked as though he had been standing up before falling straight back. Kristina noticed his yellow tint and wondered aloud if David was an alcoholic. One of the officers said he checked the fridge and there was only ice cream. They also told her that, according to neighbors, David Spencer had not been seen since last Monday, eight days ago, enough time for fluids to leak and the body to start to bloat.

Kristina was soon joined by forensic attendant Michael Sanchez, who would transport David's body back to the medical examiner's facility and assist Kristina in her investigation. Kristina noticed a lump in David's neck and worried that it might pop, but Sanchez didn't think so. They volleyed theories about David's health and possible causes of death. Sanchez, who also worked as an instructor in the emergency medical technician program at UCLA, thought that there might have been congestive heart failure because of some swelling in David's legs. He also wondered whether the decedent had been overweight at some point because there was a lot of loose skin. Together they wrapped David in a white sheet, then slid him onto a clear plastic tarp, each grabbing an end of the tarp to carry the body to a gurney set up in the front doorway. They lifted David onto the gurney and tied the ends of the tarp around him before placing him in a black body bag. Kristina asked one of the officers to use his boot to steady the gurney. When homicide is suspected, they are careful about DNA contamination, but not in a trash run. The bigger risk was disease. (One colleague had been pricked by a discarded needle at a homeless camp, requiring him to get tested for HIV.) "Don't use your hand," Kristina advised the officer.

Sanchez and Kristina were about to take him through the complex when Kristina heard children. She asked one of the officers to check where they were. "I don't want to scar anybody." When the coast was clear, Sanchez wheeled David to the van.

The two police officers kept themselves busy by walking around the apartment and looking through David's belongings. One of the officers went into the bedroom and checked out a stack of DVDs.

He returned to the living room and said, "Looks like he had a pretty hefty porn collection."

"You surprised?" the other officer replied. He didn't think it strange that loner men sought excitement in porn. *Multiple Chicks on One Dick* was one of the few items in the apartment not covered in dust.

When Sanchez returned from the van, Kristina was going through David's checkbook in the kitchen. A handful of onions, a bag of potatoes, and several cans of cat food covered the counter. Kristina looked around, wondering who David Spencer had been. The apartment was grimy and dark. The stovetop was too cluttered to have been recently used, and the small fridge looked better suited to a college dorm room than the kitchen of a grown man. The sink was dirty, but the dishes stacked on one side were clean. The micro-wave was clearly the newest appliance in the place. On a sideboard David had fastened a vise and meat grinder. He had also screwed a homemade wooden handle to a rusted cast-iron pot. When San-chez saw the contraptions in the kitchen and the bikes on the living room floor, he commented to Kristina, "This guy is a hobbyist." He imagined David spending his days alone with his tools.

Kristina switched gears to look for what she called the "impor-tant stuff," like birthday cards and letters. Greeting cards are trea-sure maps for scene investigators because they point to family and friends—people who might care enough about the decedent to claim the body. A pile of cards sat on one of the desks, but they were all generic season's greetings from banks and other institutions. There wasn't much else in the front half of the apartment except stacks of books that lay flat on a small wooden bookshelf: a well-thumbed paperback copy of *Dr. Atkins' New Diet Revolution,* a Jap-anese cookbook, and a large coffee table book with paintings by the French impressionist Pierre-Auguste Renoir. She did not find any records of medical visits. If David had been under regular medical care, she might have been able to convince his physician to sign the death certificate and write down a cause of death without an au-topsy.

Kristina moved to the two back bedrooms. The closets in both rooms were fairly empty, especially on the upper shelves. She realized that it would be hard for David to reach anything high up. A laundry basket in the main bedroom contained unfolded clean clothes, including underwear. The bedroom closet had a well-cared-for black leather motorcycle jacket, and the other bedroom closet held only three suits. One was plaid; all looked like they were from the 1970s. There was an empty blood pressure monitor box in the spare bedroom and a bottle of glucose tablets next to David's twin bed.

When she moved closer to the bed, Kristina stopped and shouted at the officers in the other room. "I got a 911!" When they entered, Kristina pointed to a pistol by the bed stand. She then found more guns, including a .22 and a semiautomatic, all loaded and stored in unlocked soft cases. "He was gonna kill anybody who tried to steal his bicycle," Kristina said with a laugh. "I like this guy." One of the officers sighed loudly. Booking evidence, like weapons, meant more work for them. "I just want to keep Monrovia safe," Kristina joked, knowing that the officer was annoyed by her discovery.

The only personal correspondence Kristina found was a letter from Susan, postmarked three years earlier. Kristina put it in a small brown paper bag, along with a tattered Scientology ID she found in the apartment. The ID could explain why David didn't seem to have a regular physician. Scientology's "mind over matter" philosophy discouraged seeking medical care and encouraged members to wean themselves off prescription drugs. The police officers had interviewed David's neighbors before Kristina arrived. The officers reported to her that he was Native American, but Kristina found no sign of such heritage. All that was left was the paperwork, much of which she could complete back at the office.

Kristina sealed the apartment and climbed back into her white sedan for the twenty-two-mile ride back to the medical examiner's facility in Boyle Heights. The drive was nothing compared with her 111-mile round-trip commute every day. She had purchased a three-bedroom house in Lancaster, close to her sister and mother. Deaths like David's had a way of reminding her what mattered in life, and Kristina valued family above all else.

Kristina imagined death everywhere, her mind often landing in this dark place on long drives after scene investigations. She would find herself thinking about other cases where the decedent had been dead for days, weeks, or sometimes months before anyone noticed. She remembered one house in the suburbs where the decedent had been dead for two months. It was a nice neighborhood, but no one said anything when the man's mail started to pile up. She made a mental note never to use lights on a timer. Neighbors won't know you're dead if your lights turn on and off on a regular schedule.

Kristina's landmarks were not highway intersections or iconic Hollywood buildings but memories of dead bodies. Passing a water treatment plant, she remembered a woman's body that had been swept with other debris against a grate after her boyfriend had dumped her through a manhole. Off the highway, she glanced at a dilapidated house that still seemed inhabited and flashed back to a drug overdose. A little farther up, she wondered whether the case of the body burned beyond recognition by the side of the road had ever been solved.

The morbidity carried into her personal life. When she was hiking with friends in Malibu, she saw a group of teens climb a fence and clamber down a rocky cliff at the base of a waterfall. Kristina turned to her fellow hikers, as they watched a particularly clumsy girl try to get down and said, "Okay, when she falls, she's going to fracture her skull on that rock." Her friends looked at her, startled. When a friend posted a picture on Facebook of her newborn swaddled and face down on a blanket, Kristina wrote: "Flip that baby over before you suffocate her." She could no longer enjoy the beach because she had seen too many people pulled out of the water, lifeless. She realized she had become a killjoy, but she couldn't help herself. Every day, she saw how life could end in a millisecond.

Back in the office at Boyle Heights, Kristina typed up her case notes. She was required to notify David's relatives. She searched Accurint—a database compiled by LexisNexis that contained personal information collated from public records, including addresses, real estate transactions, arrest records, and potential family members—but did not find anyone related to David. Having come up empty, she looked at the envelope with Susan Spencer's name and used Accurint to find a Nevada address and phone number.

She reached Susan at home. Diana Lynn, the apartment manager, had already alerted Susan of David's death, soon after Jesus discovered him. Susan was eager to help, but Kristina quickly figured out that Susan was an ex-wife and therefore not legally responsible for the body. Even though Susan was one of the people closest to David, divorce had removed her from the next-of-kin chain. Susan assured Kristina that David had no children. Kristina typed in her notes that Susan mentioned a possible sister, now estranged, but she couldn't recall a name (there was nothing about a brother). Susan also told Kristina that David was a veteran and had Native American blood. Kristina thanked Susan for the information and added the details to the case notes.

The medical examiner's office encouraged its investigators to notify next of kin in person, but it was the most difficult part of an already difficult job, and many didn't comply. Kristina remembered a seventeen-year-old who died in a car accident on Mother's Day. His birthday had been the day before and he had been hanging out with friends. His SAT test-prep books and college applications were on the back seat when he crashed the car. Kristina knocked on the door of his house. When his mother answered, she thought Kristina's uniform meant she was law enforcement and her boy had been arrested. Once she realized the truth, she went into shock. First, she began to laugh, saying that she had no time for this because she was in the middle of selling her house. And then suddenly she collapsed. Kristina held the mother for a long time and shared her cellphone number. The mother called her the next Christmas talking about her son as if he were still there with her.

In an ideal world, Kristina would have dug deeper into David's life and exhausted all possible leads, but she was needed on another case: a three-car accident with fatalities. Kristina quickly copied the paperwork containing all available contact information and added it to David's file. She highlighted in red that David was a veteran, then she transferred David's case to her department's notifications unit. Her coworkers would have to locate and notify David's next of kin.

· ·

A FEW DAYS AFTER THEIR FINAL LUNCH, CLARA TEXTED BOBBY, "What are you doing on the 4th of July?"

Bobby's reply was curt. "I'm alone."

Clara didn't know how to respond.

Bobby had only been in his new vet-subsidized apartment for a week, but he'd already befriended some of the other residents. On July 5, when a group of them knocked on his door and received no answer, they figured Bobby was taking a nap and left. More days passed and still no one had seen Bobby. A nurse was scheduled to retrieve a medication cart and entered the studio, where she found Bobby in his bed, without a pulse. How long he'd been dead was difficult to decipher because the air-conditioning had likely slowed the natural cycle of decomposition. It was July 8, 2019.

Police and paramedics were dispatched and, once the death was confirmed, the responding officer tried to call Clara. She was listed as Bobby's emergency contact. Clara was at work and, seeing an unknown number, chose not to pick up. The police officer found Bobby's cellphone and used it to try Clara again. This time she answered. When the officer told her that Bobby was dead, Clara froze. She knew this day was coming, but she wasn't expecting it to come so soon. At work, fearful that others would see her crying, she hung up and ran out of the office. She spent the rest of the afternoon sitting in the sun alone and weeping.

Back in El Monte, the police officer started looking for other family to notify. He scrolled through Bobby's phone and found a contact listed as "Son." The man who answered confirmed that yes, he was Bobby Ray Hanna's son. His name was Donnell Wells.

Encouraged by New Directions therapists, Bobby had sought to make amends with the people he had left behind in Gary, Indiana. Bobby was especially interested in connecting with his son, whom he had never met. In 2011, while in New Directions, he sent a message through Facebook, writing, "I don't know how to say this, but I think I'm your dad."

Donnell was shopping inside a Sam's Club in Indiana when he heard the ping from the app indicating a new message—a message that thirty-three-year-old Donnell had long ago given up on ever receiving. Bobby had followed up his first message with another one offering the name of Donnell's mother and details about where she had grown up, to prove he was who he said he was. Donnell scrutinized the profile picture. "Yeah, this is my dad because we look exactly alike." He turned to his girlfriend, who was standing next to him in the aisle, and asked her to look at the photo. She confirmed the resemblance.

Donnell believed the man messaging him was his father, but he wanted to be sure. He showed the messages to his mother, Deborah. "Yes," she told him. "That's your dad. He found you." Donnell had mixed feelings, excitement but also a little resentment. *Why did it take this long?*

Years before, when Donnell first joined Facebook, he had tried to find his birth father. He knew his mother had lived across the street from Bobby as a teen and had been madly in love and pregnant when, without any warning, a nineteen-year-old Bobby stuffed his dirty laundry into a duffel bag and joined the air force. Deborah kept newspaper clippings of Bobby's days as a high school track star, leaving them out from time to time for Donnell to see, to the annoyance of her parents. They were furious at Bobby. When he returned to Gary, they forbade him from seeing their daughter and, later, their grandson. But that was decades ago. Donnell felt that if his dad had wanted to find him earlier, he could have. Donnell had even given his number to some of Bobby's old friends in Gary, with instructions for Bobby to call if he wanted. Years passed and still Donnell heard nothing.

After Bobby finally established contact with Donnell through Facebook, he made an effort to visit his son. In 2013, while on tour with the New Directions choir, Bobby took a side trip to Gary. He saw his sisters for the first time in decades and drove by the house where Michael Jackson had lived. When his family decided to hold a cookout, Bobby invited Donnell. Bobby's sisters couldn't get over how much the father and son looked alike. They squeezed Donnell, telling him they felt like they were hugging a younger version of Bobby. Donnell returned the love by introducing his two daughters, who were eleven and eighteen. Bobby lit up like a roman candle when he saw the girls. He and Clara had never had children, but not for lack of want on Bobby's part. He spent as much time as he could at the cookout with his new "grandbabies" before he had to leave early to rejoin the choir. He hugged Donnell and told him that it had been the best day of his life. He promised to make up for lost time.

Bobby and Donnell settled into a rhythm of weekly phone calls. Bobby told his son about growing up in Gary in the 1960s alongside the Jackson kids. He bragged that his grandmother—Donnell's great-grandmother—had done the hair of Michael Jackson's mother, Katherine. In the bleak Rust Belt city, the Jacksons were akin to royalty. Bobby shared how he would try to play basketball with Michael and the other Jackson boys, but the siblings weren't allowed to play outside. They were too busy rehearsing under the watchful eye of their famously strict father.

Donnell shared some of his girlfriend problems and the struggle of working seven days a week for minimum wage. Like his father, Donnell had spent time overseas. His mother had sent him to live for a year with an uncle who was stationed in Germany. Donnell said he was headed down a "dark road," tempted by the fast life that had sucked in many young men in Gary, when his mother intervened. While in Europe, Donnell traveled, visiting WWII museums and vacationing in Italy. "I'm glad she exposed me to that different scene, different vibe. Life is not all about this." Donnell told his father that the experience changed him. "I became a whole different man." Bobby could relate to his son's dreams of escaping Gary, as well as the way he romanticized Europe. Bobby hoped that his son could turn his life around sooner than he had.

WHEN THE POLICE OFFICER called Donnell in 2019 to notify him of his father's death, Donnell felt he had crashed into a brick wall. He couldn't think clearly, couldn't comprehend how the man he had known as his dad for eight years and had seen only twice was suddenly gone. He had been robbed of a father a second time. Donnell did not know how sick Bobby had been—he had wanted to visit Bobby in Los Angeles, but Bobby discouraged him.

Donnell had no one to share his grief with. He and his girlfriend had broken up, and he had seen Bobby's sisters only a handful of times. He knew about Clara because Bobby had talked about her, but Donnell had never spoken to her.

As Donnell tried to process the news of his father's death, he faced a litany of decisions. The apartment manager in El Monte needed him to authorize transport of Bobby's body quickly, before it became noxious. The manager recommended a nearby funeral home, Funeraria Del Angel West Covina. Donnell knew nothing about Los Angeles or how to hire a company there to handle his dad's body. Perhaps more important, Donnell didn't know how he would pay for a funeral. He was making $10.50 an hour working in a grocery store and could barely pay his monthly bills, let alone cover a steep out-of-the-blue expense like this. Adding to his stress, the apartment manager needed someone to come in and clear out Bobby's belongings. Donnell would have to figure that out later, he said. As for his father's body, he gave the manager permission to call the local funeral home, telling himself he could put off thinking about the expense. He planned to get his father cremated and assumed that the U.S. Department of Veterans Affairs would cover the full costs.

Donnell also wasn't sure that it was his responsibility alone to figure out what to do. He wasn't Bobby's only son. Donnell knew of a half brother, Isaac, who worked somewhere in Minnesota as a fashion model and was only one month younger than Donnell. Donnell's mother had told him he might have a sibling somewhere, but Donnell hadn't known a name, and they'd never met. He chuckled when he heard how close in age they were. It meant Bobby had left not one but two women in Gary pregnant when he took off for the air force. Donnell called his half brother, but Isaac wasn't interested in helping with a funeral for a man he'd met once. Donnell was on his own, again.

· ·

LENA'S BODY LAY UNMOVED.

Le Bleu Chateau, like most nursing homes, lacked refrigeration facilities to store bodies or vehicles to transport them—a considerable problem when you are in the business of boarding older adults. The facility needed to get Lena's body out before decomposition set in and the smell became a nuisance. Usually, a nursing home would call the emergency contact in a patient's file and the family would arrange for a private funeral home to remove a loved one's corpse. But no one had visited Lena in years. Her family had long ago stopped returning calls. Nursing homes knew that private mortuaries preferred not to pick up bodies unless they obtained family authorization. So, Le Bleu Chateau did what most nursing homes do in similar circumstances—they turned to the county.

Every day, long-term-care facilities across Los Angeles County request help from the Office of Decedent Affairs. Private facilities are supposed to notify relatives when one of their residents dies, but that can take days and sometimes weeks, especially for older patients with no emergency contacts listed. These dead patients occupy beds that could be generating income, and the sooner a county employee ferries a body away, the sooner a nursing home can start charging again. Patients pay, corpses don't.

The Office of Decedent Affairs operated from the basement of the main county hospital, the LAC+USC medical center. The six-hundred-bed public teaching hospital was the largest healthcare provider in Los Angeles County, serving the county's lowest-income populations. Only 4.5 percent of their patients were privately insured (compared to the California average of 28 percent); the hospital shouldered the financial burden of the rest. By default, the Office of Decedent Affairs, itself stretched financially, interacted mostly with poor families. The office received about eleven bodies per day, three from within the hospital and eight from outside. Most of the outside cases came from nursing and convalescent homes. Staff then coordinated with the public administrator to be sure that families were notified and to determine whether assets existed for private burial.

In 2012, the year Lena died, the Office of Decedent Affairs paid its cemetery caretaker, Albert Gaskin, overtime wages to pick up bodies and bring them back to the morgue. He knew from these retrievals that nursing homes didn't always notify next of kin. Once, wheeling a body out of a nursing home, he ran into the dead patient's surprised relatives. They were bringing in a new TV, unaware that their loved one had died and that the nursing home had called Decedent Affairs to remove the body.

Albert backed the van carrying Lena's body into the loading dock at the LAC+USC building. He handed the paperwork to one of the office staff, then opened the door to the refrigerated space that held the county's unwanted bodies. He slid Lena inside. Morgues inevitably take up a hospital's least desirable space, often, like at LAC+USC, in the basement. Unlike the cavernous crypt at the medical examiner's office, with bodies stacked on racks, the county morgue had metal roll-in storage cabinets that held individual bodies and trailer-like refrigerated buildings in the parking lot for any overflow. After placing Lena in one of the cabinets, Albert closed the stainless steel door.

What would happen next with Lena's body depended on family and money. The easiest way to avoid a common grave was for a legal family member to claim the body and hire a private funeral home to organize a burial or cremation. They could also pay the county's cremation fee of $365 and collect the ashes. If neither happened, and Lena's estate had enough funds to pay for a private burial, the public administrator's office could arrange for one. It was up to the Office of Decedent Affairs, in conjunction with the public administrator, to decide how to proceed.

While Lena's body remained in the basement crypt, staff in the two offices went to work. The first step was to reach out to Lena's next of kin.

LENA CECILIA BERUMEN WAS born into a Mexican family with at least nine and as many as seventeen children (the genealogical record is unclear). Her parents, Eliseo and Josefina Berumen, had married in 1889 in Tepetongo, Zacatecas, and moved to the United States around 1905. Some of the children stayed in Mexico, some moved with their parents, and some, like Lena, were born in the United States. Whatever the actual number of Berumen children, family lore was that Lena grew up alongside five siblings, including three girls (Consuelo, Mary, and Anna) and two boys (Guillermo/William and Martin). Lena was the youngest daughter. She was closest to her sisters Mary and Anna, bonds that deepened after they became orphans in their early twenties. In 1934, their father—who had worked as a fruit vendor in East Los Angeles, where the girls grew up—was struck by a speeding motorist and dragged 125 feet. He was buried in L.A.'s Catholic Calvary Cemetery. The girls' mother suffered a mental breakdown soon after and was institutionalized. The sisters had no other family nearby: Their brothers were incarcerated, dead, estranged, or living in Mexico. Lena, Mary, and Anna were left to fend for themselves.

Mary felt responsible for the younger Lena. The sisters had grown up as Jehovah's Witnesses, and Mary became a pioneer, committed to making weekly rounds to spread their gospel. Lena boarded with Mary in the tight-knit Mexican community of

Chavez Ravine before it was razed to make way for Dodger Stadium. They worked together as laundresses, sewing their own petticoats and dresses to wear, and would go out at night together. Though Ben Brown, Jr., at first courted Mary, he eventually shifted his attention to Lena, and when they married and moved to Hawthorne, ties between the sisters became strained. After Ben Jr. passed, the sisters reconnected, keeping in touch by phone, until Mary, who then lived in San Francisco, died from breast cancer in 1971. She left one daughter, Marlene Avila, and two sisters, Lena and the older Anna (mother of Rudy and Marjorie).

Court records indicate that the county morgue mailed a letter to Marjorie (Rudy would receive a mailed notification of Lena's death from a different county agency the following year). The letter informed Marjorie that Lena was at the county morgue and that she would be cremated by the county if Marjorie didn't respond within thirty days. No one contacted Teena Colebrook, who still hadn't shaken the guilt of letting Lena down. Teena's role in Lena's life was no longer visible in the records.

Across town, a deputy for the public administrator glanced at the file for Lena Brown and saw that, because she had been under public guardianship before her death, everything about her assets was well documented.

The public administrator and public guardian shared office space at the Hall of Records in downtown Los Angeles, three miles west of the LAC+USC medical center in Boyle Heights. The public administrator deputy pulled Lena's assets up on her computer screen. In June 2004, Lena's account had been flush with $148,726.66, funds that had come from her lifelong savings and the 2003 sale of her house to Philip Kirkland. That year she was also receiving a monthly Social Security check of $569, which increased over the years to $759; in 2010, she received an extra $347 a month in Supplemental Security Income. Yet by the time of her death in 2012, Lena's Bank of America account had been drawn down to zero.

The detailed list of charges to Lena's bank account, which totaled hundreds of pages over the years, told a story about the cost of growing old in America, with medical costs compounded by the drain of an expensive legal system. Rudy had used Lena's funds to pay for her food, her DirecTV, and a onetime subscription to the *Daily Breeze* newspaper. He had also bought her a couch, a refrigerator, and clothes from J. C. Penney. These expenses, totaling $17,236, included four $200 payments directly to Lena for spending money, three in 2006 and one in 2009.

Had Lena been able to live on her own and keep her expenses down, she likely would have remained in the middle class. But Lena, like many older people, eventually needed round-the-clock care. Estimates are that 70 percent of Americans over sixty-five will require long-term supportive care and, of those, 48 percent will need paid care (such as a home caregiver, nursing home, or residential facility; the other 22 percent rely mainly on relatives). The majority of Americans do little or no planning for future care needs.

Lena's monthly bill for the caregiver who came to her home prior to her move to Le Bleu Chateau came to $1,120. Over three years and nine months, this cost Lena's estate over $44,795. Rudy also allocated money to pay for a medical alert service, medications, and doctor's visits. Then, when Lena entered Le Bleu Chateau in February 2008, Rudy paid the facility $2,400 every month with a check drawn from Lena's account. Doctor's copayments, diapers, and prescription medicines that Lena needed while living at Le Bleu Chateau were billed separately. From the time she left her home in February 2008 until she died in July 2012, Lena had been charged more than $95,000 for her medical care.

While he was still conservator, Rudy had transferred $4,890.60 from Lena's account to his own. Perturbed by Rudy's siphoning of Lena's funds, Leona Shapiro wrote in her 2010 report to the probate council that Rudy's payment was made without court order, and if it was for Lena's benefit, there should have been written justification. In response, Rudy's attorney acknowledged in court records that the "petitioner did not have order to pay himself, but he is waiving his fee. His services for the period in question would far exceed what he paid to himself." The court did not pursue the matter, and the money stayed with Rudy.

When the public guardian took over, the county charged fees for their services (about $11,000), as did attorneys, trustees, and the probate investigator. Rudy's lawyers submitted bills for $40,216.50, stating it was a "reasonable amount" for their work. Not all of it would be paid—the public guardian had determined that Lena's savings were insufficient—but an unspecified amount went to the law firm that had represented Rudy. The county counsel billed at a rate of $295/hour. Their total compensation came to $5,192. Leona Shapiro charged what she called her pro bono rate of $125/hour, roughly one-third of the $350–$450 per hour she normally charged, which amounted to $5,502.50. Altogether, attorneys billed Lena's dwindling estate over $61,000.

Before Lena died, Shapiro, sorting through her finances, also discovered $8,500 in a trust fund. The money had been paid by Philip Kirkland when he settled the court case for the house. Those settlement funds were never transferred to Lena's bank account. Rudy by then had stopped communicating with his own lawyers, and they put the check in a trust before it expired. Shapiro recommended to the court that they keep a portion of the funds for emergencies. The bulk of the money ($6,000) went to Rudy's attorneys. In the final accounting, Lena had no funds left for a private funeral.

Lena's accounts had been depleted by the cost of living a long life and having no family to manage her estate. But her fall into poverty late in life is not uncommon.

Americans over sixty-five are automatically entitled to Medicare, even if they have billions in the bank. For uninsured Americans, it may be the first time they qualify for health insurance. The program allows these Americans to receive much-delayed medical care, including cancer screenings that lead to more diagnoses and improved mortality rates. But there's one major—and intentional—gap. Medicare, the largest social program for older adults in the United States, doesn't pay for long-term stays in nursing or convalescent homes (though it does cover incurred hospital and medical costs). The average monthly cost of nursing home care in California is $9,794 (above the national average of $7,908).

Medicaid, on the other hand, will pay for long-term care, provided the enrollee has no funds to pay for private health insurance. Medicaid is jointly run by both the states and the federal government, and the benefits vary from state to state; in California it is called Medi-Cal. The critical difference between Medicare and Medicaid is that while Medicare serves everyone over sixty-five, Medicaid is an assistance program serving low-income people of all ages.

Medicaid has grown into the country's largest funder of nursing home care. People over sixty-five make up only 8 percent of the California Medicaid population, yet they use 19 percent of the program's resources. About one-third of that money goes to long-term care.

To qualify for nursing home benefits through Medicaid, Lena would have had to prove that she had no available funds. That's the reason Shapiro recommended that Lena keep only a "small portion" of the $8,500 from the trust fund for emergencies. Shapiro was concerned that a larger amount would make Lena ineligible for Medicaid benefits. Some people start moving their assets to relatives long before they anticipate needing nursing home care, deliberately bankrupting themselves. But for most patients, the policy gap means that they will be forced to exhaust their funds to pay for nursing home care, ensuring that they die penniless.

Shapiro was confident that the outcome for Lena would have been the same even if she had sold the house for more. Shapiro knew that any extra money would have been eaten up by the nursing home or lawyers' fees. As it was, she thought Lena was fortunate that Le Bleu Chateau had allowed her to stay once she switched over to Medicaid, since Medicaid pays about 25 percent less than private insurance. Shapiro knew of nursing homes that turned people out once public funds kicked in. The practice was illegal but common—it was as simple as calling an ambulance and sending residents to hospitals and then refusing to readmit them. Despite Rudy's missteps, Shapiro didn't fault him. When she compared this case to others, Lena had at least avoided a disorienting move to a lesser facility in her final days.

When Rudy was Lena's conservator, he could have earmarked funds for a burial service or directed Le Bleu Chateau to purchase burial insurance—but he hadn't planned that far in advance. And by the time Lena died, four years after the death of his wife and three years after the death of his son, Rudy had retreated into life as an urban hermit, refusing to answer the phone or door. He hid in his house, a bell attached to the outer gate to alert two loud blue-mottled Australian cattle dogs of any visitors.

None of Lena's family seemed to realize they were on the verge of repeating history. Martin Berumen, Lena's younger brother, had worked as a laborer in Los Angeles after their parents died. He married in 1938, but the couple had little time to build a life because, two years later, Martin was arrested for selling drugs and sent to San Quentin State Prison. After that, he lived as a drifter, wandering through Northern California. In 1966, Martin was sleeping at a construction site of a freeway extension near Watsonville, southeast of Santa Cruz, when he was run over by a bulldozer and crushed to death. Martin was buried in an unmarked grave in Santa Cruz. If Lena's family didn't step up soon, she would be the second in the family to be buried in a potter's field.

As the Office of Decedent Affairs waited for Marjorie or Rudy to respond, Lena's body remained in the morgue, a thick sheet of plastic wrapped around her, the temperature a chilly 36 degrees.

. .

NORA AND PASTOR HUDDLE SAW MIDGE'S FACEBOOK POST ON Thursday, February 4, 2016, the day after she wrote it. They knew that Midge had dialysis on Thursdays, and they agreed that Huddle would go by the house in the evening to check on her and bring dinner. He knocked on the door at six-thirty P.M., but there was no answer. He called Nora.

"I don't hear Midge. What do I do?"

"Let her sleep." Nora knew that dialysis sapped Midge's energy. "Put her stuff in her refrigerator, and I'll check on her in the morning." There was no lock on the main entrance to the apartment, only to Midge's bedroom. Huddle put the food in the fridge and left.

If anyone would know how to handle Midge's funk, it was Nora. She'd helped Midge in her most vulnerable moments, bathing her when she couldn't shower on her own and sitting by her bedside on nights when she didn't want to be alone.

On Friday morning, Nora used her key to enter the bedroom. When she entered the small room, she found Midge nude on the bed, the dialysis port visible on her left upper arm, and no sign of life. Nora grabbed a towel and covered Midge's dead body and the soiled sheets. She walked over to the Pattis' back door. She didn't bother to knock.

Lynne was homeschooling her two oldest children in the family's kitchen. Nora intentionally kept her words vague. "I need you, Lynne."

Lynne was puzzled by Nora's sudden appearance. She usually noticed when a visitor came up the driveway, but Nora must have come in while Lynne was getting her son ready for preschool. Before she could ask what was going on, Nora said, "No questions." She turned to Lynne's two girls and told them more softly, "Kids, stay here, please."

Nora and Lynne had never been close or even friendly with each other, but Nora was especially firm that day. It caught Lynne off guard. She stepped outside and squinted at the low February sun. The sky was hazy and gave the yard a glow. It was the kind of sunshine tourists found pretty but Angelenos thought of as angry, like the sun was trying to burn your eyes.

Out of the children's earshot, Nora said, "I need for you to call 911. I don't know your address. They're going to ask for the address."

"Why?" Lynne asked, still confused.

"Midge is gone."

ONE OF KRISTINA'S COLLEAGUES, coroner investigator Jorge Posada, arrived at the Pattis' Westchester house at one thirty-two P.M., nearly three hours after paramedics had declared Inez Gonzales, Midge, dead. Posada spoke with Mike Patti and Pastor Huddle, who had come when Nora called him. Posada asked whether they were related to Midge. Pastor Huddle responded that they were her church family. That wasn't good enough for Posada. He asked about Midge's biological family. Midge had always been private about her relatives, even about the years prior to joining the Westchester Church. Her best friends there knew little about entire decades of Midge's life. They only knew that she had grown up in New Mexico and moved to L.A. as a young adult. Mike explained to the investigator that he understood Midge to be adopted and that her adopted parents were deceased. Posada wrote it all down. He also noted in his files that Mike and Pastor Huddle were willing to make private funeral arrangements.

No foul play was suspected, and Posada was able to wrap up his investigation in a swift seventy-one minutes. After the forensic attendant had taken the body out of the apartment for transport to the medical examiner's facility, Posada sealed the property and told Mike that the public administrator would sort out Midge's assets.

Back at the medical examiner's office, Posada logged Midge's many medications. Although Midge often rejected Nora's offers of an aspirin for a headache, saying she preferred a natural approach to her health, she had a small pharmacy of drugs for anxiety disorders, high blood pressure, depression, acid reflux, insomnia, and the side effects of dialysis.

Posada spoke with the DaVita Dialysis Center in Inglewood and confirmed that Midge went every Tuesday, Thursday, and Saturday. Her last appointment had been three days earlier. She had missed Thursday. Nora was listed as the emergency contact.

Posada then checked the voicemail on Midge's cellphone. There was a message from a woman named Joan Flowers: "Mom says hello." Perhaps it was a family member? Posada rang Flowers but found out that she was only a friend who had been relaying a message from her own mother. Flowers told Posada that Midge had "never mentioned any family." Posada had done what he could with phone records and public databases. Like Kristina, he had exhausted the obvious leads and needed to move on to other cases.

ON FEBRUARY 16, ELEVEN days after Midge was found dead, an investigator in the medical examiner's notifications unit picked up the case. At fifty, Joyce Kato was the senior member of the unit. Her job was to track down next of kin and try to compel them to claim. Joyce excelled at finding families, especially the ones that didn't want to be found. The unit as a whole was so good that it was able to survive on a skeleton staff despite processing hundreds of cases every year. Only two of the unit's eight fluorescent-lit cubicles were occupied most workdays.

Joyce had started at the medical examiner's office as a scene investigator. In her first years on the job, she arrived early to observe autopsies, which was not required but helped her understand the processes in the office better. She lifted weights to help her remove bodies from scenes more easily (no small feat given her five-foot frame). But it was the way she handled families that earned her the most praise from her bosses. She could communicate life-changing news, the kind that turned a wife into a widow or a child into an orphan, with a level of kindness and compassion that people remembered forever. A profile in the *Los Angeles Times* in 1997 described her as "part detective, part grief counselor, and part body pickup worker." Her most memorable case came early in the job, when she had to retrieve a plastic bag with a severed head and legs that had been tossed in the mountains north of L.A. during the drug wars of the 1990s. The work was thrilling, but the night shifts became exhausting. She could be called out during the last thirty minutes of her shift for a complex investigation forty miles away in L.A. traffic. The only way to get a day shift—and someday have enough predictability in her schedule to have a family—was to work in notifications.

The move allowed her to train with Doyle Tolbert, a no-nonsense veteran and former police officer who was well respected in the office. Joyce sat alongside Doyle as he taught her how to comb databases and make calls to potential next of kin. Doyle liked the young Asian American woman, and he worried the job would grind her down—it was demanding, and the place never seemed to change. He advised Joyce to find a better job. She liked the work and stayed anyway. But she later learned that Doyle was right—the place never changed, no matter who was in charge.

Joyce cared about notifying families of the fate of their loved ones but resented the lack of administrative support. Her supervisors expected her to handle fifty cases at a time, without acknowledging the fact that she often caught relatives off guard, and they needed time to process the news. From what Joyce could tell, her work was seen as a legal box to check—families could sue if they were not notified of a loved one's death in a timely manner, especially if the county had already cremated the remains. Her direct supervisor, Captain John Kades, liked to tell reporters that Joyce and her colleagues saved the county millions of dollars in lawsuits. Once when she heard this, Joyce looked up from her computer and quipped, "Maybe we should get a raise if we are so important."

Joyce's job seemed straightforward: Find the next of kin, notify them of the death, and ask about funeral arrangements. In reality, it involved a complicated mix of genealogical research and persuasion all while under intense time pressure as folders kept piling on her desk. The years of being a messenger of death had taken a toll. She did what she could to counteract the stress, taking a walk at the start of every workday. But strain was visible among most of the senior investigators.

Every morning Joyce received a pile of new cases on her desk in red and blue folders. A red folder indicated that someone was presumed indigent, while a blue folder meant that the dead may have had assets. Many of the red folders were transients. The medical examiner's office handled disposition when a body identified in a red folder wound up unclaimed. Blue folders were jointly investigated with the public administrator. In such cases, after the medical examiner determined a cause of death, it was the public administrator's responsibility to assess who would pay for disposition. If assets were sufficient for a private burial but no family was found, the public administrator arranged a funeral. If assets were insufficient, the public administrator volleyed the job of ordering county cremation back to the medical examiner's office. Midge's case appeared on Joyce's desk in a red folder.

Midge's body had been stacked on one of the metal racks in the refrigerated section at the medical examiner's facility for eleven days when Joyce opened the folder, labeled case number 2016-01010. She read Posada's notes, but they offered little to go on. The details about Midge that were relevant to her friends—that she was generous, a talented artist, a gifted storyteller, and an animal lover—were irrelevant to the medical examiner. Joyce saw Midge as another in an increasing number of transient people who died in Los Angeles, up to four each day.

Joyce always started by trying to track down next of kin. She had a chart pinned on the wall of her cubicle showing an abstracted family tree with kinship ties to twenty-six levels. The most important person to find was the one designated by the decedent to have power of attorney in health and financial matters (though few people designate such a person). Second in line was the spouse or registered domestic partner, followed by adult children. But then, rather than moving on to grandchildren, the tree shoots up vertically to parents, then to siblings, then grandparents, aunts, and uncles. Only then does it move back down to grandchildren, nieces and nephews, and first, second, and third cousins. The nuclear family is privileged and the quality of the relationship is irrelevant:

Midge's church family, even though they had felt close to Midge and wanted to give her a fitting send-off, did not qualify as next of kin.

Joyce knew that almost everyone had a hidden past; it was her job to uncover it. Finding family could mean that a person on the path toward being unclaimed would ultimately be claimed. It wasn't easy: Despite the proliferation of social media, plenty of people managed to live off the grid. They used aliases and fake addresses, and would sometimes simply refuse to answer phone calls or letters. But Joyce was determined. And she had tricks. She anticipated data entry mistakes by changing the birth date to a range of years, dropping a middle initial, or searching for a last name and a birth state. Unusual names were a blessing. She and her colleagues were so good that they could find secret spouses, secret children, even secret agents. "How did you find me?" one man had asked, incredulous. "Seriously, how did you find me? I'm a federal agent, you're not supposed to be able to find me." The investigators joked that if they'd gotten a dollar every time someone asked how they'd tracked them down, the department's budget would have been balanced.

Joyce didn't put much stock in the adopted orphan story Midge had given her friends. Los Angeles drew people who wanted to start over, and people who were starting over often invented pasts or took on different names. One woman's file included forty aliases, small variants of six similar names, and an arrest record pages long. "She has been busy," Joyce's cubicle neighbor joked. Often, the earliest arrest record was the likeliest to contain the deceased's original name. People often wised up after a number of arrests.

Joyce ran an Accurint search on "Inez Gonzales." The database showed a handful of addresses, the most recent being 7299 W. Manchester Avenue, where the Westchester Church of the Nazarene was located. No arrests, no marriages, no indication of any relatives. Joyce noted in the medical examiner's digital case system that an employee in the Social Security Administration told her that Gonzales was born in Grants, New Mexico, to Francisca Madrid and Andres Gonzales. There was no record of an adoption, and it would be difficult for Joyce to obtain official confirmation without a court order. The Social Security Administration employee said that Midge's middle name was Maria and confirmed that her last known address was the W. Manchester Avenue one. Midge had received $875 in Social Security funds and $24.40 in Supplementary Security Income every month via direct deposit.

Next Joyce turned to Ancestry.com, the same genealogy database used by hobbyists. It didn't take long to find information; someone in Midge's family had created a family tree, complete with published obituaries, and Joyce used it to confirm Midge's parents. Her mother, Francisca Madrid, had died in 1976, and her obituary listed Midge as a surviving daughter, along with a son, Ernie. When Midge's father, Andres, died in 1978, his obituary listed only the son. In the two years between their parents' deaths, it seemed that Midge had been written out of the family records. According to the Ancestry family tree, Midge's brother, Ernie, passed away in Albuquerque in 2015. Midge reappeared as his surviving sister in that obituary, suggesting a tale of estrangement and reconnection.

Joyce saw that Midge's brother had been married and, hoping she could reach a relative, called Ernie's last known phone number in Albuquerque. Ernie's widow, Veronica Gonzales, confirmed that Midge was indeed Ernie's younger sister, and that she had been adopted as a child. Ernie was their parents' biological son and thirteen years older. Midge had been in touch with Ernie off and on over the decades. She had last reached out to him three years earlier, before Ernie became sick with cancer. Veronica sounded confused, and Joyce did not press her for more details.

Joyce knew that family relationships could be contentious. She often put relatives on the spot when asking them to make final arrangements and, under pressure, bitter family secrets would spill out. She flagged these in her case notes to warn Captain Kades that the body would likely end up unclaimed: "Relationships fell apart," she noted in one file, "when the decedent switched to crack cocaine." In another, she wrote that a wife was "very angry with the decedent because he was violent." A brother who had not been in touch with a decedent for thirty-nine years stated that he has "scars all over his body from his brother beating him." A brother from a different family told Joyce over the phone that "they were raised around alcohol. He himself started drinking at 13 and the decedent started about 10. He abused crank. Prior to leaving Oklahoma, he stole their sister's car." Another decedent "had three daughters but had not contacted them for decades. The daughters did not have the funds nor the desire to make arrangements for the decedent as they didn't know him and what they remember was unkind."

Each statement offered only a snippet of explanation as to why the chasm had developed, but each one served as a justification for not taking care of final arrangements. In many cases, people expressed relief or even joy that their tormentor had passed away. Letting them go unclaimed was in a sense karmic justice—a biblical eye for an eye, applied postmortem.

The next-of-kin hierarchy used in the medical examiner's office rested on a basic assumption that the closer a relative was to the decedent (by blood or legal tie), the more willing that relative would be to handle disposition. But, in reality, many relationships had completely unraveled by the time Joyce reached the next of kin. Family estrangement is fairly common but difficult to trace; it doesn't enter vital records the way divorce does. Researchers estimate that more than 40 percent of families in the United States will experience a form of estrangement at some point—frayed relationships with fathers are the most common. The medical examiner's files were saturated with stories of severed family ties, enough for Joyce to know that the next-of-kin approach was flawed. But state law dictated the hierarchy. She had no alternative.

Later in the day, after her conversation with Midge's sister-in-law, Veronica, Joyce received a phone call from a woman who introduced herself as Veronica's daughter and Inez's niece. Barbara Gonzales Fuller wanted to make sure her mother, who had dementia, had given the medical examiner the correct information. She also hoped to find out more about her aunt, who had left New Mexico when Barbara was four or five years old—she couldn't remember exactly. Barbara had been looking for her Auntie Inez. An amateur genealogist, Barbara was the one who had created the family tree on Ancestry.com, and had used online research tools to try to find out where Inez lived. But the name Inez Gonzales was too common, and Barbara wasn't even sure that Inez still lived in California. Barbara told Joyce she was especially interested in any photos of her auntie.

Joyce listened with her headset on while she took notes. She found reactions like Barbara's gratifying. Her digging had reconnected a severed link, even if the news of the death was not what Barbara was hoping for.

Joyce asked Barbara whether she would be willing to make arrangements, explaining that she had a couple of days to contact a funeral home. Barbara was interested in claiming but said she needed to think about it.

Meanwhile, Joyce called Nora to say that Midge had kin who were still alive, a courtesy call because Nora had seemed ready to finalize funeral arrangements. Nora took notes on her desk calendar, but the words were hard to process. "All the years we were told she didn't have a family, and the state found a niece."

In that moment, Nora realized, "We never knew anything about her."

7.

COUNTY DISPO

. .

NORA AND HOWARD, THE PATTIS, AND PASTOR HUDDLE had been willing to organize a funeral for Midge. As church secretary and Midge's best friend, Nora would have been the one to call funeral homes for quotes. But the revelation that Midge had relatives in New Mexico—and that the church wouldn't be able to claim her—had thrown the community's plans into doubt.

Mike spoke with Barbara and offered to send all of Midge's possessions to her, but Barbara didn't want the car or any money. She asked only for photos and anything that offered clues as to why Midge had left Albuquerque. She gave Mike permission to sell Midge's personal items and donate the proceeds to the church.

To close out Midge's bank accounts and sell her car, Mike needed a death certificate. But only family members could obtain one. When he went to vital records, the woman behind the counter took pity on him.

"You're her brother, right?"

"No." Mike never lied.

"You're her brother, *right?*"

Mike got the hint. "Oh, yes." He justified the white lie by telling himself he was Midge's brother in Christ.

Mike sold Midge's car for $3,000 and gave the money to the church. He was prepared to cover the costs of a funeral, but he didn't want trouble with Barbara. At every step, the law discouraged friends' involvement. The form Mike would have had to file with the court to claim Midge included a signed declaration that "the decedent has no living relatives." A false declaration, according to the form, was subject to perjury laws. Barbara had been deferential on the phone, but Mike and others at the church worried about being sued if Barbara changed her mind, or if another relative appeared. Along with the rest of Midge's church family, he decided to hold off on a funeral. Instead, determined to honor her, they organized a celebration of life service.

Church of the Nazarene was house rich but people poor. The church sat on more than two million dollars' worth of real estate, but few would have guessed it based on appearances. Wooden panels around the front door and windows had splintered, the sky-blue stucco exterior had been touched up in mismatched shades, and cracks stretched from the tops of the side arched windows toward the roof. The congregation had never been large, about one hundred regulars at its peak, and in recent years membership had dwindled to forty-five parishioners.

On Saturday, March 19, 2016, four weeks after Midge had died, the church sprang to life. People who had not been at the church in years returned to pay respects to their beloved Midgey. The kids from Youth First, the Wednesday night youth program that Midge had helped organize, came. Even the pastor whom Huddle had replaced made a rare return to Westchester to say goodbye to Midge. Like a lot of churches struggling to survive, Westchester rented space to other Christian groups, including a congregation called Hope Chapel, and some of their congregants attended the service for Midge, too. Joan Flowers, the woman the scene investigator had called after retrieving her voicemail on Midge's cellphone, brought her mother to the service. Flowers remembered passing Midge in the parking lot on her way to Sunday worship every week. It had always stuck with her that this "very sweet person" didn't have any family besides the church.

In all, nearly two hundred people attended Midge's memorial service. When they entered the foyer, they saw tables lined with

Midge's writings and drawings, realistic sketches of tigers and her cats staring intently at the viewer. Inside the sanctuary, Nora Spring and Lynne Patti had set up displays with photos of Midge and her artwork. Nora was heartbroken. For all her foibles, Midge was still the person Nora had spent every day with for two years, sitting in the living room, watching TV, and eating. She was still the person who had been an aunt to Nora's sons and held Nora's hand when her parents died. Nora did not want her friend to be forgotten.

Lynne, for her part, spent the week after Midge's death in a deep depression. She went over what she could have done differently or sooner to help Midge. She tried to block from her mind the sight of her friend lifeless on the bed, and regrets welling up inside of her.

At the service, the church's worship band played several songs, with Nora's husband, Howard, keeping the mood light by jamming on bongo drums. Lynne sang Midge's favorite song, Leonard Cohen's "Hallelujah." *But listen, love, love is not some kind of victory march, No, it's a cold and it's a very lonely Hallelujah.* People were invited to share memories of Midge, but few did. Nora and Lynne were both too overwhelmed to speak. Instead, it was Nora's shy son, Justin, now an adult, who gave the day's most memorable speech. Through tears, he reminisced about the love Midge had given him, how she taught him how to care for animals and how she would sit with him when he was sad. Justin's girlfriend also took to the microphone. "Midge was the real deal," she said. "When I look at her and what she's been through and how she lives out this grace, this redemptive story; *that* I believe. I can lock into that." Later, they ate Midge's favorite food—beans, rice, and chicken from El Pollo Loco—and browsed the display of art and photographs.

By the end of the service, it was clear: As far as the congregants of the Westchester Church of the Nazarene were concerned, they had been Midge's actual family.

MEANWHILE, BACK IN THE medical examiner's office, Joyce Kato waited to hear whether Barbara would claim her aunt's body. Even though Joyce's view of humanity had darkened over the years, she knew she couldn't predict what estranged families would do. Once in a while a death revived a family tie. Almost a year after she opened Midge's case file, she received a red folder concerning an Asian woman who had been found unresponsive at the bottom of an apartment stairwell. Police officers recognized her as a local transient who snuck into the building at night to sleep, but they did not know her name. It took six weeks until fingerprints and body X-rays identified her as Da-Som Pitino.

Joyce ran Pitino's last known addresses in Accurint and located a husband, Walter R. Pitino, now deceased, who had married Da-Som Kim in 1978, two years after she had arrived in the United States from Korea. One year later, they had a daughter named Daria. Hopeful, Joyce called Daria and confirmed that Da-Som was her biological mother. After her parents divorced, Daria's mother had developed mental health issues, and her father went to prison. Daria and her sister, also Da-Som's daughter, were placed in foster care and later legally adopted. Daria assumed her mother had returned to Korea, because she had heard nothing in thirty years. The sisters' adoptions meant they were no longer legal next of kin. Joyce still didn't have anyone to claim Da-Som.

Knowing that Da-Som had been hospitalized, Joyce searched for additional medical records. Da-Som had suffered from chronic paranoid schizophrenia, which had been triggered by "residual effects of severe marital and family problems." At one point, Da-Som believed that her psychiatrist was the president and was going to marry her and take her to Washington. At other times, she believed that he would whisk her away to Palm Springs where her mother and daughters were waiting for her in a house the psychiatrist had purchased. The file was stacked with hospitalizations: one for a year and a half, then another for four years. The hospital staff administered psychiatric medications each time Da-Som was discharged, with a note that the patient was stable but needed to remain on medication to keep her delusions at bay. Joyce googled Da-Som's name and found a 2012 article in a local newspaper that identified a disoriented woman with the same name wandering into a Monrovia restaurant. The article noted that the woman did not communicate with anyone.

Joyce had no legal responsibility to share the information she had found with Daria. But Joyce empathized with the sisters. She thought that if fate had dealt a different hand, she could have been born to Da-Som and put in foster care. She called Daria back and shared what she had learned about Da-Som's medical and legal problems. Daria consulted with her sister and together they decided they would take the necessary steps to claim their birth mother, which included obtaining a court order. After the burial, Daria wrote to Joyce. "The information you sent is helping me fill in the story a bit more and I am gaining some closure as a result. Thank you again for the important work you do and for the empathy and kindness with which you do it." Joyce pinned the postcard to her cubicle. Among the waves of bitter estrangement, cases like Da-Som's were rare. Joyce held on to reminders that some people came together against the odds.

TO MIDGE'S FRIENDS, BARBARA had seemed invested in her aunt. She had posted a query on Midge's Facebook page, asking urgently: "Is there anyone on this page that can tell me what happened to her when she left Albuquerque? Where did she go, where did she live, how did she make it? Anything you can tell me would be so appreciated and would fill the gaps in my heart that I have felt since the day she left."

Nora saw the posts and called Barbara. She told Barbara that Midge identified as Native American—she would say, "I'm not a Mexican. I'm not Spanish. I am Native." Barbara asked if her aunt had married or found God. Nora could confirm the latter, but she only knew about the last decade of Midge's life. The details of her earlier years remained shrouded in mystery.

Barbara got off the phone, considering the few facts she had about her disappeared aunt. She cherished her memories of Midge playing with her and reading *The Three Little Pigs*, and she had spent the last four decades scanning people's faces in crowds, hoping for a chance encounter. Barbara had asked her dad as many questions as she could, but he didn't like to talk about his sister. To complete her family tree on Ancestry.com, Barbara had started calling cousins and other extended family members. She concluded that Midge was indeed adopted, likely after Francisca Gonzales had suffered multiple miscarriages. Ernie had an older biological half sister, Vidalia, who had already left the house by the time Midge arrived. Francisca, who was in her early fifties at the time, seemed desperate for another daughter. But once she had the girl she had longed for, something snapped. Francisca just couldn't translate the longing into love.

Through her genealogy sleuthing and reading into the history of New Mexico, Barbara surmised that Francisca herself was adopted and may have been a Navajo child raised in servitude. It was common in New Mexico during the time for families to adopt Native children to have access to unpaid labor. Francisca seems to have moved from family to family, until she was married off and had Vidalia at age fourteen. Vidalia's father died in a railroad accident, and Francisca later married Andres, who was the son of a Latino family she was working for. Vidalia herself became a bride at sixteen, in what Vidalia's daughter, Virginia, called an "arranged marriage."

Although Virginia was Midge's niece, only a year separated them, and the girls were raised more like cousins. They lived nearby to each other and spent their early years playing together, often in Virginia's backyard. Virginia recalled how even as a girl of five or six, Midge tried to avoid being at home with her mother. When Vidalia divorced, she moved Virginia and her brothers to another part of Albuquerque, and Virginia saw less of Midge, who by her early teens started talking about her desire to leave home.

By all accounts, Francisca made life difficult. If she wasn't yelling at Midge, she was locking her up or withholding food. On birthdays and Christmas, Francisca showered Ernie with gifts, while

Midge, like the eleven-year-old Harry Potter living under the Dursleys' staircase, often went to bed empty-handed. Andres could be loving toward his adopted daughter, but he also didn't do much to defend her; he was quiet and preferred animals to conversation. He took Midge outside of the home when he could and taught her woodworking, but his attempts to intervene made Francisca more jealous, and she punished Midge for the attention her husband gave her. Midge, in turn, acted out against authority figures. Once, she broke her principal's windows, as payback for getting in trouble at school. She also dressed like a boy, which became a recurring source of conflict with her mother.

According to Barbara, Ernie was Midge's main source of love growing up. He called his sister Hita, which was a play on the Spanish word *hijita* ("little girl"). Even when he became an adult and moved out to live on his own, he tried to care for Midge. All of it came to an end in 1964, when Midge was sixteen and drove off on a stolen motorcycle. Her brother paid the dealership, but the incident soured their relationship, and Barbara—whom Midge had nicknamed "Lulu"—lost any connection to her aunt. Midge returned once but Francisca ran her off the property, cursed her, and told her never to come back.

Years later, after her adoptive parents passed away, Midge contacted her brother and asked him to send her adoption papers. Ernie found them in his parents' estate and mailed them to Midge. It's unlikely the documents included the name of her birth mother or father, since New Mexico was a closed adoption state. But the Final Decree of Adoption, if Midge saw it, would have told her where she was born—not Grants, New Mexico, as the Social Security Administration had in their records, but Gallup, New Mexico, near Navajo tribal lands. Midge did not show her church friends the documents her brother had sent, but soon after she received them, she deepened her reading of Native history in New Mexico.

By the time she dug into her aunt's genealogical roots, Barbara considered herself an expert. She wasn't sure that Midge would be recognized as Native American because documentation of tribal membership likely didn't exist for an orphaned infant. But it was possible that Midge had Native ancestors. In the South Valley of Albuquerque, Native American and Hispanic residents had inter-married for generations. New Mexico had a long history of *genízaros*, Indigenous people who had been captured by other tribes and ran-somed to Spanish colonial families. They were forced to pay their debt to their liberators through decades of servitude. Some gained their freedom and worked as day laborers, and a few became land-owners. Because *genízaro* was an ambiguous ethnic category and over time many people passed into the general Hispanic popula-tion, were baptized as Christians, or intermarried, it is difficult to trace back Indigenous ancestry. And descendants of *genízaro* were less likely to be recognized as tribal members by the Pueblo Indi-ans, who felt the *genízaro* had lost crucial aspects of their Native language and culture.

If Midge had been Native American and her friends or family could have proven it, she might have been eligible to receive burial on tribal land. But no one seems to have mentioned it to Joyce Kato. In the medical examiner's files, Midge was listed as "Hispanic/Latin American."

As important as the research on her aunt's history was to Bar-bara's peace of mind, the medical examiner's office was concerned with just one thing: Would she claim the body? Unbeknownst to her church family, two days after receiving the call from Joyce, Bar-bara had requested county cremation for her aunt. She agreed to fill out online paperwork that authorized the county to proceed—with the option to later collect the ashes. Then she failed to return the forms. Nor did she inform other family members of Midge's im-pending cremation. When Joyce located a next of kin, she expected the person to inform other kin. The office simply had too many cases and, by finding Barbara, they had fulfilled their state mandate. There was no record of anyone in the office finding Midge's other niece, Virginia. Barbara, meanwhile, did not immediately reach out to her cousin. It would be several years before Virginia found out about her aunt's death.

Two weeks after her last conversation with Barbara, Joyce typed a note into the medical examiner's electronic record system that the next of kin had failed to return the paperwork. Joyce had no choice but to authorize county cremation. With the click of a computer mouse, Midge became unclaimed.

．．

MARIA DIAZ ABSENTMINDEDLY TOUCHED THE TOP OF HER belly while looking at her computer screen. She was only in her fifth month of pregnancy but already the twins she was expecting made her uncomfortable. She readjusted her red bracelet with a beaded evil eye charm, which she'd started wearing when she found out she was pregnant—anything to prevent the envious looks of *mal de ojo* rendering her vulnerable babies sick and cranky.

Maria was one of two dozen deputy investigators in the office of the County of Los Angeles Public Administrator. The office ran investigations to locate heirs and assets, sometimes working in tandem with the medical examiner's office. Though the two offices did many of the same tasks—investigating scenes and searching databases for next of kin—their motivations were quite different. The medical examiner had to act quickly to determine the cause of death and avoid a lawsuit over mishandled bodies. The public administrator could take months (and sometimes years) to process an estate. During the itemizing of assets, the public administrator also notified relatives of a death and queried whether they were willing to organize funerals.

If its deputies found no relatives willing to make funeral arrangements, what happened next depended on the decedent's assets. If they totaled less than $5,000 (after paying off debts, which included taxes and healthcare costs), the office would green-light a county cremation at Boyle Heights. The deceased would then be included in the county's official numbers of unclaimed dead. The public administrator cleared hundreds of these indigent cases for county cremation every year. With $5,000 to $13,500 in assets, the deceased could receive a county cremation, and a niche memorial plate would be purchased for placement at a contracted private cemetery. If the estate was worth more than $13,500, the public administrator siphoned off whatever funds were needed to pay for a burial in a private cemetery and returned the remaining assets to legal next of kin. The office organized about sixty of these private funerals every year. In this way, people with assets dying lonely deaths escaped mass interment in Boyle Heights. The county did not include them in its census of unclaimed dead, even though these bodies were also, in effect, abandoned.

Wealthy estates with "unknown heirs" were often skimmed off by a shadow group of private investigators, called *heir hunters,* some of whom had previously worked in the public administrator's office. They knew there was money to be made amid the county's heavy caseload, and they conducted detailed research to locate heirs, sometimes even contracting with local genealogy clubs and detectives abroad to locate people. In exchange for a share of the estate, heir hunters liaised with county officials and courts on behalf of family members to distribute the inheritance. While heir hunters often discovered relatives that the public administrator might have missed, due to the extensive resources these private firms brought to a search, the consequence was that the most lucrative estates were often tapped before the public administrator had even opened their case. In practice, this meant that private companies stepped in to deal with abandoned dead millionaires and left the smaller estates for the county. These wealthy deceased could still end up unclaimed— with the county responsible for organizing a funeral.

Compared with heir hunters, who spent much of their time on the road to locate distant kin, Maria spent her days running investigations from a sun-soaked cubicle in the Hall of Records in downtown Los Angeles, in a building designed by acclaimed modernist architect Richard Neutra. Office lore held that the architect used vertical aluminum louvers after consulting with an ophthalmologist on ideal light levels, out of concern for the well-being of the workers. The natural light made working here far better than in the basement morgue or cramped medical examiner's office.

Maria had stumbled into the job. While majoring in psychology at Cal State, she dreamed of becoming a marriage counselor. She changed her mind when she found out that her marriage counseling professor was divorced. She tried working at a residential foster home for teenage girls but was frustrated by how little impact she could make in the girls' lives. A friend told her the public administrator was hiring. Tallying the assets of the dead sounded easier than managing the drama of teen girls. Maria applied. After four rounds of interviews, she and four other candidates beat out more than five hundred applicants. Within four years, two of those colleagues had already left. All the probing into dead people's business took a toll.

To lessen the risk of burnout, every morning Maria posted an inspirational quote on the small whiteboard outside her gray cubicle. The day she started looking into Bobby Hanna's case, the quote was from Honoré de Balzac: "All happiness depends on courage and work." Underneath, Maria had taped gold stars with the names of nine of the twenty junior deputies who had gone beyond the call of duty. If you are going to work together for nine hours a day every day, Maria thought, you may as well make it enjoyable. She kept a stack of party games and supplies in a cabinet in her office for retirement parties and baby showers.

As an office veteran even at age thirty-three, Maria usually took the difficult cases, such as when probate courts appointed the public administrator to mediate between feuding heirs. But she also helped with more run-of-the-mill cases, like Bobby's, when the junior staff was shorthanded.

Bobby's body had been in limbo for two months. Donnell had authorized the transfer of his father's body from the El Monte apartment under the assumption that the military would cover most if not all of the funeral costs. But when the funeral home sent him a large bill, Donnell became confused and overwhelmed. He stopped returning their calls. Convinced Donnell was never going to pay, the funeral director then referred the case to the public administrator, where it was assigned to Maria on September 5, 2019.

Maria looked at the case file and highlighted Donnell's name, along with Isaac's. Maria also circled Clara's name, even though, as an ex-wife, she was not next of kin. Maria noticed that the funeral home's last phone call with Donnell was August 14, just over a month after Bobby died. She knew that funeral homes did not like to be stuck with bodies, especially if it looked like they were not going to get paid. After checking in with the funeral director to confirm that they still had Bobby's body, Maria called Donnell and left a message. Then she tried Clara, whom she found both friendly and informative. Clara told her that she did not have the financial means to take care of the funeral, but that she would call Donnell to see whether she could persuade him. Clara made clear that she wasn't the mother of either of Bobby's sons.

Like Joyce Kato in the medical examiner's office, Maria often used the Ancestry.com database to find family members not listed in the case file. This time, Maria almost immediately found several women who might be Bobby's sisters living in Indiana. She started with Cynthia Woods. Through Cynthia, Maria learned that Bobby had come from a family of nine siblings, some of them half brothers and sisters and others foster siblings. Cynthia was surprised that the body had not yet been claimed. She said she would consult with another sister who lived close by and then go to Donnell's house. But she warned Maria that it was a delicate situation. The sisters didn't know Donnell well; he had seen his father's side of the family only a couple of times. And Isaac had only recently learned that Bobby was his father. Like Clara, Cynthia said that she did not have the funds to pay for a funeral.

THE NEXT DAY, MARIA managed to reach Donnell. He was annoyed, both at the funeral home and the VA. He started talking about getting his father's body transferred to another, cheaper fu-

neral home, even though he hadn't lined up any alternatives. The
funeral director explained they would do so, provided Donnell paid
refrigeration and transport fees. The total for forwarding remains to
another funeral home came to $2,495. Donnell told Maria that he
felt the funeral home was keeping his father hostage.

He wasn't wrong, at least not in a moral sense. The practice was
unsavory, though technically legal. Funeral homes regularly picked
up bodies without signed contracts, aware that they might get stuck
with a body if families couldn't pay. But it wasn't a real financial risk.
If families couldn't pay, the funeral homes could call the county, say
the body had been abandoned, and arrange to have it picked up
(which was why Maria was dealing with Bobby's case). The funeral
home would only have to write off the cost of the initial collection
and storage. Since the funeral home that had retrieved Bobby was
part of the Dignity network, itself part of Service Corporation International, the largest funeral home and cemetery company in the
United States, they had in-house vans and drivers, meaning the
original transport fee ($695) charged to relatives likely included a
hefty markup.

On the phone with Maria, Donnell said that he wanted his father cremated and the ashes shipped to his hometown of Gary, Indiana. He didn't understand why the U.S. Department of Veterans
Affairs wouldn't take care of it.

Maria was sympathetic; her husband had been in the military.
She gently explained that like all next of kin Donnell had two options: Either he could claim the body and make his own funeral
arrangements, or he could leave the body to the county for an indigent burial. As an honorably discharged veteran, Bobby had the
right to interment and a grave marker in one of the nation's 155
national cemeteries. Donnell would still need to hire a funeral home
to store, prepare, and transport the body. He could request a "burial
allowance" from the VA, which would (partially) reimburse him for
these expenses. If he preferred cremation, Donnell would need to
arrange to have Bobby's body cremated by a private crematorium

and Bobby could be placed in a columbarium at a national cemetery at no cost to him. Either way, Donnell would have to front the cost of getting his father's body moved from the Dignity-owned funeral home to a new facility. If he couldn't afford that, Maria explained, the body would be transferred to the county morgue.

Maria used what her colleagues called her molasses voice—soft and sweet—to calm Donnell. Feeling he had no choice, he gave her permission to transfer Bobby's body to the county morgue. Bobby would become the responsibility of the county. Funeraria Del Angel would receive no payment, but they would no longer need to store his body.

Donnell felt no relief in his decision. He still wanted to get his father cremated, and he made a mental note to call Veterans Affairs again. It had been difficult keeping track of the different government agencies and their procedures. In his mind, it all blended into a single office giving him conflicting advice. During these confusing weeks, he'd leaned on Clara for help.

At first, Clara hadn't wanted to do anything for Bobby. Shortly after his death, Bobby had managed to jolt her from the other side. A young woman called saying she was Bobby's girlfriend. She tried to flatter Clara by saying that Bobby always spoke highly of his ex-wife and how strong she was.

"Oh, you know, we wanted to get married," the girlfriend dropped.

"Well, now I do!" Clara was floored. She didn't have time to process her shock before the girlfriend started asking about Bobby's belongings. She wanted Bobby's Mason ring as well as his Chevy Camaro. She claimed that Bobby had promised her the ring and the car.

Clara was hurt that Bobby would suggest they get remarried while he was courting another woman—one half his age. And it stung that he planned to leave his car to this thirty-year-old, even while he was sweet-talking Clara about getting a replacement for her stick-shift Toyota. At least Clara could truthfully tell the "fiancée" that she had no idea where the Mason ring was. The Camaro was a different story. She wasn't willing to give up on the car so easily. Clara recalled Bobby's excitement when he first showed up in a pitch-black V6 Chevy Camaro—the vehicle he'd fantasized about for years. He had parked outside her apartment in West L.A. and called her to come out, the windows and sunroof open to allow his music to boom. He grinned at Clara as he revved the engine. "Your dream came true," she told him.

Clara called the El Monte apartment manager, who immediately warmed to the British woman. He told Clara he had been dismayed at how Bobby's young girlfriend had yelled at Bobby when he couldn't move his cancer-riddled body quickly enough to open her car door one day. The manager offered to park the muscle car in the back where the girlfriend would not see it until Clara could get out there.

Clara flirted with the idea of keeping the car even though she knew it was a gas guzzler. But when she arrived at the El Monte apartment complex, she realized this was a different car from the one Bobby had shown her. She later found out that Bobby had sold the paid-off black Camaro and bought a cobalt-blue one with silver stripes that he called Thunder. It had unpaid parking tickets, fire damage under the seat, and, worse, Bobby still owed $21,000. The lien holder was Santander, a company that targeted people with low credit scores. (The company was later sued by thirty-four state attorneys general for issuing unfair auto loans with excessive interest rates; the company settled the case in June 2020.) The car dealer warned Clara that the Santander people would want to stick her with the debt. Clara fretted, even consulting with a friend who was a lawyer. She felt fortunate when Santander repossessed the car. *Good riddance,* she thought.

The experience with the car and the sting of the girlfriend soured Clara's mood and weakened her resolve to help Bobby's family back in Indiana. But when Donnell called days after Bobby's death, sounding confused and heartbroken, Clara's Catholic guilt kicked in. She told him she was willing to empty out Bobby's apartment—

though now that she knew about the girlfriend, she felt apprehensive about what she'd find there.

· ·

ON MAY 24, 2017, ONE DAY AFTER DAVID'S BODY WAS MOVED from his apartment in Monrovia to the medical examiner's facility in Boyle Heights, a forensic pathologist inspected the body. The scene investigation did not suggest foul play and no autopsy was required, but because David had no primary care physician who could have explained his passing, the pathologist needed to determine the cause of death. The doctor noted his height (five feet seven inches) and weight (157 pounds), then pressed his gloved finger into David's swollen legs; the dimple that appeared remained when he took his hand away. To document the swelling due to fluid buildup, the pathologist wrote "pitting edema" on the examination form. He also noticed a yellow tinge to David's body, ant activity on his face, and a full beard and mustache. He saw no marks indicating anything suspicious. The pathologist took fluids from David's eyes and femoral blood. The cause of death was presumed to be congestive heart failure due to narrowing of the arteries and high blood pressure, a default natural cause of death.

As his body was examined, the job of finding next of kin once again fell to Joyce Kato in the medical examiner's notifications office.

In her twenty years as an investigator, Joyce had worked on hundreds of cases of loners like David. Some lived in extreme isolation. Six years before David's folder crossed her desk, Joyce worked on the case of Yvette Vickers, a 1959 *Playboy* centerfold and actress who starred in the cult favorite *Attack of the 50 Foot Woman*. Vickers had died in her home in Beverly Hills in 2010 but her body lay undiscovered for nearly a year, until a neighbor did her own welfare check. Compared to Vickers, David was fortunate. He had been dead for only eight days when Jesus found him.

Joyce opened the report that Kristina McGuire had filed and

then tried David's name in her various databases. On Ancestry.com, Joyce almost immediately found a David Grafton Spencer with the same birth date as the one on the driver's license recovered in David's apartment. Then she located two possible siblings, including Judith Lee Spencer, now seventy-seven, with an address in Oroville, California, north of Sacramento. She sighed. Once again, she had located a relative without much effort. Her office was supposed to be a last resort for difficult-to-find relatives. But scene investigators didn't like to do desk work, so they were quick to forward the file to notifications. They wanted Joyce to find the relatives and break the bad news.

When she rang the phone number listed for Judith, there was no answer. Joyce also found a probable brother, Steven Spencer, with another Oroville address but no phone number. They appeared to have the same mother, Juanita Spencer. The city of fifteen thousand was too small for the finding to be coincidental. That gave Joyce confidence that she had found David's living kin. She printed the medical examiner's standard notification letter and addressed envelopes to both siblings.

Twelve days passed before Joyce received a call. It was from Mikel Clark, who used an interpreter for the hearing impaired to relay that he was David's brother-in-law. His wife, Tiffany, had been born as Steven. Both Tiffany and Mikel were deaf and living in Chico. According to Mikel, Judith had been institutionalized with dementia for some time. Tiffany hadn't communicated with David since 2001, two years before their mother died. Mikel asked about an indigent veteran burial for David, explaining that he and his wife lived off Social Security.

Joyce ran David's name in one of the state databases that contained financial information and saw that he had a retirement account with more than $40,000. That meant David's case did not qualify for an indigent burial. Joyce explained to Mikel that while *they* might be indigent, David was not.

Tiffany and Mikel were in a catch-22. To gain access to David's money, they needed a death certificate. The medical examiner's office would not release the death certificate until the couple hired a private funeral home to transfer the body from the crowded crypt. Quick access to the death certificate was one of the few carrots the office had to entice hesitant families to claim.

Joyce wanted to make this point forcefully, but she had little leverage over Mikel. The body was in the medical examiner's facility, and the county would have to dispose of it—with or without relatives' cooperation. Every day, the medical examiner's staff retrieved dozens of corpses from all corners of L.A. County, and every day they needed to sign out a similar number of corpses. Falling behind meant that the crypt—a large, cooled space with metal racks that stacked bodies six rows high, for a total of 520—would overflow.

Family members used different tactics to avoid taking responsibility. Some simply signed a form relinquishing their right to dispose of the body. Others stymied the office's efforts by making promises, running out the clock, or refusing to respond to phone calls or letters. After waiting months for a reply, Joyce would then forward a file to her supervisor, Captain Kades, who would make a final attempt to persuade the relatives. If that failed, the body would be tagged "county dispo" and sent to one of three private mortuaries the medical examiner's office contracted with to handle cremations (the county crematorium could only handle ten bodies per week, so the medical examiner had to outsource). The ashes would then be transferred to the Office of Decedent Affairs for storage.

In Joyce's experience, families often exploited the fact that the medical examiner's staff did not verify indigence, taking families' claims of poverty at their word. She had been doing this work long enough to know that people asserted financial hardship even when they had assets—she could easily look up their addresses and see their million-dollar homes. The office could file a civil suit to recuperate triple the cost of transport, storage, and, later, cremation. But for Captain Kades it was not worth it. "I'm not gonna spend a dollar chasing after a dime I might not get," he said. "At the end of the day, I can cremate that body for $160 or I can pay Joyce overtime to chase that family and rattle our saber at them. The time it would take for them to prove or disprove their indigency—thirty days is gone, and I need the space."

These days Joyce felt like she had to work harder than ever to coax families to care enough to spend thousands on a funeral. Their actions, which she saw as selfish, grated on her, and she always wondered whether they were trying to pull one over on the county. That wasn't how she'd felt when she'd started the job. Joyce remembered breaking down in tears in front of a family early in her career; she'd decided then that she would need to be more professional to survive. Professional, in the medical examiner's office, meant detached. As the years passed, "detached" had morphed into incredulousness at relatives' efforts to escape their moral and legal responsibilities.

While Joyce was dealing with Mikel, the public administrator started to tally David's assets to determine how much money the estate was worth. David had $159.63 in a checking account the day he died, but when the deputy assigned to the case looked at the account weeks later, the total was $1,285.63 (the Social Security Administration regularly made direct deposits into dead people's accounts). David also had $6,179.26 in a savings account, plus the $40,000 retirement account that Joyce had noticed.

Every year, the County of Los Angeles Public Administrator's office handled dozens of cases of people dying alone with financial resources and no one to oversee a burial. In 2013, they handled the case of Robert Bradford, a retired mathematician who lived alone. What made Bradford stand out was the amount in his savings account—over $1.3 million. Bradford was divorced but, unlike David, he had a son. In his will, dated thirty-five years earlier, Bradford had disinherited his son and wrote that everything should go to his mother. If she predeceased him, his brothers should inherit his estate. His brother, Thomas, was the only one who had survived him. The brothers talked every week and had a cordial relationship. Even so, Thomas nominated the public administrator to handle his brother's estate and burial. Thomas skipped the at-sea ceremony his brother had requested, saying Robert would not have cared if he was there. Thomas received a certified check two years later in the amount of $1,381,846.53.

In their independent investigation of David's case, the public administrator found nothing that Kristina McGuire had not already logged in her case notes. Still, the office wouldn't allow the apartment to be cleaned out until they determined who, as next of kin, had legal authority over David's belongings. (In cases where the deceased is a John or Jane Doe, an apartment can be in limbo for months until the deceased has been identified and their relatives notified.) Diana Lynn, the apartment manager at Royal Park, was eager for the investigation to wrap up. She planned to get the apartment sanitized and put back on the market. Instead, Diana received a form listing the items the public administrator had removed, including a Rolex watch, which would later bring in $7,000 at an auction conducted by the public administrator. Other items to be auctioned were four sealed bags of rare coins (sold for $595), a pair of checkered cuff links (sold for $22.50), and David's 14-karat gold ring (sold for $180). Other than that, there wasn't much of value in David's apartment. Everything else—his books, the homemade gadgets, the computer equipment—would be boxed up and trashed, eventually.

David had promised his Rolex to his neighbor Jesus, but without a will there was no way for Jesus to legally claim it. Diana pointed out to Jesus that he had David's tall oak walking stick. David had left it in Jesus's car on their final outing to the store to get cat food.

"If there was anything that would remind you of David," Diana told him, "it would be his walking stick."

Jesus nodded. The stick wasn't worth much, but it was one of David's most cherished possessions. The public administrator would have discarded it.

"You see," Diana added, "it was meant to be. You were supposed to have it."

The public administrator determined that the next of kin should make final arrangements, using the funds in David's accounts.

But this administrative conclusion did nothing to help Joyce solve her problem with Mikel. He wanted David's money but didn't want to take responsibility for the dead man's body. Joyce explained that, because David had assets, his funeral "MUST be handled privately." If David was honorably discharged from the navy, as Mikel suggested, he would qualify for a military burial. But the next of kin had to step in to request a burial through a private funeral home. Mikel did not want to do this. He wanted the county to deal with David's body. Joyce replied that if he and Tiffany could not handle the duties required of them by law, the only option would be to allow the public administrator to collect the funds and pay a funeral home out of David's estate. She explained that they would also deduct a fee for their services, and she copied the deputy in charge of the case for emphasis. Then Joyce signed off, "I hope this helps."

The next day Mikel wrote that they had no choice and would go with the option to hire the public administrator. "It is hard to trust anybody these days when money is involved."

Tiffany signed the affidavit of heirship to nominate the public administrator to handle her late brother's estate. On the form she wrote "unknown" for even the most basic questions, such as David's date of birth, and whether he had ever been married or had children. She filled in only her parents' date of death and sister's current residency. Tiffany's handwriting had a childlike quality—large and swirly, with letters punctuated with dots that looked like floating bubbles. She indicated in the paperwork that the last time she had been in contact with Judith was when their mother died in April 2003.

David hadn't wanted his family to get anything, but he hadn't drawn up a will because he didn't want to pay for an attorney. Susan knew how frugal he was and had tried to persuade him otherwise. "Just go to the bank and put me on your accounts," she had told David on one of their calls. That's what she had done, she said, listing a friend as her beneficiary because she had never remarried and had no children or living relatives. If David had followed through with putting Susan on his accounts, she might have been able to arrange for his cremation. But David had kept putting it off.

In this, he was not unusual. Fewer than half of Americans (46 percent) had a will in 2021, and those who did were more likely to be wealthy or elderly. An older study of 1998 showed that an even smaller percentage (32 percent) purchased either burial insurance, which heirs can use to pay for final arrangements, or funeral insurance, which pays a funeral home directly.

Without a will, David's wishes in life—to give his watch to Jesus or make sure his body was laid to rest under the trees—became unenforceable in death. Along with narrow assumptions of who constituted kin, the county had strict ideas about what constituted a "good" disposition. A funeral with burial was preferred over cremation, despite the rise in cremation's popularity. In 2015, for the first time in U.S. history, more Americans were cremated than buried (the rate rose to 59 percent in 2022). Still, the public administrator continued to opt for burial when funds allowed because they considered it more dignified and respectful. Some religions don't allow for cremation, and burial was a way to play it safe.

Meanwhile, even as they refused to claim David's body, Mikel and Tiffany were planning how they would spend David's money. When the estate was settled, after expenses and fees amounting to $30,000, Tiffany's share came to $10,996.71. The same amount would go to Judith. Mikel wrote to Joyce in an email that he and Tiffany had married in 1985 but had been too broke at the time to take a honeymoon. The couple longed to buy a trike motorcycle to travel the open road. Feeling no shame about benefiting from the investment account of a man they hadn't spoken to in decades, Mikel shared with Joyce, "It has been our lifelong dream, and this might give us a good chance to make it come true before we get too old!!"

. .

EVERY WORKDAY, CRAIG GARNETTE CARRIED IN ONE HAND A fourteen-ounce Styrofoam cup filled with peanuts from his dark gray Honda Accord to a park bench next to the crematorium building at the county cemetery in Boyle Heights. In his other hand, he held a mug filled with whatever happened to be his latest drink obsession. At the moment, he was mixing a teaspoon of coffee with a teaspoon of chicory, the woodsy herb popular in New Orleans coffee. His daughter had recommended the combination, arguing that it was good for his health. She was working on getting her dad to follow a vegan diet, too. She knew he needed to slim down to ease the pressure on his knees, his limp from a car accident worsening with the years.

Craig threw a handful of peanuts in the dirt and waited, the Styrofoam cup on the ground next to his heavy work boots. He could see beady black eyes in the trees watching him. He clucked his tongue against his teeth. Two squirrels darted down, then halted. One moved forward, retreated up a tree, then ventured back down again. Soon, the bravest of the squirrels grabbed a peanut and darted off. Others followed, grabbing the nuts out of the cup, picking fights, and chasing one another along the way. Craig was mesmerized. He loved the little fellows and their fussy company. The squirrels brought a dose of untainted pleasure to working at the cemetery. He counted seven squirrels on this September day, far below his record of nineteen.

Craig used to keep the crematorium's back door propped open, and sometimes an audacious squirrel would venture in for peanuts. Craig stopped feeding them inside when workers digging a new metro track nearby uncovered a small burial plot for Chinese migrants. The grim discovery led county supervisors to make unplanned visits to the crematorium. Craig had been having trouble with his supervisor and didn't want to invite unnecessary scrutiny.

Craig was a reserved man, not especially eager to make small talk. He preferred hanging out in the quiet cemetery with his squirrels over jockeying for position in the Office of Decedent Affairs. When families showed up at the cemetery to see the handwritten ledgers where the unclaimed were logged, Craig usually stuck to a script. He answered families' questions in a cordial manner, but he did not pry. He let people maintain their privacy, though at the end of their visit, he would always ask if they needed directions to wherever they were going next.

LENA BROWN HAD DIED on July 7, 2012. Four months later, on September 20, the public administrator determined that Lena had insufficient funds for a private burial. Because her family had failed to claim, the Office of Decedent Affairs scheduled her for cremation. Craig and Albert Gaskin retrieved the body from the county morgue and drove the two miles back to the crematorium. Lena was still wrapped like an unwieldy parcel, in a white bedsheet with a layer of thick plastic around her, to keep fluids from seeping out. At Boyle Heights, Craig and Albert transferred her from a discreet white van onto a white wooden board placed on a small metal rolling cart. They pushed the cart through the storage area to the cremation chamber, where two of the three ovens were roaring with gas flames. Craig had started warming up the ovens half an hour earlier. It was not the flames but the extreme heat—1,800 degrees—that would reduce Lena's body to ashes.

After thirty years working together, the two Black men still addressed each other as Mr. Gaskin and Mr. Garnette, not Albert and Craig. Albert, now age seventy-two, had recruited the younger man back in 1979, when Craig was a seventeen-year-old student doing administrative work in the old hospital building of the LAC+USC medical center, where he had been born. "General Hospital," as Craig and locals still referred to it, was the birthplace of many of the city's low-income residents from nearby South Central and East L.A. Albert knew Craig's brother, who had been hired to work in the morgue because of his height: He would boost their department's chances in the annual hospital volleyball tournament. (Craig and his brother were both well above six feet.) His brother left after an injury and later moved to Bakersfield, but Craig remained a fixture at the crematorium and cemetery, preferring to work quietly in the background while Albert, who had worked in a funeral home back in Louisiana before moving to Los Angeles, served as the complex's confident face.

Craig pushed Lena's body, still shrouded, into the furnace. It was surrounded by fire-resistant bricks that were cracked from years of heat exposure. He pulled the metal tag off the body and attached it to a hook next to the oven. Before he closed the furnace door, the body had already caught fire and lit up the dusty room. Four hours later, organs, tissue, and skin had all been vaporized.

Craig pushed a button to lift the furnace door. In the ashes, long bones were still visible, along with a seamed section of skull and parts of the lower jawbone. Hooded in a welding helmet and wearing heatproof gloves, Craig reached into the furnace chamber with a long metal rake to break up and tamp down those last remaining bones. Unlike most county employees, he could not wear an ID tag: The heat would have melted it as soon as he opened the incinerators. When the furnace was cool enough, about forty-five minutes later, Craig, dressed in full protective gear, raked the ashes toward the oven's entrance, where they fell through an opening into a metal drawer. Craig scraped the ashes that had settled in the crevices of the uneven bricks with an angular tool welded to a fifteen-foot metal stick, which the county's machine shop had custom built for him. With a metal broom, he brushed whatever remains had fallen onto the concrete floor and added them to the drawer. At this point, Lena's ashes still contained several bone fragments, two to three inches in diameter.

The crematory furnace did not turn the body to gray dust like a fireplace turns wood to ashes. That required further processing. With a long metal hook, Craig picked up the metal drawer and emptied it into a cremulator. He closed the lid and put his hand on it while the machine—which he called, with morbid acuity, his human blender—ground the bone fragments into a fine, pasty-white, sand-like substance. Thirty seconds later, Lena was a chalky gray ash.

With a paintbrush, Craig carefully removed the ashes from the lid and shook the container to loosen any wayward bits. He then grabbed a screwdriver out of the top drawer of an old metal desk and pried open a dark brown plastic box where Lena's cremains would be placed. He put a plastic bag in the container and draped the edges over the box's sides. He poured the ashes into the container through a metal funnel he had designed himself to perfectly cover the brown box. Before closing the plastic bag, Craig placed on top of the ashes the metal tag with an ID number that had been attached to Lena's body. Then he closed the bag with a twist tie, tamping it down and securing the lid, so that it fit tightly. An average U.S. woman weighed seven pounds in ashes, but Lena's frail body would have been barely four.

He filled out a paper label with Lena's name, the date, and cremation number under the crematory's address and affixed it to the front of the box. He had done the same for three others that day, and there would be four more tomorrow. Those numbers did not include the bodies that the Office of Decedent Affairs or medical examiner's office outsourced to private cremation companies.

Craig picked up the box with Lena's name and case number and carried it into the storage area, where thousands of similar boxes filled with ashes were waiting on shelves thirteen rows high. On each shelf was a sign with the year of cremation. The crematory had enough space for about 6,500 boxes.

Not all cremains ended up in boxes. A separate group was stored in a metal filing cabinet in the main furnace room, the postcard-sized brown envelopes sealed shut with white packing tape. Two drawers held more than one hundred such remains—the infants and over-twenty-weeks-old fetuses that had been left unclaimed at hospitals and cremated by the county.

When Craig first started working at the crematorium, he saw it as "just a job." As time went by, he began to view it differently. People sometimes came to him looking for their relatives, years and even decades after their death. As long as families had a name and an approximate date of death, Craig could locate their loved one in the ledgers—the name usually handwritten by Craig himself, using the careful penmanship he'd learned in drafting and engineering school. It could take time to work through the delicate pages, but he liked to see the joy in a person's face when they found their family member—joy infused with sadness. Looking at a yellow house across the street from the crematorium, Craig recalled how its previous occupant had come by the cemetery on a whim one day. The man had lost touch with his father decades earlier and had been trying to find him ever since. But the entire time he had been searching, his father was right next door, having been cremated and buried in the county cemetery.

After putting Lena's box on its shelf—2012—Craig went outside for some fresh air. The cremation furnace contained a pollution control chamber that eliminated smoke and odor, a feature added after some of the cemetery's neighbors had complained of an offending smell (an investigation would later attribute the odor to a nearby car-painting shop). The noise of the fiery machines was also dampened. There was nothing here to suggest the radical reduction of human bodies. Just some green grass, trees, and tame squirrels set amid five acres. Craig sat on the bench and watched a squirrel rummage with its nose through the peanut shells looking for something edible. It found a morsel and sat up, holding the nut between its front paws as it nibbled. Craig smiled.

MARJORIE RAMOS RECEIVED THE letter from the Office of Decedent Affairs alerting her of the county's procedures to claim cremains, but she ignored it. She'd been close to her cousin, Marlene, who had since died, but not Lena. She and Rudy had moved on with their lives.

PART THREE

..

REMEMBERED

For if you always think of me,

I will never be gone.

—MARGARET MEAD,

"REMEMBER ME"

8.

THE DEAD DON'T VOTE

· ·

FATHER CHRIS PONNET HELD HIS PATIENT LIST UP AGAINST a hospital room doorframe and drew a small cross next to a name. The sign served as a reminder to note later in an electronic record that he had given the patient a blessing. Father Chris headed the chaplaincy program at LAC+USC, and he spent his workdays making rounds among the patient rooms in the large public hospital. Balding, his beard a neatly trimmed mix of gray and white, the affable Catholic priest had the look of a friar when he wore ecclesiastical garments. But he intentionally avoided robes when visiting patients. On this late December day, he wore black khakis and a black shirt that read CHAPLAINS ARE PRAYING FOR YOU in both English and Spanish, with an illustration of two gloved hands forming a heart with thumbs and index fingers. The other exception to his no-religious-clothing rule was a pair of red-and-green-striped Christmas socks, a hint of whimsy he combined with his signature dark brown Birkenstocks.

When Father Chris joined LAC+USC in 2009, he discovered that the Office of Decedent Affairs—located on the same grounds as the hospital—held a small burial ceremony for the ashes of the unclaimed dead each year in Boyle Heights. Typically, the only attendees were Albert, Craig, an official from the medical examiner's office, and Father Chris's predecessor, Chaplain Phil Manly. The ceremony lasted five minutes, time for Manly to offer a quick prayer and a Psalm reading but little else. It irked Father Chris that, in a religiously diverse city, a burial service for 1,600 Angelenos only offered brief, generic Christian blessings. He saw an opportunity for a larger interfaith service that could become a model for the nation.

In all his work, Father Chris was guided by Catholicism's seven corporal works of mercy, a set of practices—from feeding the hungry to visiting the imprisoned—that bestow kindness on all, even (and perhaps especially) those who might seem undeserving of our love. Burying the dead is one of these corporal works. Tending to the sick, part of Father Chris's day job, was another work of mercy, and it was intimately connected to his efforts on behalf of the departed. Father Chris knew that many of his patients were at high risk of going unclaimed.

He glanced at his list and saw the name of a new patient, a forty-three-year-old man. He knocked on the door. "Ethan, I am Father Chris, one of the chaplains. I am just stopping by."

"Oh, man. I need to see you, bro." Ethan didn't sit up; both his ankles were wrapped up in casts. He could only turn his bare-chested, densely tattooed body toward the door to signal a welcome. Father Chris asked Ethan how he was doing. "I could be better, I could be worse," Ethan answered, adding that he had been off heroin for six days, after ten years of using.

"Well, praise God," Father Chris responded.

"Praise God," Ethan agreed.

"One step at a time."

More at ease, Ethan began to confess. He had run with gangs since he was thirteen, had been shot three different times, and spent more of his life in than out of prison. He gazed intently at Father Chris and said, "I've done enough shit. I ain't killed nobody." Ethan had been out of prison for over four years but struggled with a heroin addiction that had started while he was incarcerated. Father Chris listened and nodded. He had learned not to judge.

"Every once in a while, we need a kick in the back," the chaplain said. "Right?"

Ethan looked down and responded that a lot of people were afraid of giving him a kick in the ass. Father Chris nodded and said that sometimes friends think that they are helping you, but they aren't.

"A man without a sense of direction is lost, and . . ." Ethan's voice trailed away. So far, only his girlfriend and brother had visited him. He had yet to see his four-year-old daughter, whom he'd had with another woman.

"Well," Father Chris said, "you have an opportunity now." He pointed at a crocheted brown and orange blanket that Ethan clutched under his arm. "You've got one of our quilts?"

The previous week, the hospital chaplains had distributed more than five hundred handmade blankets throughout the hospital. Ethan said that he found it on his bed when he woke up. It happened to be his birthday. He didn't know where it had come from but had quickly become attached to it. Father Chris assured him that it was his to keep: Volunteers worked on them all year round and prayed for the person who received the blanket.

Ethan's eyes welled up. "I just need you . . ."

"We'll keep you in our prayers and thoughts, okay?" Then Father Chris proposed that they pray together. "How's that?" He always asked before starting a prayer for someone, and he only brought in the name "Jesus" when he knew a person would be open to hearing it, usually employing a more general "God" in his prayers. Some of his friends teased him, asking if he was still Catholic.

Ethan held out his hands, which Father Chris took. The chaplain prayed for a future of new possibilities and for Ethan's partner and daughter. He prayed that Ethan would be surrounded by people who would believe in him, challenge him, affirm him, love him, and want what's best for him. Ethan squeezed Father Chris's hands when his daughter was mentioned. After the prayer, Ethan asked for a rosary. The chaplain checked his gray felt satchel but could not find one. He promised to send one up, and wrote a cross and an *R* for rosary next to Ethan's name.

FATHER CHRIS SEEMED DESTINED to serve the lonely and down-trodden. He'd grown up in a large, churchgoing Irish-Belgian family. An aunt was a nun, and a brother went to seminary. At first, young Chris had no interest in following in their footsteps. But a nun in his Catholic school regaled him with stories of saints that piqued his interest in working for the church. The most memorable was the story of Marcellino, an orphan boy abandoned on the steps of a monastery. The monks raised him, and he grew into a rowdy boy. The monks told him not to enter the cloister's attic, but Marcellino snuck in at night and found a statue of Jesus. The statue came alive and spoke to him, telling him how to be a better person and giving him religious instruction. The boy kept returning to the attic. One day, the monks followed him and, seeing the miracle of the statue coming to life, they welcomed him into their religious order. Even as a nine-year-old boy, Father Chris saw the story as a parable about serving the invisible people in our midst, including orphans and lost souls.

Sixteen years later, in 1983, he became an ordained Catholic priest. Almost immediately, he started to minister to HIV patients, at a time when AIDS was seen as an exclusively gay disease and just punishment for immorality. Such patients were discriminated against both inside and outside the hospital. The diocese of L.A., under a young archbishop named Roger Mahony, boldly recognized Father Chris's work and established an official ministry to welcome those with HIV/AIDS into the Catholic Church and treat them with dignity and respect. Later, the ministry split into separate LGBTQ and HIV groups. Father Chris remained involved as a spiritual leader in both ministries.

Over the years, Father Chris's bottom-line belief that every person deserved to be treated with dignity had led him to become

active in anti-war protests. In 2003, he was arrested for civil disobe-
dience while protesting the invasion of Iraq. To underscore their
"No Blood for Oil" protest slogan, Father Chris and the activists
drew some of their own blood and mixed it with petroleum, then
dramatically poured the mixture into an intersection in downtown
L.A. Even though they had told the police in advance what they
intended to do and explained what the fluid was, LAPD made a
spectacle, closing off the intersection and four surrounding blocks.
Father Chris spent a couple of days in jail before his sentence was
reduced to house arrest.

It wasn't the only political fight that Father Chris waged. For
years, he convened a group of Catholics Against the Death Penalty
every month in his home parish, St. Camillus, a short walk from the
hospital. The group included a retired judge, an attorney, prison
chaplains, and an exoneree who had served more than twenty years
for a wrongful conviction. In 2016, the group was finally able to put
a ballot question in front of California voters. If Proposition 62
passed, it would abolish the death penalty in the state. They gathered signatures, mailed out postcards to parishes, hired a speakers'
bureau, and organized phone banks to get their word out. The California bishops issued a statement of support. Father Chris believed
fervently in the cause: It was easy to protest executions of the innocent, but the real challenge for the faithful was to abolish even
executions of the guilty. Asking "Who Would Jesus Execute?" followed with "Thou Shalt Not Kill," the interfaith coalition hoped to
rally voters to support the legislation. But they lost. Even worse,
voters approved a competing measure that limited the time for
death penalty appeals. Not even the likelihood of executing an innocent person was sufficient to sway the electorate, including some
in his parish who were unified in their opposition to abortion but
not the state murder of adults. "We're at a time when mercy is not
as high a priority," he lamented.

He refused to give up, though. Ever the idealist, Father Chris
was heartened by an influx of new activists, giving him hope that

they could someday try again. Before an execution, he would hold a mass to pray for the victim. The day after, he would hold one for the family of the executed.

IN HIS ROLE AS head chaplain, Father Chris oversaw the chaplaincy training program at LAC+USC. He told his students that regardless of their own faiths and beliefs, they should try to meet patients where they were, spiritually. With a large Spanish-speaking immigrant population, many of LAC+USC's medically underserved patients were Catholic, but the intern chaplains were taught a range of prayers for the sick and dying. In a pinch, they could consult an iPhone app, Interfaith Care for the Ill, to remind them of what was appropriate for certain faiths.

Father Chris also cared for his students. Every day, he conducted a daily self-care session for trainees. Normally a dozen or so attended, but on that late December morning, close to the Christmas holidays, only three other chaplains showed up. Father Chris asked the group to keep a homeless patient in the ICU in mind. LAC+USC saw more than its share of homeless patients: 10 percent of its patients were considered homeless, compared to 3 percent in hospitals across the state. The man was scheduled that day for what the hospital staff called a compassionate extubation, which would result in his death. Father Chris had been struck by how tenderly the man's girlfriend, also homeless, caressed her ailing partner.

Father Chris's chaplaincy students and chaplains responded to about four hundred yearly pager calls and made ten thousand visits. Before he let them go into patient rooms on their own, he encouraged them to visit the Boyle Heights crematorium and tour the facility with Albert and Craig. Father Chris told his students that chaplains will often encounter a desperate person in the hospital who, as death approaches, says, "Just dump my body in the street." The homeless, Father Chris thought, internalized society's disdain and believed themselves social pariahs. He instructed the chaplains to tell these lost souls about the staff at the public cemetery and to say, with complete honesty, "Your body will be treated with respect."

Indeed, no society that we know of has ever "dumped" bodies in the streets. Even in times of upheaval, such as war, one of the first acts of recovery is to bury the dead. For cultures without burial traditions, such as the Zoroastrians in Mumbai, who leave bodies out for vultures to devour, ritual prescriptions guide their practice. A special group of pallbearers places the bodies on rounded platforms for a designated amount of time, before gathering the bones afterward and placing them in a central ossuary. The Zoroastrians adopted sky burials because they believed that burying a body in the earth contaminated the soil.

In ancient Greece, the philosopher Diogenes, a founder of Cynicism, exposed his countrymen's attachment to "proper" disposition by telling his disciples that he wanted his remains to be thrown over the city walls and devoured by wild beasts. When they asked whether he would mind being mutilated, he told them to give him a stick to chase the animals away. When they pointed out that he wouldn't be able to use the stick after he died, they proved his point: "If I lack awareness, then why should I care what happens to me when I am dead?" His contemporaries, like people throughout history, did not listen. When Diogenes died, the Corinthians erected an elaborate marble pillar in his honor.

When Father Chris's students met Albert and Craig, they were relieved to discover that the poor and unclaimed dead of Los Angeles wouldn't be trashed. However, this didn't mean that all unclaimed Americans are guaranteed a dignified send-off. Without a federal policy in place, each local government is left to decide how to handle their unclaimed bodies.

In Imperial County, California, in the desert lands at the U.S.-Mexico border, unclaimed bodies were buried in a local cemetery until the late 2000s. Then, in what an assistant public administrator said was a cost-saving measure, the county started cremating unclaimed bodies—which includes unidentified migrants—and sending their ashes 110 miles west, to the San Diego coast, to be scattered in the Pacific Ocean. In San Bernardino County, which borders Los Angeles, urns were collected until there were enough to fill a concrete vault, at which point there was a burial. But there was no announcement or ceremony. In the most famous American potter's field, Hart Island, prisoners buried New York's unclaimed in plain pine caskets with little fanfare. The public was prohibited from witnessing interment or visiting the gravesites.

Father Chris wanted more for the unclaimed. After all, they were people who, like anyone else, had had dreams and setbacks, who'd enjoyed life's pleasures while struggling with its obstacles. They were people whose deaths should mean something to those left behind.

After his planned rounds, Father Chris left the medical ward and made a detour to the ICU, to see if the homeless man he had prayed for earlier that morning was still there. The chaplain leaned into the ICU's keyless gate with his lanyard. He glanced in the first room, where the man had been the day before. The room was empty, except for a made-up hospital bed and unplugged pumps and monitors pushed to the side. He was too late. The man had passed away and was likely already in the basement county morgue.

Father Chris said a short prayer, then saw that it was almost noon, time for him to lead mass at St. Camillus, and headed downstairs. Before he left the hospital, he stopped at a memorial displaying pictures of staff members who had died in the past year. He joked with an orderly passing by that he was checking to see whether his own name was on it. Not yet, the orderly replied with a smile. Over the previous few years, Father Chris had had four heart stents implanted and suffered two strokes. He was more easily winded, but he did not share his health problems with patients unless they asked him directly.

Walking down the hill, Father Chris stopped to catch his breath. He turned to look at the San Gabriel Mountains shimmering in the far distance. He thought of the homeless couple. There was a good chance the man who had been extubated would go unclaimed, and it would fall on Father Chris to oversee his burial in the county cemetery in Boyle Heights in a few years. One more soul among the tens of thousands the city had laid to rest.

. .

BY LATE NOVEMBER 2015, IT WAS OBVIOUS TO ALBERT THAT no one would come for Lena Brown's cremains. The brown plastic box bearing her name had collected a thin layer of dust over the nearly three years it had sat in storage, untouched. Marjorie Ramos, Lena's niece, lived just two miles from the crematorium, but she had no interest in claiming her aunt's ashes. *After all,* she thought, *she'd never really known Lena that well.* Rudy was also a no-show at the crematorium. They weren't alone in this neglect. Families came by to pick up ashes in only about one of every six cases. The overwhelming majority of those cremated by the county—more than 82 percent—remained unclaimed.

Disheartened by the apathy he saw, Albert cherished the days when families came looking for ashes or visited the common graves. Their visits assured him that his work made a difference. With piercing round brown eyes, he listened intently as family members recounted stories of their loved ones.

On an early March day in 2015, someone came in for one of Lena's shelf-mates. Karen Rosoff had died at age fifty-nine on December 21, 2012, five months after Lena, in an assisted living facility in Lancaster. An autopsy determined that the cause of death was the effects of methadone (an overdose can be lethal), exacerbated by an enlarged heart. The medical examiner's office sent Karen for cremation the following February, and her ashes were later transferred to the county crematorium, where Albert placed them in a plastic box for storage. More than two years passed before he would touch the box again.

Like many of the unclaimed, Karen's relationship with her next of kin—in her case, her adopted sister, Susan Rorke—had frayed. Karen had been a hell-raiser from an early age, never letting up on the party life. Their mother kept a firm grip on Susan, out of fear that she, too, would fall in with a "fast crowd." The restrictions made Susan resentful, and the sisters frequently fought. As adults, they spent much of their lives distanced from each other, though they reconciled at a Thanksgiving dinner shortly before Karen died.

Susan had wanted to claim her sister's body because, despite everything, they were the only family each had left. She was cash-strapped; the year that Karen died, Susan earned $57,000 from a clerk job in an L.A. County office, enough to cover her bills but only barely. She didn't know how she would pay for a burial or cremation. It also took her a while to process Karen's sudden death, and by the time she was ready to retrieve the body two years later, Karen had been cremated and the ashes stacked for storage in Boyle Heights.

The thought of having Karen's remains dumped "like she was garbage" in a mass grave was too much to bear, and Susan was motivated to act before the three-year clock ran out. It took repeated phone calls to the Office of Decedent Affairs for Susan to learn that she could retrieve the ashes after she filed a burial permit and paid an administrative fee. She started the paperwork, comparing the bureaucratic journey to Dorothy's in *The Wizard of Oz.* "One step at a time, follow the yellow brick road." When it was time to pay the $350 fee, Susan balked. She had lost a week's wages earlier in the year after a suspension at work, and she was still recovering from the financial hit. She called the Office of Decedent Affairs and received a fee waiver, which she had learned the office would grant in cases of indigency.

When Susan came to pick up her sister's ashes, Albert welcomed the thin, gray-haired woman warmly. She smelled like a bouquet of fresh roses and lilacs, and the flowery aroma was a welcome break from the industrial staleness of the crematorium. Albert guided Susan around the facility, showing her the furnaces and explaining how they worked. Then he walked her to the facility's unused chapel, a white-washed room at the front of the crematorium with simple dark wooden benches and an old piano. He unlocked a fireproof cabinet in the corner and searched through the heavy ledgers that contained names of the unclaimed going back to 1896. After he found the volume with 2012 deaths, he placed the ledger on a wood lectern at the front of the room and used Karen's day of death to locate her entry, on page 361. He waved Susan over and pointed to the line where she needed to write her name and the date and then sign.

Albert retrieved the ashes from the storage area. He had wrapped the box in brown paper earlier in the day. He opened a corner, showed Susan the white label, and asked if the name was correct. Susan nodded, through tears. Albert put a piece of tape on the brown paper to rewrap the box. He gently asked her whether she would like him to carry the box to her car, since the ashes were heavy. Susan shook her head, reached for the box, and held it to her chest.

It was a simple exchange, but Albert lived for these moments. "I don't think I could sleep at night if I didn't honor these individuals," he said. It made all the difference to him that Karen had been returned to her sister rather than disappearing into a mass grave.

ALBERT SAW CARING FOR the unwanted as his life's work. He had started out as a driver, transporting bodies. Then he was promoted to supervisor. When he became a senior supervisor, he felt he had earned a right to help steer the cemetery's policies on engaging with the public. He wanted to be able to call up relatives, to encourage them to come by. He would have told them about the fee waiver for indigency. He would have held ashes longer if they asked. He would have installed park benches, so they had a place to sit as they visited the graves of loved ones they had found too late. Instead, families had to make their way through a bureaucratic maze to find him, persisting when repeated phone calls to the Office of Decedent Affairs went to voicemail.

"Our boss now, she's not a public person."

Albert was talking about Estela Inouye, who had run the Office of Decedent Affairs since 2007. She was in her forty-third year working for the county, but her office looked like she had just moved in. The space had none of the usual personal touches—photos, cards, paperweights, inspirational sayings, or jokes. She was guarded at work.

Estela and Albert disagreed about what the county owed the unclaimed. Estela saw her job mainly as bringing in the right bodies and releasing them as quickly and quietly as possible—to relatives, to the medical examiner's office, or to one of the crematoria. Her crypt held only four hundred bodies, and every day she received an average of eleven new ones. Her two nightmare scenarios were a backlog of dead bodies and the cremation or release of the wrong one. Either way, she was eager to get rid of bodies with as little scrutiny as possible.

At her desk in the bowels of the county's death bureaucracy, Estela checked the morgue's inventory every morning and every evening. It took a lot to care for the bodies that came through her morgue, and she didn't receive enough resources to do it the way she wanted. The dead had to be counted, tracked, and kept between 36 and 39 degrees twenty-four hours a day, seven days a week. Estela knew that state inspectors could show up at any time. She pointed out that her office handled thousands of bodies every year and she received less than 0.00006 percent of the Los Angeles County Department of Health's $7 billion annual budget.

As is often the case in resource-strapped workplaces, the lack of funding turned people against one another. Estela resented how little she had to work with; Albert, on the other hand, thought Estela used the budget as an excuse to strip him of control. He used to be able to ship cremains to family members out of state, but Estela put an end to that. She thought it was too much hassle and risk. She required that relatives come in person to retrieve ashes, but also closed the office on Fridays and weekends. It baffled Albert. He believed that as a public service agency, the Office of Decedent Affairs should try everything in their power to help reunite the deceased with relatives.

As the number of unclaimed began to rise in the early 2000s,

Estela's mood worsened. She doubled down on protecting the people she called "my dead," withholding the names of the unclaimed and refusing to release information that should have been publicly available, citing privacy concerns.

Paradoxically, the move drew more attention to her office. Jon Schleuss was a data reporter for the *Los Angeles Times* and an expert in infographics. He'd grown up in rural Arkansas and had been in Los Angeles only a few months when he learned that the county buried 1,600 people a year with no relatives to claim them. For Jon, who had been more focused on earthquakes and wildfires, the unclaimed were a new kind of natural disaster. His small-town roots helped him see the city through a different lens, as a place bathed in loneliness and hyper-individualism, and the unclaimed became his vehicle for exploring the dark side of L.A. On a hunch, he called the Office of Decedent Affairs.

Estela was immediately irritated by the eager newspaper reporter. She tried to keep Jon away, telling him that he needed to go through the hospital's public information officer as part of standard protocol. What she didn't say—to Jon or the other reporters and researchers who called—was that the public information officer deferred to the Office of Decedent Affairs on all matters regarding the unclaimed. Every request went through Estela for approval. And she always declined.

Jon persisted. After several tries, he had arranged to meet her at the county crematorium. But as he made his way on the Metro's Gold Line to Boyle Heights, Estela called and left a message to say that the meeting was canceled and the records off-limits due to the Privacy Rule of the Health Insurance Portability and Accountability Act, better known as HIPAA. Jon disagreed, arguing that unclaimed were buried on county-owned land and their names were a matter of public record. Moreover, the HIPAA Privacy Rule covers individually identifiable health information, which was not included in the records. He decided to continue, hoping he could convince whoever was on-site to hear him out.

But when he got to the crematory office, next to the chapel, a clerk at the door told him politely that he had to leave. The clerk then locked the door.

Jon was more than a little irritated. Estela had ruffled the young man, his friendly southern gentility giving way to his investigative instincts. He called his editor, who contacted the *Times* attorney. The Los Angeles County counsel took his side, agreeing that the ledgers were public records, and a few days later, Jon was finally able to make an appointment to view them. Jon had a new beat: the disregarded dead of L.A.

On his return to the crematorium, Jon met Albert, who unlocked the safe and gave Jon access to the records. Jon pulled out his iPhone 4 and started snapping. There were too many names to get them all, and Jon decided to focus on the names of the people who would be buried later that year, in 2014. He hoped that publishing the names might lead families to act in time to claim the ashes. It took him several visits to capture everything he needed. Back in the newsroom, he and fellow *Los Angeles Times* data reporter Maloy Moore spent what little free time they had digitizing the names and details of the unclaimed dead from 2011 and entering them into a searchable database they had built for the newspaper's website.

His ten months poring over the records of all the people who had been cremated by Albert and Craig helped Jon realize two things: First, he had no desire to die in Los Angeles. But if he did, whether he was claimed or not, he would be honored to have Albert and Craig cremate his body. Jon had become fond of the two men at the crematorium during his months of reporting. They were, in the words of another county official, "two diamonds in a field of coal." Jon was fascinated by Albert and, in one story, noted that Albert wanted to be cremated by Craig when he died. "It's like if you go to a doctor," Albert told Jon, "you'd want to go to a very good doctor because you know he's going to take care of you."

Jon published several stories about the unclaimed in the *Los Angeles Times* in late 2014 and again in late 2015. One of them was read by Cherry Williamson, a retired YMCA employee in San Diego. Her brother, Wesley, had disappeared in 1980. He had been a professional dancer, something that most young men didn't dare aspire to in the conservative Colorado city where they'd grown up. Wesley traveled through Europe on dance tours, eventually working for Disney. When their mother's health declined, Wesley returned to Colorado Springs to help care for her. She died six months later and then, without any warning, Wesley took off again—after he cleaned out a bank account the siblings shared.

Cherry had spent decades longing to know what had happened. She suspected that her brother had likely gone to New York or L.A., but she couldn't find him. Then, by chance, Cherry read about the unclaimed dead in the *Los Angeles Times* and called Jon. He told her about Albert and the cremation registers. For the first time in years, Cherry had hope of finding closure. She said she would drive up from San Diego when she could.

IN THE WAKE OF Jon's article, Estela begrudgingly agreed to post online a searchable database of unclaimed records, starting with the dead of 2012. But she managed to keep one aspect of her work out of public view. For decades, the Office of Decedent Affairs had been providing bodies for scientific study to the LAC+USC campus of the University of Southern California's Keck School of Medicine and at Cypress College, which offered a mortuary science program. After the students were done with them, the embalmed unclaimed bodies traveled back to Boyle Heights or to an outside crematorium to be cremated.

There was nothing illicit about this: California's Health and Safety Code, which had last been updated in 2009, explicitly allowed the use of unclaimed bodies for research. But Estela realized that even if the practice was legal, it didn't look good for the poor to be dissected without having given their consent (especially when the same medical school ran a separate "willed-body" program that did require consent).

Since 1745, when the first formal anatomy course was taught at the University of Pennsylvania, medical and mortuary schools in the United States have sought to source human bodies. Schools initially obtained the bodies of executed criminals, thanks to a federal law from 1790 that allowed judges to add dissection to a death sentence. (Dissection was intended to serve as a crime deterrent because early colonists believed that the desecration of the corpse impeded resurrection.) When the supply of bodies from capital punishment was insufficient for American medical education, robbing the graves of freshly buried people, especially slaves and the poor, became rampant. Grave robbing was a fate feared by many, and with good reason. New York alone saw six hundred to seven hundred bodies snatched in 1854. In a peculiarity of American law, body snatchers could be punished more severely if they were found in possession of a dead man's cuff links than his bones; possessing a corpse carried no penalty.

Because body snatching occasionally led to mob violence, medical schools learned to tap into a set of cadavers less likely to generate public protest: unclaimed bodies. Human corpses were (and still are) classified as quasi-property, an ambiguous legal category. If corpses were treated purely as property, they could be bought and sold. Instead, limited property rights reflect relatives' right to bury their dead (right of sepulcher) but not to own the body. If relatives are uninterested in handling disposition, the quasi-property status makes it legal for the state to release unclaimed bodies for "instruction."

Massachusetts, home of Harvard Medical School, was the first state to pass laws, in 1830 and 1833, allowing medical schools to use the bodies of unclaimed people who died in prisons or asylums. Other states followed with similar laws, including California in 1927.

These laws cut out the shady body snatcher but did little to change who ended up on the dissection table. Unclaimed, immigrant, and indigent bodies had already been most likely to be dug up during midnight cemetery raids. Some lauded the fact that those who were considered a burden in life could still be of use in death, ignoring the humiliation of a dissection that the poor themselves didn't choose. Laws made exceptions for the unclaimed bodies of travelers and soldiers, underscoring again that dissection was for those on the lowest rung of society.

The county had reason to keep its cadaver program under wraps. Two years after Jon's series in the *Los Angeles Times,* New York state had banned its practice of making unclaimed bodies available for medical research and education without consent. The reason for the change was public outcry after a series in *The New York Times.* Estela, meanwhile, amped up her efforts to protect the unclaimed dead.

AT THE SAME TIME, budget pressures on the Office of Decedent Affairs were unrelenting, and Albert and Craig were becoming more alarmed at the cost cutting. When Jon published his feature on Albert in 2014, Albert and Craig were still getting to work at four A.M. and cremating about ten bodies per day. But then one of their three furnaces broke down and they didn't know when, or even if, it would be brought back online. With the reduced capacity, the two men were able to cremate only two bodies per day. The rest went to private crematoria. County bureaucrats had calculated that outsourcing was cheaper than paying Albert and Craig overtime.

Then the situation worsened. When Estela found out that Albert and Craig allowed the public to tour the crematorium, she forbade the visits, declaring that everyone should obtain written permission from the department's information officer before being shown the county's facilities. She also installed a clerk at the crematorium who was directed to call her if anyone showed up.

Albert and Craig felt they were being spied on. They knew that the public information office deferred to Estela, meaning relatives would never receive permission for a tour. One of the job's greatest joys for Albert was erased. He was reduced to a box carrier.

Pressures were coming from all sides. In 2016, the Los Angeles County Civil Grand Jury, a watchdog entity, had issued a report: *Who Cares for the Dead if the Dead Don't Vote?* The grand jury observed that having two agencies deal with dead bodies did not benefit the citizens of Los Angeles. The report proposed folding the Office of Decedent Affairs into the Los Angeles Medical Examiner–Coroner's office. It also recommended that the medical examiner's budget be increased by at least $2.3 million to account for the additional staff needed to follow the medical examiner's statutorily mandated procedures of investigation and notification. The merger plan floundered for lack of financial resources.

Two years later, Albert, then seventy-seven years old, decided he'd had enough. On an otherwise ordinary-seeming workday in February, he drove the two miles from the cemetery to the hospital morgue to clock out. He changed from his work overalls into his off-duty clothes. He walked past one of the clerical aides on Estela's staff on his way out.

"I am gone," he said, tersely.

"Okay," she replied. "See you tomorrow."

"No. I am *gone*."

The man who had advocated for five decades for L.A.'s unclaimed would take no more of the bureaucratic apathy. It pained him to think that the work had been in vain, but it could no longer be his burden to carry.

9.

A CALLING

· ·

DOYLE TOLBERT PICKED UP A DOG-EARED FILE THAT HAD been crammed in the back of his desk. It was 1998 and the medical examiner's office, where he ran notifications, relied mostly on paper to keep track of cases. The manila folder barely held together, the seam torn from repeated opening and closing. Doyle carefully opened the folder and leaned back in his chair, running his thumb and index finger down his white horseshoe mustache as he studied the contents. His eyes lingered on a paper imprinted with two tiny baby feet. It looked like the kind of memento a new mother would cherish, a reminder of how perfect her child's toes once were. These feet, though, would never grow bigger. They were a medical examiner's identification card for case number 98-02204.

The footprints belonged to Baby Doe. Doyle was unsure whether she'd ever had a real name. He called her Grace, a name for someone who honors with their presence. The medical examiner's scene investigators had retrieved her from an aqueduct in Palmdale. No one knew how long she had been in the water. What was left of her body weighed barely five pounds, and her eyes were gone. *Someone really hated her,* Doyle thought. *Not only did they murder her, they threw her into a flood channel.*

Doyle did not turn away from gruesome deaths. If he had not seen it all, he had seen most of it. Before he was a deputy scene investigator, he'd worked in communications and intelligence in the

U.S. Air Force, where he was awarded an Air Force Good Conduct Medal and a National Defense Service Medal. He spoke often about his tours in Vietnam and in Pakistan, and the thrill of jumping out of a plane, feeling suspended for precious seconds, pulling the parachute's rip cord, and landing on foreign soil. While he survived the heated conflicts of the 1960s, many of his military brothers had not. Doyle was haunted by their deaths.

After an honorable discharge from the air force, he spent nearly two decades as a police officer in Los Angeles and Fullerton before a back injury sidelined him and he transferred to the L.A. medical examiner's office. He kept a replica metal hand grenade on his desk with a number 1 dangling from its safety pin. Above the grenade was a sign: COMPLAINT DEPARTMENT: PLEASE TAKE A NUMBER. A joke, kind of. Doyle had a low tolerance for bullshit. Next to his desk, he hung a picture of John Wayne in *The Green Berets,* a staunchly pro-military and anti-communism movie released in 1968.

To the right of John Wayne, under a big American flag, hung scribbled drawings by his two-year-old granddaughter. His three small grandkids were his treasures. "Papa's girls," he called them.

Doyle was confined to a desk, but his job was an emotional roller coaster: the high of finding kin after searching for weeks through arrest records, missing person reports, and Social Security files, and then the deflating low when the family remained unmoved by the news. He received between ten and fifteen cases every day, some of which took months and even years to solve. He was a phone detective—days spent chasing leads and making calls to law enforcement agencies across the country.

Sitting next to his wife, Gilda, made the job easier. The couple had met in the medical examiner's office and married in 1992. It was Doyle's fourth marriage. Two ended in divorce, and one made him a widower after just twelve months. With Gilda, he had found his life partner. At home, they raised her children from an earlier marriage, and at work, they ran a small crew trying to get bodies claimed.

Gilda focused on identification while Doyle took the lead on notifying the next of kin.

Most of the time the work didn't bother Doyle. He had a rather dim view of humanity: His previous job as a narcotics officer had showed him how drugs and mental illness could corrode family ties. When he contacted relatives by phone, he could tell right away whether they cared. Many didn't. Doyle thought America had become a "carefree" society. Relatives acted greedily, more interested in inheritance than in honoring the dead. Even when children wanted to do something for their fathers, ex-wives were bitter and vengeful. Some people even scammed the dead. He still remembered a mother and daughter who sobbed and wailed when he showed them pictures of an unclaimed woman who had died of a drug overdose and was found next to a highway. He took their word that they were related. They quickly cremated their lost dead sister and daughter. Except it was all a con: One of the women, trying to elude creditors and probation officers, wanted a death certificate so she could fake her own death. Neither woman was related to the dead one.

The babies' deaths were different. Those gnawed at him, their tiny bodies found in trash cans, creek beds, stuffed in duffel bags and tossed out of a car, or—like Grace—floating upside down in a canal.

Doyle glanced at the print of the small feet in front of him. He kept the folders of the babies close and mentally reviewed their cases during his forty-five-mile commute from Rancho Cucamonga. Who would do such a heinous thing? He had seen babies cast aside during wartime, but that wasn't supposed to happen in *his* America. It hit close to home for Doyle. His mother had run off when he was a young child, abandoning Doyle and his siblings. Seeing the baby's little toes reminded him that his life, too, could have ended before it began.

Over time, Doyle had realized that he could not bring babies like Grace back to life, and their parents were unlikely to be held accountable, despite his and Gilda's efforts to track them down. Without a name, he had nothing to go on. But, he thought, these babies deserved more than their parents had given them. He became obsessed with trying to do something to bring dignity to their short lives. For Doyle, that meant a gravesite: a mark of a life mourned. Each year he made a pilgrimage to visit his father's grave in Santa Maria. Doyle Sr. had served in World War II, and his son considered him a hero. Visiting his grave was Doyle's way of showing his respect.

Over the years, Doyle had unsuccessfully asked cops, funeral directors, local business groups, and even the Boy Scouts to help organize funerals for abandoned infants. He thought he had scored when he located a couple in Downey, a city in the southeast corner of L.A. County, who wanted to help. The couple buried half a dozen babies, but became overwhelmed by the never-ending need for their services. Most of the babies that Doyle investigated were still cremated by the county and kept in small envelopes at the Boyle Heights crematorium until they received a mass burial.

Then, in 1996, a woman named Debi Faris called the medical examiner's office. Faris was a mother of three from Yucaipa, a small town seventy-three miles due east of downtown Los Angeles. She told Doyle that she was overcome with a strong desire to do something for an abandoned baby she had read about in the news. She was the answer to Doyle's prayers. He helped her navigate the bureaucratic hurdles, and she began claiming babies and organizing funerals in the town of Calimesa, in nearby Riverside County. In two years, Faris had buried thirty unclaimed children; Grace became the thirty-first.

Doyle and Gilda attended all the funerals and participated when they could. In one service, they carried a casket holding twin girls whose deaths the couple had investigated. The presence of caring strangers—more than fifty at many of the services—was proof to the couple that their efforts were justified. *The strangers showed these babies more love than their parents ever did,* thought Gilda. For Doyle, working with Faris was transformative, and he thought the name she had chosen for the cemetery, "Garden of Angels," was apt. Faris was an angel who had made an "old duffer" like him keep the faith.

Faris's influence extended further than either she or Doyle realized. Soon, in San Diego, another woman would dedicate herself to the burial of unclaimed babies—and would find herself going far beyond what Faris had ever imagined.

IN DECEMBER 1999, ELISSA DAVEY, a fifty-one-year-old real estate agent, sat at her kitchen table sipping instant coffee and reading that morning's *San Diego Union-Tribune.* A story caught her eye: A baby had been tossed in a garbage can and left to die. Elissa thought, *Whoever did it should be shot.* When her mug was empty, she closed the paper and expected that would be the end of the story for her. But as the day went by, playing Legos with her two grandsons, she couldn't get the abandoned baby out of her mind. A month later, she called the San Diego medical examiner.

"For my own peace of mind, whatever happened to that baby?"

"He is still here," the medical examiner told her. He explained that if no one claimed him, the remains would go into an unmarked grave in the city's Mount Hope Cemetery.

Elissa wasn't sure what prompted her, but she heard herself asking, "How do you a claim a baby that's not yours?"

"Show me you have a dignified place to put him," the medical examiner replied. The San Diego medical examiner's office was more willing than its counterpart in Los Angeles to allow outside groups to bury the unclaimed.

Elissa felt daunted by the prospect of organizing a funeral; she was more accustomed to the solitary endeavor of genealogy, a hobby she spent hours on each week. She was fascinated by long-lost connections and the fact that many people spent their days completely unaware that they had a relative living in the next town. She specialized in helping adopted adults find their birth parents, but she limited her role to providing a name and an address. When she presented the results of her detective work, she would tell her client,

"Here's where they're at. Do what you want with it because I'm not going to be involved." She searched hard because it was important to her to find answers. The unidentified baby in the trash raised questions she could not answer. No future genealogist would ever look for these kids because no one knew they had existed.

Elissa was pondering how she could convince a cemetery to bury an abandoned baby for little to no cost when she happened across an old newspaper profile of Debi Faris. The article mentioned that Debi planned to expand her services to San Diego, noting that there were seven to ten unclaimed infants there each year. Faris hoped to bury these babies in her Garden of Angels outside Los Angeles. This might be Elissa's answer. She contacted Faris, who invited her to an upcoming organizational meeting in San Diego.

By the time the meeting convened, Faris had realized the logistics of burying the San Diego babies 120 miles north in Calimesa would be unmanageable. She encouraged those present at the meeting to start their own burial place for abandoned babies. One of the women in attendance, Rebecca Melendez, was from a local cemetery, El Camino Memorial Park. Rebecca thought they might be able to bury the babies in an unused corner in the back of the cemetery. Rebecca and Elissa struck up a conversation, and Elissa arranged to visit the cemetery.

El Camino marketed itself as San Diego's "premier cemetery since 1960," offering high-priced individual mausoleums. (Jonas Salk, the developer of the polio vaccine, is one of its most famous residents.) The grass in the cemetery was lush, and the setting serene. Rebecca was almost a decade younger than Elissa, with long black hair and a solid build; Elissa wore her reddish-brown hair short around her round face. When Elissa got to the corner of the cemetery that Rebecca had proposed for the babies, near Fenton Carroll Canyon, she had to wade through waist-high foxtails. On the other side, she saw two green rolling hills and a canopy of trees. The place had potential, if it could be tamed.

"It's beautiful," she told Rebecca. "I'll take it."

Rebecca negotiated with her bosses, and the cemetery offered to donate space for 108 baby graves, though someone would need to pay for the labor to open and close them. It would cost $16,000 in total, paid in advance.

Elissa founded a 501(c)3 nonprofit organization. With Rebecca's guidance, she named it the Garden of Innocence. They assembled a board of directors, drawing from the attendees at the Faris meeting; though none of them had known one another previously, they all said they were passionate about the cause.

At the board's first meeting, Elissa put a pen on the table next to the contract of El Camino and explained that someone in the room would have to sign a promissory note. Elissa waited expectantly for a volunteer. One by one, the board members said they could not commit to the debt. Elissa looked at Rebecca and sighed. *Will this be over before we've even started?* she thought. Even though she couldn't afford it, Elissa picked up a pen and signed the form.

To finance the garden, Elissa took out a home equity loan. She figured if she asked thirty thousand people for one dollar each, she could pay off the principal and interest within ten years. But she didn't have to fundraise nearly that long. As she shared her vision with church, youth, and civic groups, donors lined up. One church donated $10,000, and several youth groups organized car washes. Elissa paid off the debt in two years and had money left over, which she used to buy the land around the initial graves. She now had enough space for six hundred graves and, more important, she had found her calling. She had always been an active volunteer, serving for years as a student teacher in her son's classrooms, but nothing on the scale of what the Garden of Innocence required. To her delight, she discovered she was good at bringing people together for a higher purpose—including the local public administrator and medical examiner.

From the county's perspective, a volunteer organization burying unclaimed babies was even cheaper than cremation and interment in a pauper's grave. The Garden of Innocence would pay for picking up the remains, store them, provide a casket, purchase a burial site, and pay for opening and closing the grave. Still, county officials

didn't want bad publicity. They insisted that the services be dignified, steering clear of politically sensitive issues such as abortion,
and that Elissa keep the details of the deaths confidential. She
agreed, and the San Diego Public Administrator gave Elissa permission to bury her first abandoned baby in May 1999—a boy found
in a trash can. Since he was the garden's first, Elissa named him
Adam.

Elissa picked Adam up on May 21 with plans to bury him in
view of a kneeling bronze statue of the biblical Rachel. Rachel sym-
bolized maternal sacrifice; in the Old Testament she perished during childbirth. The statue had been in storage in a cemetery shed
and brought out when the garden was readied. Elissa felt that it had
all come together perfectly.

She tapped a Baptist pastor as officiant. Someone wondered
whether the pastor should be briefed beforehand to keep the ceremony nondenominational, but Elissa dismissed the suggestion.
"Ministers know what to do at a gravesite service," she insisted. She
was wrong. The minister turned Adam's eulogy into a thunderous
sermon about the sin of killing babies and vilified the mother. There
was also talk of the evils of abortion and abandonment. He invited
anyone who was ready to receive Jesus as their savior to meet him
under a nearby tree. Representatives of the medical examiner's office and local media watched it all unfold.

To make matters worse, *The San Diego Union-Tribune* published
an article about the service that revealed details of Adam's death.
The paper divulged that the baby had been left in a trash can on a
college campus. A second person had found the baby, removed its
wrappings, and dumped the baby in a different trash can. Readers
quickly pieced together which college campus and in which trash
cans the baby had been abandoned. The story included details even
Elissa didn't know, but, as far as county officials were concerned, she
was responsible for the leak. They told her she could not continue
with the burials.

Elissa was devastated. She had no idea what she would tell Rebecca, her volunteers, or the dozens who had donated to the cause.

. .

CLARA STRUGGLED TO MOVE ON. SHE KEPT BEING PULLED BACK
into Bobby's life, first with the surprise of his engagement and then
by his grieving son. When Donnell had called Clara asking for help
with clearing out his dad's apartment, Clara was too nice to say no.
On the telephone, they had bonded over their distrust of the "fiancée." Donnell told Clara that the young woman had started calling
him, asking for Bobby's belongings to be sent to her. Bobby had
never said anything to Donnell about being engaged to this woman,
and Donnell was suspicious.

   With Donnell's blessing, the manager of Palo Verde Apartments
in El Monte had let Clara into the apartment. Clara braced herself
for a wave of memories. But when she entered, she found an almost
bare room with a lingering smell of medical disinfectant and human
decay. Bobby had lost most of his stuff after his eviction from the
apartment on La Brea, and what was left he had tried, mostly unsuccessfully, to sell. Clara recalled how surprised she was the previous year when she saw Bobby posting his possessions on Facebook
Marketplace, practically begging for money. *It wasn't like him,* she
thought. Now Clara wondered if it had been at the girlfriend's
prodding.

   As Clara went through what remained of Bobby's belongings,
she realized that his beloved guitars were gone. "Are you kidding?"
she fumed, her words echoing off the bare walls. Bobby didn't read
music but first noodled with a guitar when his foster father invited
musicians to jam in his childhood home. After that, he always traveled with at least two instruments, including a bass guitar that he
poured his energy into mastering. Clara couldn't imagine Bobby
without those instruments.

   But his keyboard had miraculously remained in the apartment,
along with an amplifier. Clara could sell those and give the money
to his sisters in Gary, with whom she'd reconnected in the weeks
since Bobby had passed. In the kitchen, Clara found a nice set of
pots and pans that she would donate to a neighbor.

Then there were Bobby's prized clothes—more than he could ever wear. Artfully distressed designer jeans, sports coats in flashy colors, and a curated collection of T-shirts. Clara thought about whom she could give the clothes to, making a mental note that she would call his sisters to see what they wanted. Other clothing she would give to a Jewish charity in Culver City that she knew. A few of the smaller items she planned to mail to Donnell.

When Clara came to the closet where Bobby kept his shoes, she had to smile. He could hardly walk, but he had kept dozens of pairs. It was just like him. Except his favorite pair of two-tone blue ostrich boots were gone, the ones that matched his new Chevy Camaro, with its dark blue base and light grayish-white racing stripe. Where were they? Bobby had listed the boots for sale on OfferUp.com. To her knowledge, nothing had sold. Clara wondered if he had given the boots away.

Besides the clothes, clean and neatly folded, and shoes, there wasn't much. Clara only found various pieces of paper and medical supplies.

Then her eyes caught a white-and-gold picture frame next to his bed.

"Oh my God."

She picked up the frame and gazed at her own wedding photo. There she was in a white gown, the train spread neatly in a circle in front, clutching a large bouquet of white lilies in her hands. She looked assuredly into the camera as Bobby held her from behind and smiled widely. He wore a white tailcoat with a pink boutonniere and a black silk string bow tie, Clara's prince in the making.

When she married Bobby, Clara had imagined a beautiful life with kids. But when he kept partying well into his thirties and it became clear that he was unlikely to hold down a job, she decided against children. She was afraid she would end up a single mom, and it was a struggle she didn't think she could handle. At their last meal together, Bobby had told her, "I always wanted kids with you."

"I know that," Clara had said. Then, with more honesty than she typically offered her ex, she added, "I knew it wasn't going to work."

Holding the frame with her wedding photo inside Bobby's studio apartment, Clara whispered, "I can't believe you kept this all this time." She teared up when she realized that he had lost everything when he was homeless, but had saved this. There were no pictures of his girlfriend, of the choir performances, or of the musicians that Bobby adored. Just one photo of Clara. It comforted her to know that the girlfriend would have seen it, too. Clara had been the real love of Bobby's life.

THE NEW DIRECTIONS ALUMNI Association regularly organized memorial services at the facility in West L.A., the same building where Bobby had lived during his two stints in the veterans' treatment program. The group scheduled Bobby's service for July 18, 2019, roughly two weeks after his death. Clara would represent Bobby's family, since none of his kin back in Gary could afford the trip.

Even so, Clara felt slightly out of place making her way into the treatment facility. She knew that the organizers had also invited Bobby's fiancée. It was only because Clara's two friends from her Redlands days said they'd accompany her that she found the courage to show up. They offered to run interference if the girlfriend caused trouble.

Clara entered the building and for a moment wondered whether she was in the right place. The room was packed, hundreds of veterans and support staff crammed into chairs and standing around the edges, eating sandwiches from a buffet. Clara didn't think Bobby had that many friends, and she did not immediately recognize anyone. But when she noticed a slideshow projected on the wall with pictures of Bobby, she knew this was where she was supposed to be. She found a staff member and mentioned who she was. She was ushered to the front of the room, where she sat in a seat designated for family.

On a podium sat a pair of military boots, an inverted rifle, and an air force helmet in a battlefield cross to represent a soldier gone.

The program hewed to the broad contours of a military funeral. A cadet presented a folded flag to Clara while taps played—the presentation of the flag an acknowledgment of her role as family and that she and Bobby were together even in his passing. The veterans had also taken up a cash collection for Clara totaling two hundred dollars. They told her that as "the wife" she could do with it what she wanted. Clara did not correct them. In that moment, the American flag resting in her lap, Clara felt like a widow.

True to Bobby, music featured prominently in the two-hour memorial service. A Korean violinist played a mournful song that brought people to tears. George Hill sang "It's So Hard to Say Goodbye to Yesterday," a Motown song featured in the 1975 comedy-drama *Cooley High*. Its lyrics—"I'll take with me the memories to be my sunshine after the rain"—set the tone for the sharing of memories about Bobby. Other choir members reminisced about Bobby, joking that he could be a pain in the ass about practicing, especially before the *America's Got Talent* performance. Bobby was a stickler for detail and didn't accept any slacking. "Music," Carleton said, "was his medicine."

After Bobby died, the choir decided to stop singing one of their standby songs, "Oh! How I Hate to Get Up in the Morning." It was an Irving Berlin tune that made fun of the indignities of military life, especially the hated five-thirty A.M. reveille. Carleton and Bobby used to perform an interactive skit, with Bobby taking the lead at the top, while the rest of the choir sang backup. With Bobby gone, it felt wrong to perform the song.

Other veterans in the New Directions program stepped up and shared their stories about how Bobby had affected their lives. More than one of the men disclosed that when they threatened to leave the program, usually after an altercation that bruised their egos, Bobby would seek them out. He wouldn't tell them they shouldn't go. Instead, he would sit on their bed and watch them pack. As they angrily emptied their closet into a duffel bag, he would remind them why they joined the program. "You came here for one thing, and somebody hurts your feelings and now you going to show them you're going to hurt yourself more?" Then he would walk off and let them think about what would happen if they left. Many of them decided it might not be bad to stay a little longer.

Clara sat through the songs and speeches, comforted by how much Bobby had affected people. She learned that he had given away his guitars to one of the current New Directions residents who, like Bobby, dreamed of becoming a professional musician.

Encouraged by the shared love for Bobby, Clara stood in front of the crowded room. She had prepared a short eulogy. She told Carleton that she would focus on the fun she'd had with Bobby, skipping over the lows. "Because I did have a hell of a time with him," she said, more to reassure herself than him. In her eulogy, she recounted the day she and Bobby had met, more than thirty-five years earlier, when a shy Bobby walked up to her till at McDonald's. Then she told the story of their last meeting in the New Directions cafeteria, just a few feet from where she now stood. At the end of her eulogy, Clara looked up toward the sky. She paused and then said the same words Bobby had said to her, "I'll see you on the other side." When her eyes returned to the crowd, she could see a few people wiping away tears. She scanned the audience one last time, looking at the other women in the room. But Bobby's young flame never showed up.

TOUCHING AS IT WAS, the memorial at New Directions had done nothing to solve the problem of Bobby's body. He had been moved from Funeraria Del Angel to their storage facility at Oakdale Memorial Park in Glendora, eight miles farther east. There he remained until Donnell agreed to have him moved to the county morgue in early September.

Maria Diaz in the public administrator's office had assumed when she spoke to Donnell that his reluctance to claim Bobby's body was rooted in his financial situation. She had offered advice on low-cost cremations to entice him, thinking to herself how sad it was that she had to persuade someone to take care of their family. She confirmed that Bobby's body had been transferred out of the private funeral home to the county morgue. She then closed the case using one of the office's standard administrative codes, NH04 HEIRS TO TAKE UNDER PROBATE CODE. The code meant that Donnell had accepted responsibility for disposition of Bobby's body.

Maria had hoped that the county morgue would cremate Bobby and ship the ashes to Donnell. She didn't realize both were against the rules of the Office of Decedent Affairs. Each of the three agencies followed different policies, and it routinely caused confusion.

Los Angeles County no longer cremated veterans. In 2014, the county had come under fire for allowing fifty-two bodies of unclaimed veterans to pile up in the county morgue. Some had been there for a year. The reason, as it often is in the funeral industry, was money. Rose Hills Mortuary, a private funeral home in Alhambra, had been transporting unclaimed veterans from the county morgue to Riverside National Cemetery at no cost to the county. These bodies were separate from the ones the medical examiner's office handled. They were the ones who did not die suspicious deaths and went through Estela Inouye's Office of Decedent Affairs. Though the VA handled burial at Riverside, Rose Hills said it cost $2,800 to prepare and transport each body. The VA reimbursed the funeral home $300, and Rose Hills wrote off the "loss" as charity (not missing the chance to promote the program as good public relations).

Then, Rose Hills' parent company, Service Corporation International, looked more carefully at the death certificates of indigent veterans. Company executives realized that some of the veterans had families who lived in wealthy ZIP codes. The veteran may have been homeless, but the next of kin weren't. Rose Hills stopped transporting veterans for whom family had been found, even if the family refused to claim, and bodies piled up at the county morgue. The scandal caught the attention of the Obama White House and became part of a larger national critique of the VA's treatment of veterans and their rising suicide rates. County officials brought the medical examiner's office in to sort out the problem. It took months to clear the backlog.

The medical examiner's office decided to cut out the role of private funeral homes entirely, and obtained its own certification as a funeral home, the first medical examiner in the nation to do so. That allowed them to contract directly with the U.S. Department of Veterans Affairs and reduce the waiting time to transport bodies, once a veteran was considered unclaimed. For more than a decade, a medical examiner's van made the trip to Riverside every Wednesday.

The medical examiner's office took great pride in their veteran burial program. By prepping the body, putting it in a casket, and transporting it to Riverside, they had gone beyond the narrow administrative mandate of "disposing of the bodily remains," because the men and women "who answered the call to service to their country" deserved better. The VA told Captain John Kades that, as an organization, L.A.'s medical examiner did more veteran burials than any other funeral home in the United States.

When the Office of Decedent Affairs realized that Bobby Hanna was a veteran, they quickly transferred his remains to the medical examiner's facilities. Captain Kades would have to put something in motion soon—it had already been two months since Bobby's death, and to let veterans linger was a public relations disaster in the making. Donnell's choice was either to let the medical examiner bury Bobby at Riverside or pay for cremation by hiring a crematorium.

Donnell continued to be tormented over his father's remains. Money was a factor, but it wasn't the only one. He had kept some things from Maria Diaz. He didn't tell her he was struggling to think because he had suffered a knife wound to his head earlier that year. His ex-girlfriend had stabbed him seven times: three times in his arm, once in his stomach, once in his back, and twice in his head. When the paramedics came, they found Donnell with the knife still protruding from his skull. It took him seven months to recover enough to work and function, although the pain would likely last forever, especially in his right arm where nerves were damaged. He had talked to his dad about it, who encouraged him not to focus on retaliation but "put it in God's hands."

"Whatever you do," Bobby said, "don't let your anger and your emotions take control of your actions." They had prayed together at the end of the call.

After the stabbing, Donnell's already precarious financial situation deteriorated. He had earned an associate's degree in education from Indiana University Northwest and always dreamed of becoming a teacher, but with memory lapses and constant pain, his dream job slipped out of reach. His mom kept him afloat, but he had no dime to spare. Amid the wide-spaced, overgrown lots in Gary's Midtown neighborhood, where boarded-up houses could be bought for only $6,000, he did not have a car.

Now he was coming up against a system that prioritized legal relationships. He had contacted the VA to see whether they would reimburse him for his father's cremation and, to his surprise, they agreed. There was only one issue: He had to prove that he was the next of kin by showing that Bobby was listed as his father on his birth certificate. Bobby had left for the air force before his son was born, and Donnell's mother had listed "unknown" in the box asking for the father's name. Donnell felt defeated. *How am I going to get them to do this?* he wondered.

Captain Kades made one last call to Donnell to ask whether he wanted to make his own arrangements. Donnell was adamant that Bobby be cremated. He knew it was unlikely that he would ever be able to afford a trip to California to visit Riverside National Cemetery. Because he had run out of options with the VA—he couldn't prove Bobby was his father—he tried to persuade Captain Kades to help. Couldn't they cremate Bobby and transfer his ashes to the military cemetery closest to Gary, Indiana? "No one will visit his grave in Los Angeles," Donnell pleaded.

Donnell's logic was impeccable, but it was not how the medical examiner's office worked. Their policy was to bury (not cremate) veterans at Riverside or to release them to relatives. Those were the only two options. To make exceptions to the policy was to invite trouble.

Kades, having reviewed the paperwork, decided that Donnell was unlikely to act. He scheduled Bobby for indigent veteran burial.

10.

STEEL AND SASSAFRAS

· ·

D AVID'S OBITUARY RAN IN THE *LOS ANGELES TIMES* ON Thursday, August 31, 2017, in the middle of the B-section, at the bottom of the page. "Spencer, David Grafton services on September 1, 2017 at Armstrong family mortuary at 10 a.m." The announcement cost his estate $95.

No one who had been close to David saw the obituary. More than three months had passed since David's death, and his three friends had received no information from the medical examiner's or the public administrator's office. They had no clue what was happening with his body. Apartment manager Diana and building superintendent Jesus would have liked to have known when the funeral would be held so they could pay final respects, but there was no county protocol for calling friends. David's ex-wife, Susan, assumed that David had already been buried in a military cemetery.

What Susan didn't know—and no one in the county realized until it was too late—was that the information she had given to both the medical examiner's and public administrator's offices about David's navy service had fallen into an administrative black hole. Kristina McGuire, David's death scene investigator, had retrieved his military discharge papers from his apartment and put copies in his case file. But it was the public administrator's responsibility to follow up once Tiffany Clark signed the paperwork nominating the office to handle her brother's estate. The deputy in charge of the case should have contacted the VA to confirm David's eligibility for veteran burial benefits and organized interment at Riverside (as the office had done for other veterans). But despite several rounds of review by various supervisors, the public administrator's office missed that David was eligible for a military burial.

Instead, David received one of the generic individual funerals the office organized. The public administrator contracted with a handful of private mortuaries and cemeteries, rotating their place on the list every few years to prevent the appearance of favoritism. According to the California law that guided the public administrator's policy, David's burial needed to befit the "standard of living adopted by the decedent prior to his demise"—this standard determined solely on a tally of the decedent's assets at death. Decedents were eligible for three funeral packages, each reflective of a different social class. The basic plan, which cost $2,230, skipped embalming and provided the deceased with a plain, cloth-covered wooden casket with a flat or raised top and a crepe or rayon interior. It included a simple burial without a church or gravesite service. The next level up would have sent David off in a casket of 20-gauge steel or solid hardwood, without hardware but with the possibility of a rounded top, locking mechanism, and crepe or muslin interior. Family and friends, were any notified, would have had the opportunity for visitation (up to four hours) at the funeral home and his gravesite service would include flowers with an option for music. This package would have cost $4,160.

What David ended up with was even more extravagant. His body was transferred to Armstrong Family Malloy-Mitten funeral home, where he was embalmed ($1,750) and dressed in clothing the public administrator provided from David's closet ($50). His body was then placed in a $3,000 Astral Industries 18-gauge steel casket, with the words "Going Home" and four birds flying up into clouds embroidered in the velvet interior of the cap panel. The casket had ornate decorative pillars and handles on the outside. The funeral home printed one hundred folded funeral programs for $45, even though they knew it was unlikely anyone would attend the gravesite service. No one had shown up for the four hours of visitation at the funeral home. Three copies of his death certificate cost $63, and the funeral home provided flowers at an additional cost of $75. The total charges from Armstrong Family Malloy-Mitten came to $5,495, the maximum allowed by the public administrator's contract. Anyone who had enough funds in their account (and no will or family to say otherwise) received this "premium" funeral package.

THE FUNERAL PACKAGE, HOWEVER, did not include interment. For this, the public administrator took additional funds out of David's accounts. His plot was in Odd Fellows Cemetery, a mile from Boyle Heights. Odd Fellows charged $3,000 for a single adult grave, $495 for interment, $290 for the concrete vault encasing the coffin, and $150 for long-term care of the grave. Vaults are not required in California, but cemeteries prefer them because they keep the ground from settling after burial. David's estate was charged $45 for one bronze flower vase and another $10 for long-term care of the vase. It was one of the typical up-charges that the funeral industry threw in, usually at the expense of grieving families too distraught to argue. David's twelve-by-twenty-four-inch flat granite marker cost $310, with a setting fee of $85 and, of course, an additional charge for perpetual care of the marker ($20). With recording fees and sales tax, the cemetery charged a total of $4,532.17, again the maximum allowed under the contract with the public administrator. (If David had received a veteran's burial, the cost of interment in a military cemetery would have been covered by the VA.) Altogether, David's burial cost just over $10,000, or 20 percent of his total assets.

Without question, David Spencer was a frugal man. He would have been flummoxed at the amount of money spent on what he would have called a "worthless" burial. He would also have objected to the environmental toll. Embalming fluid is a highly toxic chemical cocktail of formaldehyde, phenol, menthol, and glycerin, which can leach into the soil after bodies decompose. Each year, more than 827,000 gallons of embalming fluid in the United States are put in the ground because of interments, and about 30 million board feet of hardwoods, 2,700 tons of copper and bronze, 104,000 tons of steel, and 1,636,000 tons of reinforced concrete are used for caskets and vaults. Green burials, on the other hand, skip embalming, forgo vaults, and preserve a cemetery's natural habitat. Such a burial would have come closer to David's vision of letting his body decompose in the woods and better reflected his true standard of living.

But David wasn't alone in having his interests overridden by others', whether those of government officials or private contractors. Historically, even when wealthy people prefer a simple burial, their wishes are often ignored. The French author Victor Hugo requested a pauper's grave, but the French nation instead gave its favorite poet an extravagant burial.

None of the cemeteries the public administrator contracted with came close to the natural setting David had imagined. The website for Odd Fellows Cemetery featured cheery pictures of a wooded forest in autumn, a lush English-style garden, and a young white girl standing at the sideline of a parade. In reality, Odd Fellows was a brown, dry, flat field with a handful of trees adjacent to five freeways. The constant blare of trucks racing down Interstate 5 made David's final resting place one of the least desirable places in the county for burial.

Funerals at Odd Fellows—at least those for the unclaimed dead—were as depressing as the setting. They lasted less than seven minutes, with a series of perfunctory rituals. Carmine Sciarra, a former furniture salesman, was seventy-seven years old when he passed away in 2017 with an estate worth close to $750,000. The Italian American man died alone inside his four-bedroom, two-bath wood and stone ranch-style home in the suburban city of Azusa. The house hadn't been updated in the five decades Carmine had lived there: brown shag carpet, stained yellow counters, a broken stove. Carmine never cared. He preferred to eat out at the local Hometown Buffet. His sister in Pennsylvania, whom Carmine detested because she'd put him in the "looney bin" after his Alzheimer's worsened (he'd checked himself out), received half of the estate; the other half was split evenly among the three adult children of Carmine's late brother. No one in the family wanted any of Carmine's belongings: not the 2001 red Ford Explorer, CardioFit exercise machine, or his thirty-two boxes of collectible beer mugs. Nor did they have any interest in Carmine's funeral. Several of Carmine's neighbors in Azusa would have loved the opportunity to attend his funeral, but they weren't notified of the service. Only the funeral director who oversaw Carmine's body preparation and two cemetery workers were at Odd Fellows when the priest mispronounced Carmine's name (as "Carmino") before making the sign of the cross and sprinkling holy water from a plastic squirt bottle on the earth around the grave. (The funeral director tended to hire Catholic priests regardless of the decedent's faith, unless the public administrator instructed otherwise.)

After the blessing, for which the clergy received a gratuity of $150, cemetery workers snagged the expensive bouquet on Carmine's 18-gauge steel casket just as it was being lowered into a vault, presumably to reuse for the next funeral. The funeral director said that in the three years she had been working there, no relative or friend had ever attended a funeral ordered by the public administrator.

"It's just the two of us," she said, turning to the priest. "Always the two of us."

David's burial was similarly empty—of people and meaning. Susan chuckled in exasperation when she found out how much the county had spent on her ex-husband's funeral. She made no plans to visit the grave. If she had, she would have seen that David's headstone was located on a strip of dead grass along a metal chain-link fence, abutting a homeless encampment at the edge of the interstate.

WHILE SUSAN WAS OFFENDED by the money wasted on David's body after his death, Jesus was haunted by how David had died. He couldn't stop replaying the image of his friend's body lingering for days unnoticed. Jesus had lived at Royal Oaks longer than David; he, too, had no children and no spouse.

"That could be me," he lamented to Diana over more than one cup of tea. She said she understood. She didn't need to see David's sad grave to know that the outcome was the epitome of a lonely life.

David's death served as a warning to Jesus. After his thirty years as the behind-the-scenes troubleshooter for the Royal Oaks Apartments, who was going to care what happened to him when he died?

Psychologists have a term for the fear of dying alone: monatophobia. In the sitcom *30 Rock*, Tina Fey's character Liz Lemon panics after she chokes on a piece of dehydrated meat from a frozen meal, her coworker having taunted her earlier that day with the comment, "I would think a single woman's biggest worry would be choking to death alone in her apartment." But the real fear is more existential—it's what a lonely death says about the lived life. F. Scott Fitzgerald made brilliant use of this insight in *The Great Gatsby*. No one attends the funeral of the enigmatic multimillionaire Jay Gatsby, who entertained hundreds of people at his extravagant parties. No one attends because there is nothing to gain.

Jesus was determined to avoid a fate like David's. His diabetes worsening, he told Diana, "I want to see my mom before I die." He had spent his adult life living in the United States without formal papers. He hadn't seen her in decades because if he returned to Mexico, it was a one-way ticket. Diana knew that she would never see Jesus again and tried to convince him to stay. L.A. was his home. She pleaded with him to wait before making any major decisions, knowing that Jesus had recently undergone eye surgery. But he was adamant.

"I want to see my mom."

Diana didn't want to lose her friend, but she accepted that this was what he needed. *You have to let a grown man do what he's going to do,* she told herself. Diana asked her on-site manager to drive Jesus to the border. From the Mexican side, Jesus took a flight to the small city where his mom lived. One year later, he was dead.

After he died, Diana went through Jesus's belongings. He'd left most of what he owned back in L.A. There she found the wooden staff that David had left in Jesus's car in the days before his death— the last remaining item that connected David to those who had known him.

. .

WHEN DOYLE TOLBERT RETURNED TO CIVILIAN LIFE IN THE late 1960s, he found a nation embroiled in anti-war protests. It was a marked contrast with the country he had left in 1962. At the start of the Vietnam War, most Americans believed that military action was warranted to stem the spread of communism. By 1968, public opinion had shifted. Doyle, who was born on the 4th of July and seemed destined to become a patriot, didn't know what he should have expected from a war-weary public, but it wasn't open hostility. In Doyle's mind, veterans were heroes who guaranteed everyone's freedom. He and his fellow servicemen took an oath to defend the United States, often at heavy personal cost. In return, they deserved recognition and respect.

His frustration with America's treatment of veterans continued when he became a patrol officer. While working in the Fullerton Police Department, he befriended a homeless man who had been a decorated WWII veteran. The veteran had a GI pension, but, from what Doyle could tell, it mostly went to alcohol. At the end of the month, when the man ran out of money, he would accost Doyle and ask to be thrown in jail for "three hots and a cot." Doyle didn't want to arrest a fellow veteran, especially not one who had served in WWII. One particularly difficult month, the man tried three different times to get Doyle to take him into custody. Doyle refused. The homeless man then called police dispatch to report a man down on the street. Doyle looked on as the squad car arrived and the man, seeing the police coming, lay down in the street. Doyle said, "You win this one. We'll go in." Then one day, the man was gone. Doyle never found out what happened, and it bothered him.

When Doyle left the police force in 1986 and started working in notifications, he discovered that many homeless veterans went unclaimed. Although the medical examiner's office had an in-house program to make sure unclaimed veterans received a military burial at one of the nearby national cemeteries, the office took a haphazard approach to checking decedents' veteran status. The office would call the VA only if they found obvious signs of military service, such as dog tags or a discharge card.

Doyle knew that many veterans did not "look" like veterans—or if they did, it was only to someone with military experience. He suspected that scores of indigent veterans were missing out on honors they had earned. In one case, Doyle examined autopsy photos of a man who had died by suicide and noticed that he was covered in marine tattoos. Doyle checked to see whether the man had served and, lo and behold, he had. The man's twenty-year-old military records revealed a living son. The son, Doyle learned through his sleuthing, was also a marine. It was 1991 and the son was stationed in Saudi Arabia. He was slated to be part of a U.S. ground assault on Kuwait the following day. Doyle rang the International Red Cross, who located the marine and notified him of his father's death. The son was able to travel back to the United States to take care of his father's body. If Doyle hadn't been determined, the dead marine could very well have ended up cremated by the county, his ashes later interred in a mass grave in Boyle Heights.

Over the years, Doyle personally helped many indigent veterans avoid a pauper's grave, but unless he could change the system, he knew that some men and women would always slip through the cracks. Inspired by his success organizing funerals for unclaimed babies, he decided to do something for his fellow soldiers.

Using his administrative acumen, he put rules in place to check the military status of every decedent the medical examiner's office received, male or female. (The public administrator had a similar system, but the failure to check David's records showed that it was not fail-safe.) The number of bodies scheduled for cremation dropped, and more veterans ended up at Riverside National Cemetery.

WHEN DOYLE RETIRED FROM the medical examiner's office in 2006 at age sixty-three, he devoted even more time to veteran causes. An avid motorcycle rider, he started making cross-country trips on his Harley from Southern California to the Vietnam Veterans Memorial in Washington, D.C., where the names of military brothers who died in Vietnam were etched into black granite. The rides were part of an annual campaign to promote healing among veterans.

Doyle also joined a local branch of the Patriot Guard Riders, a group of motorcycle enthusiasts who came together in 2005 after members of a Topeka, Kansas, religious sect, Westboro Baptist Church, started to disrupt soldiers' funerals to protest the military's "Don't Ask, Don't Tell" policy. Westboro trafficked in virulent homophobia, anti-Semitism, and Islamophobia. At military funerals, members carried signs reading THANK GOD FOR DEAD SOLDIERS and GOD HATES FAGS. They shouted to grieving families that soldier deaths were divine retribution for America's tolerance of homosexuality. Some protestors wrapped American flags around their shoes to symbolically stomp on the nation.

Members of the American Legion Riders in Kansas, learning about the disruptions, agreed to form a human wall at funerals where Westboro was expected to protest. The riders and their supporters linked arms and held up flags to shelter relatives from the sights and sounds of the protestors. Other Patriot Guard Riders groups soon sprang up across the country, with tens of thousands joining the cause, including hundreds of members in Southern California.

The So Cal Patriot Guard Riders expanded their operations to escort funerals at the families' request, by motorcycle and "cages" (cars). These "missions," as members referred to them, were promoted on the group's website and via social media, drawing dozens of attendees. Doyle cherished the moment in the military funeral when a flag would be presented to relatives thanking them for the deceased's military service "on behalf of a grateful nation."

Doyle dreamed of bringing this kind of appreciation to unclaimed veterans. While he took credit for changing how the medical examiner's office checked the military status of veterans, he didn't think his former employer had done enough. For instance, there was considerable dissension over the caskets used to transport the veterans. Some of the private funeral homes had slapped together boxes from plywood or used cardboard shipping containers in lieu of coffins. When the medical examiner's office took over transport, they had to decide what kind of container to use. They could have ordered metal caskets from the VA, but the reimbursement process was cumbersome and took six months. For a while, the medical examiner had used simple wooden caskets, made locally and delivered weekly to the county for $150. It wasn't perfect, but it was better than burying soldiers in what looked like oversized U-Haul boxes. Still, the cheap-looking caskets remained a sore point for veterans. Some believed that private funeral homes would provide better ones, but the medical examiner's office did not want to lose control over the process, given the 2014 scandal. It worsened later: At some point over the years the medical examiner switched over to cheap, mass-produced industrial gray plastic caskets that looked like giant Tupperware containers.

Unable to solve the casket problem, Doyle turned to *how* the veterans went in the ground. He wanted to give each unclaimed veteran a dignified funeral that recognized them individually for their service, and he thought the riders offered a model. He proposed that a group of motorcycle-riding veterans escort unclaimed veterans to Riverside National Cemetery. His plan drew consternation from his former coworkers in the medical examiner's office, who did not want a "motorcycle gang" involved in funerals. Lieutenant David Smith, who oversaw the medical examiner's veteran program after Doyle's retirement, said it was disrespectful. Senior administrators never gave Doyle an explicit no, but, typical of bureaucracies, they delayed a decision.

If they were hoping that Doyle would give up and go away, they underestimated him. Age had emboldened Doyle, and he went over his old supervisors' heads and pleaded his case directly to elected county officials, arguing that indigent veterans deserved better. The officials, seeing a political win, supported Doyle's plan. On March 3, 2008, Doyle's newly formed offshoot of the So Cal Patriot Guard Riders, called Veterans Without Family, began escorting unclaimed indigent veterans from Los Angeles's medical examiner's office to their final resting place inside Riverside National Cemetery.

This still fell short of what Doyle thought the nation owed their veterans. He recalled the marine covered in tattoos and the man's anguished son. Doyle felt he had helped ease the son's pain by making sure he could be present at his father's burial. He wanted to give each unclaimed veteran a dignified funeral that recognized them individually for their service. Sitting at his desk at home, Doyle used the law enforcement databases that he had combed through when he worked for notifications to find relatives and invite them to the service. The arrangement he had with the medical examiner's office prohibited him from contacting relatives, but Doyle didn't care.

When he called someone, the reactions varied. Some greeted the news with sadness. Others slammed the phone down after shouting that "they want[ed] nothing to do with that drunk." Some relatives lashed out. They hated how the man who'd passed away had made their lives difficult and said it was good that he was finally dead—that giving him a funeral with military honors made a mockery of their pain. Over the years, Doyle had even received death threats from furious relatives.

Doyle was unfazed. Whatever happened in a veteran's life after their military service was background noise to him. Occasionally, he persuaded families to attend the ceremony—though it was against Riverside's rules, which instructed relatives to skip the interment and come back in the afternoon or even later, after the grave had been sodded and marked with a gravestone. Yet things didn't always go as planned. A few times, families had shown up in limousines, as if to flaunt that they had the money to claim and had decided not to. It burned Doyle that families had abandoned their military relatives, but he knew they would have to live with the choices they'd made.

Wherever Doyle went, he told fellow former servicemen and -women about Veterans Without Family. He left business cards in veterans' resource centers, recruited fellow Patriot Guards, and found volunteers at whatever military-related events he could attend. He didn't obscure the truth: Their mission was emotionally daunting; every week, they would need to mourn fellow soldiers, disconnected from or unwanted by their families of origin. Veterans, Doyle knew, would have to take care of their own.

. .

ELISSA DAVEY RECEIVED A CALL FROM A COUNTY OFFICIAL. IT was 2017 and another deceased baby had been abandoned in a local San Diego hospital. "We are turning it over to you."

"Thank you," Elissa responded. "We'll take care of it."

Elissa had been given a second chance after the failed funeral for Adam. She had learned that the reporter for *The San Diego Union-Tribune* who had published confidential information about Adam had a source within the medical examiner's office. Elissa had provided the county with proof that the Garden of Innocence wasn't to blame for the leak and promised that the people who gathered at the gravesites would not fixate on the past but rather celebrate the present—the baby's embrace by a family of strangers. The following years had not been easy, but at least she had proven to the county that she could be trusted. She had buried more than four hundred babies, surpassing the one hundred and ten that Debi Faris had interred at Calimesa. By 2012, Faris had started closing the Garden of Angels to new burials. She felt that she had helped prevent unclaimed babies by lobbying for the passage of a "safe surrender" bill in California, which allowed a parent to confidentially surrender a newborn baby within seventy-two hours of birth.

That didn't sit well with Elissa. She knew abandoned babies hadn't vanished. She drove the thirty-seven miles from her small ranch house in the northern suburbs of San Diego to the hospital where the newest baby for the Garden of Innocence, a girl, awaited her.

When the attendant on duty met Elissa at the morgue and opened the door, he stood back, motioning her to continue on her own.

"You're not going to get it for me?" Elissa had expected that the morgue attendant would retrieve the baby.

The man quickly shook his head no. "You can get her."

A morgue attendant afraid of the dead? Elissa sighed.

She entered the room and found several bodies stacked on top of one another on the refrigerated shelves. The baby was hard to find. Eventually she found its small form between two adults. Elissa made sure the tags matched the case number the county had given her and opened the homemade casket she had brought from home. It had a blue absorbent lining on the bottom, to soak up any liquids. She had dozens of these caskets stored in her garage, donated by volunteers. She wrapped the baby in a receiving blanket, then a second comforter blanket, and placed the baby gently in the casket.

When she left the cold room, Elissa signed out with the morgue attendant and carried the casket to her car. She placed it in the trunk and drove to a local funeral home that had agreed to store the body for free. It might still be several weeks or even months before the GOI could finalize plans for the funeral.

Elissa was the only member of her group of volunteers who knew the backstory of the babies. She received the hospital or medical examiner records and entered them in a database, keeping a hard copy in case her computer crashed. Babies who died from homicide or neglect, like Adam, made up a third of the burials in the Garden of Innocence. Others were infants who died during childbirth or soon after at local hospitals, their bodies left behind without instructions from their parents. The rest were fetuses. Some had been used in medical schools to study fetal development. The majority were fetal remains from nearby hospitals. California state law mandated that any fetus over twenty weeks of gestation had to be disposed of as human remains, like any other child or adult.

Birth parents had three options: They could organize their own burial; they could fill out a form that turned the remains over to San Diego County's Indigent Burial and Cremation Program, which disposed of unclaimed adults; or they could leave the hospital without making any arrangements. The third option was considered by the county to be "abandonment." Those were the remains that Elissa received.

Elissa understood that some young women hid their pregnancies from their families; others lacked money for a funeral. Many parents struggled with addiction. She was empathetic, to a point. But in the end, the reason didn't matter to Elissa. The babies had been abandoned. Like the neglect of veterans, this abandonment represented a terrible injustice. But unlike veterans, who often left a trail of broken relationships, babies entered the world as innocent beings. They had done nothing to warrant ire—they hadn't been given the chance to—so Elissa found it easy to rally to their defense.

Yet this same purity posed its own challenge. How are we supposed to make sense of this tragedy? When an adult dies, a piece of the past is lost. How do we mourn a "piece of the future"? The abandonment of a deceased infant also violates expectations of parental love and, in certain ways, the very purpose of human life. Now, Elissa was asking strangers to take on the burden of mourning one of the hardest kinds of death. And she needed to keep politics out, especially after what had happened with Adam. Other groups in the United States and United Kingdom had sprung up to bury abandoned babies as part of an explicitly anti-abortion mission; the Garden of Innocence stayed out of that.

In her confidential database, Elissa had legal names of each child buried in the garden. For stillborn babies left at hospitals, she might have only a family name, such as Baby Boy Devereux, but using it meant that those families could be identified, so she renamed each infant that came into her care. As Elissa told her board, renaming was important, both to separate a baby from its difficult past and to prevent unnecessary harm to parents. She didn't want a young woman shamed by someone calling her out in the future for abandoning her child.

The new names came from a second list she maintained—names suggested by garden volunteers and inspired by a dear uncle or grandparent, or, often, a child or teenager who had passed away. The new name filled two needs—it integrated the baby into a new community and, by being etched in granite on a headstone, it left a mark to say, "I once was here." Looking over her list, Elissa picked a name for the baby girl now in her hands: Tessa.

Elissa had not realized when she impulsively called the county to ask about burying babies that so many people were carrying unresolved grief from their own loss. The Centers for Disease Control and Prevention's National Center for Health Statistics counts about 23,500 stillbirths and miscarriages (of fetuses over twenty weeks) in the United States annually. Healthcare providers often regard such losses as less traumatic than other deaths, even though when these babies die, their parents experience profound grief. For decades, hospitals disposed of the remains of miscarriages and stillbirths as medical waste, never offering the mother a chance to hold her infant. Even today, the hushed, hurried way infant deaths are handled can make the loss ambiguous and even shameful. Western cultures provide few opportunities to mourn these deaths. The grief caused by them is further minimized, often unintentionally, by friends and relatives. Not knowing what to say in such dark moments, they may fail to recognize and legitimize a pregnancy loss, especially since most women give birth to another child within a year. What they don't realize is that the new birth doesn't erase the previous death.

LAURA JOHNSON WAS A clueless new mother when she adopted a baby boy in 2004, nearly a year after his birth. She named the infant

Keegan. Keegan's birth mother had come into the hospital in labor with drugs in her system during a time when the nation was in a moral panic about poor pregnant women exposing their fetuses to illegal substances and alcohol. Addicted mothers were publicly vilified and often punished rather than supported. But even if Keegan's birth mother had received prenatal care, she might not have known she had contracted CMV, a herpes virus. The virus is common in adults, and symptoms are rare. When passed in utero, however, it can be deadly. In addition to a rash and lung problems, Keegan was at risk of growing up with hearing and vision loss, limited coordination, seizures, and intellectual disabilities. He spent the first year of his life in the neonatal intensive care unit.

After the adoption was finalized, Laura noticed in Keegan's paperwork that he was a twin. Laura told her husband, "There's a big chunk of history missing here." She felt an immediate attachment to Keegan's sister and needed to know more. She started making calls to find out if the baby girl had survived and, if so, where she was. It didn't take long for Laura to learn that Keegan's sister had been stillborn. Knowing then that she was looking for a body, Laura called the San Diego medical examiner. The office suggested that Laura contact the Garden of Innocence.

In 2005, Laura called Elissa, who confirmed that Keegan's twin sister, renamed Jeanette, was indeed buried in the garden. Laura and her family visited the Garden of Innocence soon after; at the time, Keegan was three and running around, a security blanket in one hand and the thumb on his other tucked into his mouth. He was too young to understand where he was, let alone whom he was visiting. But as the family continued to make visits, Keegan eventually realized he had a twin who was buried there. The family laid a flower on Jeanette's headstone with each visit. Laura felt relieved that a mystery had been solved and grateful to the GOI for giving Keegan's sister a loving burial.

Stories like Laura Johnson's helped Elissa better understand her mission. It wasn't just about the babies and their abandonment. It was also about the people who would be coming to mourn them.

Even people living far from San Diego found comfort in the idea of the garden. Elissa recalled one story in particular: A woodworker in Arkansas had sent her a "beautiful" urn carved out of sassafras. In a letter that accompanied the urn, the man told Elissa that he and his wife were married young, and about six months later, she became pregnant. Then, six months into the pregnancy, she had a miscarriage. The man had been grieving the loss for twenty-five years and had made the urn to mark his daughter Daisy's death. Elissa could feel the care the woodworker had put into crafting the cremation vessel, which he had adorned with a carved daisy. The urn represented all that Elissa hoped to bestow on the babies: dignity, honor, respect. And, as a bonus, it smelled like root beer.

The babies coming into the garden would have no shared connections, and there would be no stories about them to tell. In Elissa's words, GOI volunteers and participants were there to bury "other people's dead." But she had learned something profound in her conversations with people like Laura Johnson and the man who had made the sassafras urn. Grief has ripple effects. If a loss is not acknowledged, or grief remains unresolved, it haunts not only the bereaved but those around them.

Joan Didion wrote that grief is "a place none of us knows until we reach it." She continued, "We might expect if the death is sudden to feel shock. We do not expect the shock to be obliterative, dislocating to both body and mind." The absence, Didion declared, is "unending." Elissa found that leaning into loss, rather than running away from it, allowed people to heal, even if they never fully recovered. The key was grieving *together.*

A month after retrieving Tessa from the morgue, Elissa took her tiny body out of the funeral home refrigerator and wrapped her in a new receiving blanket, added a hand-knit comforter blanket on top, and then gently placed Tessa on a small pillow in a casket. She added a beanie baby. Tessa was ready to be buried.

STANDING IN THE GAP

· ·

THE LOS ANGELES COUNTY MEDICAL EXAMINER—CORONER'S office had scheduled Bobby Ray Hanna for burial at Riverside National Cemetery. He would be the third of five veterans interred there during the week of October 9, 2019. Members of Veterans Without Family posted the names on their website, and one of the women who helped Doyle organize the Wednesday services, Cora Gilbertson, ordered commemorative dog tags engraved with the names of all the servicemen who would be receiving funeral honors. She would sell the tags at the cemetery for three dollars, using the earnings to fund care packages for soldiers. Meanwhile, the medical examiner's staff lined up a plain casket for Bobby's body. Come Wednesday, he'd be loaded in a white coroner van for the sixty-three-mile trip east to Riverside.

Two thousand miles east, however, Bobby's son refused to give up hope that he could claim his father. Donnell had taken on as many hours at the grocery store as his managers would allow, but it didn't get him close to $2,700, the amount a private funeral home had quoted him for cremation.

Donnell's mother, Deborah, saw her son's anguish and took a risk. She applied for a high-interest loan under her name, with the expectation that Donnell would pay her back in monthly installments. They were running out of options.

Deborah called Clara and said they were thinking about a lawsuit against the VA. It didn't make sense to Clara, who thought, *In their defense, you all haven't done anything.* But she kept her opinions to herself. Even if she knew Bobby better than anyone and felt that an indigent veteran's burial was his best option, she understood it wasn't her decision to make. Donnell was the next of kin in the eyes of the county. Clara rang the medical examiner's office and told them the family was threatening legal action. Captain Kades called off the transport the day before the scheduled burial.

The following month, Donnell had scraped together the money he needed to cremate his father's body. He had managed against the odds. But the pride he felt in claiming his dad was dampened by the feeling that the private funeral home was screwing him. On their website they advertised $648 for a complete cremation—but the true total included substantial costs and fees (storage, shipping, permits). It was too much for Donnell to understand, both because he struggled to think clearly and because he lacked the wherewithal to fight. He cursed the company but paid the bill. He told himself he was doing his best to navigate a bullshit system. He included the VA in that system, angry that he'd been denied Bobby's veteran benefits, since his name was not on Donnell's birth certificate.

Donnell was hurt that no one but his mom had offered to help with the costs. Not Isaac, who shared his blood. Not Bobby's sisters, who wanted some of the ashes. Not even Clara. Worse, Donnell's family in Gary mocked him for paying for ashes of a father he had seen only twice.

He decided that the sacrifice was worth it. He was, after all, Bobby's oldest son, and now he had had a chance to prove it. Donnell and his daughters would struggle that winter without a financial cushion, but Bobby had called on him to get it done, and by God, he had.

Three years later, he had lost his job at the grocery store and moved in with his grandparents, taking care of them after his grandmother's stroke. It stung to live with the people who had forbidden his mom to marry his dad, but Donnell was desperate. With no income, no car, and thousands of dollars in debt, the future looked bleak.

To ease his sadness, he put up a string of colored Christmas lights in a corner of his bedroom and placed Bobby's black plastic urn in front of it. Next to the urn, he put a small clear bottle of purple cologne that Clara had sent after she cleared out Bobby's apartment. Except for a few photographs stored on his phone, they were all Donnell had left of his father. Every now and then, when memories of Bobby surfaced, Donnell opened the cologne. He didn't put it on, just breathed in the distinct mixed-berry scent. It reminded him that he'd once had a father.

· ·

A WHITE VAN, EMBLAZONED ON ITS BACK PANEL WITH A SEAL of Los Angeles and the word CORONER inscribed in royal blue below, traveled east on I-10, out of Boyle Heights. On this summer morning, the driver was carrying four bodies. Waiting for the van at a concrete and wood shelter in Riverside National Cemetery was a group of about fifty men and women, many clad in leather jackets and vests. A neatly arranged row of chrome and black motorcycles stood sentry beside them. The bikers' jackets were decorated with pins and patches: JANE FONDA COMMUNIST AT HEART TRAITOR BY CHOICE; THE NATION WHICH FORGETS ITS DEFENDERS WILL ITSELF BE FORGOTTEN; PATRIOT GUARD RIDERS STANDING FOR THOSE WHO STOOD FOR US. Some had sewn on a small round patch with a sketch of Doyle Tolbert's face and his nickname, "Popeye."

Many of the men were Vietnam veterans, five decades out of the jungle but still struggling with war injuries or trauma. Some of the older men had served in Korea, while the younger ones had been stationed in Iraq and Afghanistan. Almost all of them moved with observable pain. Their grief, too, was visible—wrapped around their wrists in the form of remembrance bracelets and etched in their skin with the tattooed names of soldiers left behind.

This June day promised to be sweltering, but with the sun still low, the air had a chilly bite. Dew had moistened the wood beams supporting the shelter. Flags from each branch of the military and the Coast Guard were pinned to the shelter's stone wall. A large American flag hung, too. At the center of the shelter sat a stone lectern, draped in a dark red cloth with FREEDOM IS NOT FREE embroidered in white thread. Atop the cloth was a thick metal ring holding hundreds of black dog tags, the ones that Cora ordered each week to capture the names of unclaimed veterans.

Riverside National Cemetery held an average of sixty burials per day, a pace that required factory-like efficiency. Families who held funerals at shelters in the morning were asked to leave while cemetery staff laid caskets into concrete vaults. Close family members could return at three P.M., after the graves were covered. Doyle's group followed their own schedule. He and his fellow veterans held their honors ceremony at eight-thirty A.M. without caskets (which were still making their way on I-10). At ten A.M., the group convened at the gravesite to watch the interment.

Before the ceremony began, Doyle held a quick briefing. He wore a black SPECIAL FORCES AIRBORNE trucker hat and aviator sunglasses, his cheeks ruddy above his thick white mustache. A snug blue T-shirt accentuated the swell of his stomach, and its short sleeves revealed a large boil on one elbow and, on his left forearm, a faded tattoo with stars and stripes. What skin wasn't inked was covered in sunspots.

He tried to break up the multiple conversations going on around the shelter, but his voice was unsteady. Someone standing nearby saw the struggle and shouted for him.

"Meeting! Everybody! Meeting! Be quiet!"

The crowd formed a semicircle around Doyle, some taking a seat on a concrete bench. Doyle spoke haltingly, searching for his words and taking long pauses. He had not been feeling well of late. One of the onlookers whispered to another, "Vietnam is still killing him."

Doyle reminded those gathered to turn off their phones and

raise their flags. He demonstrated the correct way to hold a flag: The left hand supporting the bottom of the tilted staff at the waist, the right hand higher up on the pole and upside down. Then he led the group in the Pledge of Allegiance, with the marines in the audience adding "Oorah!" a couple of times.

"Anybody new here? Newbies?"

A man stepped forward.

"Right here, sir," Doyle ordered. "Are you a marine, too?"

"Yes, sir."

Doyle knew it. He could spot a marine from the way he carried himself. "Tell me your name, why you're here, and who paid you." The joke fell flat.

"Both my grandfathers were veterans and they both passed, so I wanna support the cause."

"Thank you for their service," Doyle said. Then it was oath time. "Raise your right hand and repeat after me."

The crowd stirred, becoming visibly animated. "Raise your right hand!" they shouted.

Doyle continued, "I, insert your name here, do solemnly swear to honor veterans."

The man started, "I, Cesar Aranda, do solemnly swear . . ."

The crowd burst into laughter.

"Now what did I say?" Doyle mocked.

Cesar caught on. "I, insert your name here, do solemnly swear. . . ." More laughter from the crowd. They had witnessed the same exchange many times, but this joke did not get old.

Just then, a car with military cadets arrived.

"Come on," Doyle told the crowd as the cadets emerged, in dress uniform, and began to unload their gear. "We better get ready, guys."

The group quickly dispersed and re-formed, lining up in two front-facing rows, their flags raised just as Doyle had showed them. To the side of the shelter, three of the cadets fired guns toward the sun—an evocation of the battlefield, when fighting paused to allow each side to attend to their dead. One of the cadets put a bugle to his lips, though instead of blowing into it, he pressed a button on the side to activate a mechanical device in its bell to play taps. (Not enough musicians in the military knew how to play the original brass instrument.) The veterans kept their flags upright throughout, in saluting position. Even though Doyle had seen it more than a thousand times, the cadets' ritualistic folding of the burial flag— folded thirteen times on the triangles to represent the original American colonies—still moved him. A single flag, reused each week.

Doyle stepped in front of the crowd. Holding a white binder, his arms noticeably shaking, he slowly read the soldier's creed. Then he brought up the story of a twenty-five-year-old army veteran, Dionisio Garza, who had recently fired 212 rounds into a Texas gas station, killing one person and leaving six others wounded, before being shot himself by responding officers. Garza's family said he was suffering a mental health crisis, brought on by his time in Afghanistan. Doyle speculated that the young man thought he was killing the enemy. Looking off into the distance, Doyle lamented, "I feel for [him] because he couldn't be helped in time."

Turning back to his audience, he urged: "You see a vet that needs help, please, please, step forward and help him no matter what his problem might be. Help him." Then he moved to the side.

A veteran in a black beret and long goatee stepped up next and named the men they'd be honoring that day. A volunteer then rang a bronze bell, and a retired military chaplain gave a homily. The chaplain often wore leather chaps to these ceremonies, but today he was dressed less memorably, in faded blue jeans and a long-sleeve Harley-Davidson T-shirt under a leather vest. He asked the Lord to provide the dead veterans a safe passage home.

Doyle closed the short honors ceremony as he always did, slowly reciting the last verse of a poem by Larry Vaincourt, "Just a Common Soldier."

> *If we cannot do him honor while he's here to hear the praise,*
> *Then at least let's give him homage at the ending of his days.*
> *Perhaps just a simple headline in a paper that would say,*
> *Our Country is in mourning, for a soldier died today.*

At nine twenty-seven A.M., the group adjourned to a nearby Farmer Boys fast-food restaurant for breakfast, where the conversation ranged from politics, like changing gun laws in California, to personal matters—one man spoke of having to sting his wife with bees each week to ease her pain from multiple sclerosis. Several men were caregivers: to sick wives, children with special needs, orphaned grandchildren, and elderly parents.

Most days, Doyle sat next to his friends, enjoying the comradery inside the crowded restaurant. This time he sat on the Farmer Boys patio, away from the chatter. He was savoring his black coffee, taking slow, deliberate sips, when Ray Gould, an African American former marine who went by the nickname T-Bone, walked up.

"Hey, sir," said T-Bone. He wore a camouflage baseball cap, leather vest over a neon-green T-shirt, and khaki cargo shorts. He had tied a black resistance strap around his right calf.

"What's going on, my man?" Doyle asked.

"Oh, you know. Missions out there." T-Bone served as a ride captain for the So Cal Patriot Guard Riders. He'd been to twenty-seven missions so far this year, and it was May. One year, he did 540. "That's what keeps the heart pumping," he added.

Doyle nodded. "As long as you're keeping things running smoothly, can't ask for anything else." He asked if T-Bone wanted to join a mass paratrooper jump—"over two dozen C-17s" (military cargo planes)—in North Carolina that Sunday.

The other man looked uneasy. "Yeah. I don't know. That last jump didn't go so well." In 2001, T-Bone had been on a routine surveillance run as a door gunner of a utility helicopter in Iraq when it came under fire. The pilot had made a sharp ninety-degree turn to avoid getting hit. T-Bone and a fellow marine had been thrown out and had fallen the equivalent of thirteen stories to crash on the rocky desert floor. T-Bone had broken his back in three places. He had also broken all of his limbs, lost most of his teeth, and suffered a debilitating skull fracture. His fellow marine had died on impact. Hearing Doyle talk about jumping out of a plane gave T-Bone goose bumps. "You're gonna jump, too?" he asked.

"Shit, I wish I could," the older man said. Like a lot of the men in the group, Doyle longed for action. Back in his heyday, Doyle had done four missions a day for the Patriot Guard Riders. Now, his worsening health left him in constant pain, able to do only a handful of missions each month.

DOYLE HAD EXPERIENCED A considerable share of "ups and downs," as he called them. One of the "major downs" was a recurring bout with cancer. But he wasn't interested in reflection. He was a firebrand who preferred to act first, think later. It was how he'd made Veterans Without Family happen, going over his former bosses' heads. Every now and then he watched the veterans digging into their pancakes and bacon and wondered if the group wasn't just a coffee club, the funerals an excuse for the men to hang out and rib one another. Then he caught himself. These folks were serious about coming out to honor men and women who would otherwise be forgotten. If he was remembered for anything after he died, Doyle thought, *let it be this.*

Doyle finished his coffee and headed back to the cemetery. At ten forty-five A.M., the coroner's van arrived. The Veterans Without Family members on motorcycles were waiting, prepared to escort the van from the front office to the gravesite: eight motorcycles ahead of the van, one behind. As they moved at the posted speed limit, 5 mph, the convoy passed large swaths of green grass and an artificial lake. Riverside was a manufactured oasis in the desert, and only the areas of fresh interments revealed the natural taupe landscape. A ride captain made sure the Harleys in the front were evenly spaced out in two rows, flags rippling in the breeze. When the van reached the gravesite, it drove onto the cemetery dirt while the escort riders parked their motorcycles on the road.

Earl Bagley, a sixty-seven-year-old African American member of Veterans Without Family and an occasional chaplain at the Wednesday services, said that of all the veteran events he participated in, the Veterans Without Family ceremony was the most difficult. "There's such a weight of loss there that you feel more compelled to stand in the gap, rain or shine." Standing in the gap was military lingo for taking the place of a fallen soldier to keep the line of defense strong.

Earl felt that a lot of men in the group suffered in silent sorrow—some, like Doyle's friend, former national guardsman Craig Breskin, weren't that different from the men they buried every week. Craig was divorced with no children. His only family was a brother in Pacifica, outside of San Francisco. He was one health mishap away from a funeral, and if his brother couldn't bury him, Craig had no one but Veterans Without Family to mark his death. "Inside, they're needing and wanting help," Earl said. He understood men like Craig felt society's pressure to be strong and not show weakness. "Those are just deceptions that we live with."

A crew of three cemetery attendants positioned a casket-lowering device over the first dirt grave. An excavator had already removed the concrete covers of the pre-dug cement vaults. The veterans had given a cemetery worker four small bouquets of carnations and baby's breath to place on each casket, to spruce up the cheap-looking gray boxes. A last check of the name, and the cemetery attendants turned a crank handle that slowly lowered the casket, the splash of red from the carnations disappearing into the ground. Members of Veterans Without Family, flagpoles raised high, bowed their heads and saluted. They did this for each casket. And each time, Doyle announced the soldier's name—Ralph George, Jr., Oliver Hardge, Bennie Alonzo, Clifford Breed—and closed with the same line.

"May he rest in peace. We are his family."

· ·

IN 2003, A FEW YEARS AFTER ELISSA HAD BURIED ADAM, SHE received a call from an eighty-five-year-old woman who made an unusual request. When she was in her midtwenties, the woman had given birth to twins and one of the babies, a boy, had died. While she was in the hospital recovering, her mother-in-law and husband placed the baby in a box and "just buried it somewhere" near their home on the East Coast. It was not unusual at the time to whisk away a newborn's remains, reasoning that it would protect the mother from her grief—especially when there was a surviving baby. The woman had been haunted for sixty years by the thought that her baby had received such little care. She wanted to return to New Jersey, exhume the body, and bring him to Southern California, where she now lived, so that "when I die, he can go with me." She asked Elissa's permission to bury him in the garden.

Elissa delicately explained that, even if she opened the garden to babies that hadn't been abandoned, infant bones are soft. "You may find a tiny fragment of a box, or a blanket, but more likely there's nothing there," she said. "Why don't you come to one of our services instead and let us help you?" The woman didn't think it would be the same, but she promised to attend.

Since the GOI's founding, the people aching from infant loss and in search of healing had only grown. By 2017, when it was time to bury Tessa, Elissa had started gardens in ten other California counties and hoped to expand further. She was turning seventy soon and worried about what would become of the organization when she was too old to run it. Her sons had no interest. Maybe her cofounder, Rebecca Melendez, who preferred to help behind the scenes, would decide she was up for the challenge? Elissa tried to shake off her negative thoughts and focus on Tessa.

At the edge of Fenton Carroll Canyon in El Camino Memorial Park, Elissa approached the microphone. Without preamble, she leaned in and sang a short tune a friend had written about the garden: a place with "quite enough love for the world," "quite enough peace for all the world," and "quite enough power, to help us through horror and fear."

Elissa wasn't much of a singer, but she had grown up singing hymns in church and sang with confidence. Even if she no longer attended church, Elissa still found comfort in the familiar sequence of music, silences, and gestures of religious rituals. She saw no reason to mess with centuries of tradition.

When she stopped singing, a background chorus of birds and crickets took over. More than thirty women and men—a mix of races and ages—watched as an honor guard of sixteen members of the Knights of Columbus marched in step across the cemetery, escorting a small wooden casket from the administrative building to the tree-dotted clearing where the group was waiting. The knights wore plumed chapeaus and capes in red, white, purple, or green; black tuxedos with white shirts and black bow ties; baldrics; and white gloves. Swords rested in scabbards at their sides. The knights' involvement had been accidental—the local chapter had heard about the GOI's work and volunteered to be part of the ceremony. The project fit with the knights' pro-life mission, even though the GOI explicitly avoided any mention of abortion. For her part, Elissa thought they added pomp to the proceedings.

The lead Garden of Innocence officiant that Saturday morning was Becca Ferguson, a retired naval officer. She thanked the attendees for helping to send baby Tessa home, and then invited them to join the circle of love.

"As with each child that comes to the Garden of Innocence, we form a chain of love and pass that child from one person to another, so that we can say we have touched this child, and this child has touched our hearts."

People stood, shaking out stiff knees and hips. Becca's longtime friend and one of the GOI's spiritual advisers, Reverend Jerry Moore, took the small casket from the knights and handed it to the woman on his right. It was made of varnished pine wood and had a small maple-stained carving of a baby on the top and on each side. It was surprisingly light, a reminder of Tessa's short life. One woman made the sign of the cross prior to receiving the casket. Another wiped her eyes as she passed it along. Some took time to whisper what might have been a small prayer. The casket made its way around the oblong concrete footpath, which enclosed more than fifty infant-size graves. Each headstone bore a child's first name inscribed inside a heart, with an angel holding a basket toward heaven. It was early February 2017, and someone had placed small markers with pink valentine hearts next to the graves. "When that child gets passed from one person to another," one volunteer reflected, "I know for me and I know for many others, that child becomes part of our life." When the casket had made it around the circle, the Knights presented their swords, and Jerry placed the casket next to the open grave. Becca invited people to take their seats.

For Tessa's service, eleven-year-old Zeke Oakley strummed "Amazing Grace" on his ukulele before a pastor from a nondenominational church connected a biblical story about King David, who had remained steadfast in his faith despite losing his son, to "our daughter" Tessa. "We cannot bring Tessa back," as King David could not bring back his son, "but we have complete confidence that she is in perfect peace," the pastor added. One of the cemetery workers stood over the grave while the other lowered Tessa's casket.

After another musical interlude, participants lined up and grabbed handfuls of petals from a white wicker basket to gently scatter over Tessa's small grave. Reverend Jerry stood at the edge, lending a hand to any older guests who seemed unsteady. As the procession of attendees waned, a man with a red, white, and blue trucker hat took a handful of petals, brought them to his mouth, and then made a cross in front of his chest before releasing them. A cascade of colorful rose petals fell into Tessa's grave, the wind catching a few and spreading them in a half circle around the dirt hole.

In this way, Tessa's new family was part of an ancient tradition: sage, mint, and figwort lined graves during Paleolithic times, while Victorian Christians chose roses to convey particular emotional states—crimson for mourning, red for eternal love, pink for appreciation, white for hope and innocence, yellow for friendship, and black for change and courage. Tessa's blanket of white, pink, red, and yellow petals had been donated by a local florist.

At last, it was time to let go of the baby. Susie, a garden regular, took the microphone and announced, "As we are gathered here today for Tessa, we encircle her with our love. We give dignity to her birth, yet we know we must say goodbye."

Four volunteers from the audience held small white doves in their hands, the birds' fast-beating hearts a visceral reminder that life continues, even amid death. Susie said, "We release a dove as a symbol of the spirit of Tessa being set free."

A volunteer launched her dove into the air. But instead of taking off into the clarion sky, the dove made a beeline for the nearest tree and perched on a branch. Susie, uneasy, muttered in the microphone, "Or not."

Someone yelled, "Fly away!"

Tessa's dove remained in the tree. Then three more doves were released, one at a time. These performed as expected, winging out across the cemetery. The first dove joined the others eventually, but now one of them was being chased by a Cooper's hawk. People tried to encourage the dove. "Come on, bird!" Fortunately, the hawk was too slow.

It wasn't the first time a hawk had chased the doves at one of the GOI's ceremonies. When asked about the possibility of shooting the predator, Reverend Jerry replied drolly: "It's a $20,000 fine. We already thought about that."

In a final act of remembrance, the names of all the babies that had been buried in the San Diego garden were recited, in order of burial, starting with Adam, and ending, 162 names later, with Tessa. The incantation of the names of the dead linked the garden ceremony to vigils that honor victims of mass casualties. On the anniversary of 9/11, relatives of the victims recite their names at eight forty-six A.M., which is when the first plane struck the north tower of the World Trade Center. Every five years, more than two thousand volunteers gather in Washington, D.C., to read the names of 58,281 fallen soldiers chiseled in the Vietnam Wall. Similar public rituals memorialize those who perished in slavery and the Holocaust, even if not all victims' names have been recorded. It's a relatively recent ritual; memorials used to consist of a single image that stood for the multitude of dead. But publicly reading the names of victims marks every life as significant and every death as a tragedy. The litany of names evokes personhood and emotional resonance in a way that statistics cannot. Activists rally around *#sayhername* to raise awareness of Black women victims of police murder, for example. Saying a name out loud guards against forgetting individual lives. Because Elissa's volunteers took turns selecting names for the babies, every time they attended and heard their baby's name recited, they felt connected again to the garden.

Reverend Jerry Moore had named four babies in his more than ten years as a volunteer. "All my family's names are written there, my wife, my kids." He didn't find having his children's names etched on gravestones morbid. Rather, it was "powerful to feel that much love." He pointed out that he wasn't alone. Susie, the volunteer who announced the releasing of the doves, brought her 101-year-old father to many ceremonies. "He comes to the garden," Jerry said, "because he loves to see how we love."

Jerry had been the first person to arrive at the cemetery that morning, and he would be the last to leave, lingering just in case someone wanted to talk. He had long dreadlocks tied in a low ponytail, a silver stud in his left ear, a graying beard, and preferred pressed African-themed dress shirts to the business suits other clergy wore. People found it easy to confide in him, to share losses that they had carried—sometimes alone—for years. He had perfected the long, full-bodied hug, and readily handed people he'd just met his phone number and invited them to call. He knew all the cemetery workers by name and asked about their kids.

For Jerry, the garden was a place of wonder, beauty, gratitude, and healing. Even so, he knew it wasn't an easy place. "My parents died when I was a child, so I know what it feels like to be alone in the world." He knew it professionally, too. During his twenty-four years of active military service, Jerry counseled male violence victims, accompanying them to the hospital and sitting with them through the forensic exam and the police investigation. It might take weeks, months, or even years before a victim felt like a survivor, but Jerry remained present, putting reminder stickers on his calendar when it was time to check in with them.

At his first ceremony in the garden, Jerry realized the power of burial rites to help the living process and heal. *We need more of this in our crazy world*, he thought. When people pushed back, wondering why someone should attend a funeral for a baby they didn't know, Jerry had his answer ready. "That's the wrong question to ask," he said. "The right question to ask is why did God bring these babies into my life?" The way he saw it, the ceremony was a conduit to light amid the suffering that darkened the human landscape.

Once, after a ceremony for a baby boy, Jerry drew an athletic-looking young man sporting dark aviator sunglasses into an impromptu prayer circle. Thomas had been fidgeting, working through nervous energy by rotating his wrists. Jerry turned to him and said that he was now connected to this community and that they would pray for him and his family. Put on the spot, Thomas explained to the group, "I lost my daughter when I was on deployment. My wife had to deal with that by herself. When I came back, it was all already done." It had been five years, but the veteran still suffered. Men can experience "lasting grief" after miscarriage and child death, but tend to find their experiences marginalized and their emotional needs unrecognized. Putting a baby to rest in the garden was therapeutic for Thomas, as were the nods from the others in the prayer circle. He had invited his wife to attend a ceremony in the garden, but the thought of seeing the small caskets was too much for her. Thomas came alone.

OVER THE YEARS, THE GOI had widened its responsibilities: The ceremony was not just about burying babies but also about helping people heal. Elissa vividly remembered the eighty-five-year-old woman who wanted to exhume her twin boy in New Jersey. When she reluctantly attended a garden burial, she took her place in the circle to pass around the casket. She glanced down and realized that she stood above a grave marker with the name Michael, the same name she had planned to give her son. After the service, she told Elissa that she no longer felt the need to return east to locate the grave.

"My baby's here," she said.

She placed a blue rosary on Michael's gravestone. The cemetery's grounds crew later moved it to the bough of a nearby tree, where it stayed for many years.

12.

PRESENTE

..

MIDGE WAS SCHEDULED FOR CREMATION ON APRIL 4, 2016. Her body was sent thirty miles southeast, to a private crematory in Orange County. On April 18, her cremains returned to Boyle Heights, where Craig Garnette registered them in the leather-bound log at the county crematorium. Using his careful penmanship, Craig wrote Midge's legal name, birth date, sex, race, date of death, and her medical examiner case number in the book. He placed Midge's cremains in a brown plastic box, labeled the box, and put it on a storage shelf. The nickname she had gone by for most of her adulthood, irrelevant from a legal standpoint, was nowhere in her record.

Slowly, memories of her began to erode as well. At the Westchester Church, where she had once been prominent in the children's ministry and neighborhood outreach, her community began to drift apart. In 2018, the Pattis sold their home and moved to a larger house in Santa Clarita, north of Los Angeles. By then, they were no longer members of the church. Not long after Midge's memorial service, Mike and Pastor Huddle had gotten into a disagreement about what the church should do with its valuable real estate (Mike wanted to sell; Huddle said no). After their departure, the Pattis lost contact with most of the members in the congregation. What they had kept of Midge's art and writings went into a box in their garage. Two years later, Huddle resigned as pastor and moved to Oakland. His replacement, a husband-and-wife team from Co-lombia, knew of Midge but couldn't recall anything specific, other than that she had lived in her van in the church parking lot.

In Albuquerque, Midge's next of kin had also moved on. Her niece, Barbara Fuller, was offered a chance to claim Midge's ashes upon cremation—a clerical assistant in the medical examiner's office mailed the notification letter on April 21, six weeks after Midge would have celebrated her sixty-eighth birthday. But Barbara was unable to do anything about it. Shortly after her aunt's death, Barbara was diagnosed with breast cancer and underwent an aggressive treatment plan that left her with little energy. Chemotherapy treatments made traveling to Los Angeles impossible; she couldn't risk an already compromised immune system. She called and asked the Office of Decedent Affairs to have Midge's ashes shipped but was told that the county didn't offer this service.

Barbara received another chance to collect Midge's ashes two and a half years later, in the fall of 2019. By then, Barbara was in another round of cancer treatment and confronting her own mortality. She was curious about her aunt's life but had come to terms with their estrangement. Midge had chosen her life in L.A. It was where she'd found Christ and where her church friends were. If Midge had not wanted to come back to Albuquerque, it didn't make sense to Barbara to bring her there now. She comforted herself by saying that Midge was a "simple woman" who hadn't wanted much. She decided that an indigent burial would be most fitting.

For Midge's closest friend, Nora Spring, the grief was still sharp and raw. In her mind, Midge had not gone unclaimed. Nora associated going unclaimed with being unwanted, and the church had wanted to bury Midge. When Nora received the call from the medical examiner's office saying a niece had been found, Nora believed that was the end of the story. She had no idea that Barbara had not picked up Midge's ashes. Even years later, she refused to believe her friend's remains had been abandoned.

The denial did not ease her grief. In the years that followed, Nora would cry whenever she talked about Midge. Loss took hold of her in waves—at Thanksgiving, when Nora remembered their messy attempt to deep-fry an unfrozen Snickers bar. Or when Nora sank into her sofa to watch HGTV and remembered how Midge would dream aloud about a home of her own.

Other reminders were less expected. Nora was sitting at her home computer one day when she heard, "Knock, knock!" in a voice that was unmistakably Midge's. Then again, "Knock, knock!" Nora stood up and walked to the door. No one was outside. She was steadying herself with one hand against the wall when it hit her. She went back inside.

"Sparky, is that you?"

The parrot bobbed his head up and down. "Whatcha doing?" he said, again in Midge's voice. Nora walked over and scratched her bird's head.

"You miss her, too."

· ·

ON DECEMBER 2, 2019, CRAIG INTERRED MIDGE'S ASHES, ALONG with 1,456 others, in a grave at Boyle Heights, just as he had done with Lena's cremains in 2015. He worked alone. After Albert had retired, Craig expected that he would be promoted from crematorium operator to cemetery caretaker. But Estela had announced in a staff meeting that Albert would not be replaced, nor would anyone else be hired to work alongside Craig. He wondered what else the county would cut. After he emptied the last plastic box of ashes into the grave, Craig went home and made himself dinner.

Two days later, he woke to pounding rain. A storm had slammed into Los Angeles, dumping up to two inches of rain and causing traffic pileups throughout the city. A flash flood warning was in effect until three P.M. Craig drove to work and, once there, put on a full-length yellow raincoat. The ceremony to commemorate the people he had buried a few days before was scheduled for ten A.M. He didn't expect anyone to show.

The grave where Craig had placed Midge's ashes was now a

muddy mess. Under better weather conditions, he would have laid teal hospital sheets around the gravesite before the ceremony—the county's low-budget substitute for the fake grass that private cemeteries used to hide freshly turned dirt. Rain had made that impossible this year. The only pops of color were two floral wreaths standing on easels in the mud (one donated from Rose Hills Cemetery, the company that had transported unclaimed veterans to Riverside before the scandal) and a large arrangement of orange roses, yellow lilies, and magenta chrysanthemums from the public administrator's office.

In past years, Craig's main role on the day of the ceremony was to greet cars as they arrived at the top of the cemetery hill. He would sip coffee or tea out of a thermos while using his other hand to direct drivers. This year, Estela had closed the small parking lot to visitors, worried that car tires would tear up the soaked gravel. Only preapproved county workers were allowed to bring their vehicles inside the gates. Everyone else would have to park in the neighborhood and walk up the steep driveway before sloshing through the grass to the burial spot.

Father Chris was one of the few drivers allowed past the security guard. He pulled his gray Toyota RAV4 into the crematorium's twelve-car lot and popped the trunk. Earlier in the day, he had gathered the items he'd need for the ceremony: the manila folder that held copies of the burial's program, a bowl for incense, and a stole. Father Chris viewed stoles as another means of expression, using his extensive collection to connect with different audiences. For this service, he alternated between two: one embroidered with animals from Noah's ark and a diverse mix of smiling children's faces; the second made of dark purple silk with symbols of other religions—everything from a Star of David to a Hindu wheel of dharma. Unable to decide, he had brought them both along. He exited the small SUV, reached for the stole with children's faces, then changed his mind. He draped the purple multifaith stole over his beige hooded robe, his black-and-white clerical collar peeking out. He looked out at the rain and said a short prayer. Then he walked toward the grave, saying hello to Craig as he passed.

Twenty feet from the grave stood four small portable canopies, set up that morning to provide shelter. They were designed to protect from the sun, not storms, but because the county didn't have rain gear readily available, they would have to do. Father Chris took his spot near a microphone stand beneath one of the canopies. Next to him sat a smoldering stone bowl that would be used in the ceremony for a Native sage blessing, to cleanse the land of negative energy.

Father Chris shared Craig's concern about the weather deterring people. Attendance was vital to sustaining the event. If few Angelenos showed, Estela could persuade county officials that people didn't care about the unclaimed, and it was therefore a waste of her department's time to organize a large public gathering. Funding cuts and the squabbles between Estela and pretty much everyone else had made the ceremony increasingly precarious. Every year, Father Chris felt he had to prove it was worth having. What he really wanted was to expand the event and show the rest of the country how communities could care for the unclaimed.

Estela stood away from the action, with a clipboard in hand, watching Father Chris. She had no desire to take part in any aspect of the ceremony. Even so, she was more dressed up than usual. She wore a camel coat over simple black slacks and blouse, and her hair was tied back into a chic French twist.

At nine-fifty A.M. Father Chris looked up from his notes and stared in astonishment. A steady stream of dark-clad mourners was marching up the hill in the rain. Some came in small groups, but most were alone. When they arrived, the strangers stood close together under the canopies. A second circle formed around the edges. Then more, fanning out in wider circles. They reflected the diversity of the country's second-largest city: Black, white, Latino, Asian, Native American, long black hair, short gray hair, purple hair, full beards, faces too young to be bearded. More than a handful wore jackets or name badges that revealed their affiliations with various county agencies. These were people who had interacted with the unclaimed before and after their deaths, including clergy in Father Chris's chaplaincy program at the hospital. They wore maroon LAC+USC lanyards over clerical robes and suits. Altogether, there were almost two hundred mourners. Most knew nothing about the people they were about to honor.

· ·

WHEN MIDGE ATTENDED LOYOLA MARYMOUNT UNIVERSITY IN the early 1990s, she submitted an essay for an ethics class that focused on how one can improve the self. The essay, which she typed on an electric typewriter and titled "A Better View," provided a glimpse into the missing decades of her life, between leaving New Mexico and arriving at the Westchester Church. She began:

> When I was a child I knew already what it was
> that I wanted to be and what I wanted to do.
> I wanted to be a healer, a neurosurgeon. I
> also wanted to play the violin and to be a
> singer. But this was not to be, because of
> the obstacles that were set before me from
> the very beginning. We be come [sic] who we
> are by the actions we take, but first we
> become who we are by the actions that others
> take around us.
> I grew up in a household filled with
> violence and hatred. Most of it was directed
> my way. Fr seventeen years, from age 1 yr.
> & 8 mos., I was emotionally, physically,
> spiritually, and sexually abused. I learned
> to numb my emotions so that I wouldn't hurt.
> This isn't much for a human being to begin
> with. The most critical goods missing in

```
this environment was [sic] love, kindness,
tenderness, and just an over all [sic]
general goodness. We were poor, but I never
knew that as a kid. Most basic material
things were provided for most of the time;
things like food, clothes, a roof over my
head and a bed to sleep in. Development of
virtues was not possible under the circum-
stances. There was only time to brace myself
for the next blow.
```

. .

AT NINE FIFTY-EIGHT A.M. FATHER CHRIS ADJUSTED THE microphone and gestured for people to move closer. He reminded the mourners that the 1,457 people they were there to bury had died three years earlier, in 2016. "They come to us and our city as coworkers, veterans, immigrants, homeless people. They are infants, and they are elders." While in past years much of the sound from the portable speaker was absorbed into the ground, this year the sound echoed off the top of the canopy above the microphone. It felt powerful to Father Chris, as if the souls buried underneath the mourners' feet—including the thousands of bodies buried before the county began cremating in the 1920s—might also hear what would be said about the unclaimed on this day.

Father Chris told the mourners that he had recently seen *A Beautiful Day in the Neighborhood*, the movie that starred Tom Hanks as beloved television personality Fred Rogers and recounted Rogers's friendship with a troubled journalist, Lloyd Vogel. "At a key moment in the story, Mister Rogers says to [Vogel], 'We need a moment of silence to think of all the people who loved you into being.' And that's what we're about today. We're thinking of these 1,457 individuals who were loved into being."

He was referring to a scene in the film in which Rogers and Vogel sit across from each other in a Chinese restaurant. Vogel was estranged from his father, and his professional life was unraveling. In the film, Vogel tells Rogers that he is broken. Rogers disagrees. He describes Vogel instead as "a man of conviction," who knows the difference between wrong and right. "Try to remember that your relationship with your father also helped to shape those parts." Then he asks Vogel to take one minute to think of the people who loved him into being. Vogel hesitates but then goes along with it, and soon the entire restaurant is quiet. Sixty long seconds of total silence. It was signature Fred Rogers—awkward and unsettling in the most welcome way. For Rogers, loving others, even those who challenge us and those we pass by without much notice, was a way of learning to love oneself. Rogers himself had grown up sickly and overweight, the target of school bullies who chased him home from school. He said he cried when he was alone after school. His life changed for the better once he started to seek out others who needed help, cultivating what would become his trademark mixture of empathy and radical kindness.

Feeling broken is a universal experience, one the people who surrounded Midge's grave shared with the people buried in it. Often, this brokenness is a symptom of a deeper malaise—one that comes from feeling alone and unloved. It was a malaise that Midge knew well, and Mister Rogers, too. The cure that Mister Rogers found for himself and later preached to millions of American children was the same lesson that Father Chris wanted to teach the mourners that rainy day: what has broken us makes us who we are.

. .

Most of my life I spent it going in and out of some institution or another: youth detention homes, jail, and hospitals. This was my way of asking for help. Most of the time no one really listened or tried to find out what was wrong. I couldn't take care of myself. I

went from one home to another, from one person to another trying to find an answer for
myself.

Change did not come to me as a result of
some gradual awareness or understanding that
I had acquired over time. It came as a
result of an attempted suicide. When I was
twenty-eight years old, my roommates had
gone on a vacation weekend and I was left
behind. I had gotten myself a gallon of
cheap wine at Vons and proceeded to drink it
within a twenty-four-hour period. I began on
Friday evening and ended on Saturday evening
when I got up from where I was and went to
the bathroom. There I took a razor blade and
put it in the pocket of the jacket I had
just slipped on. I got on my Kawasaki 400
motorcycle and started out for my friend
Gary's home. This was not a premeditated
action. I felt nothing and I thought
nothing.

Half way [*sic*] to Gary's home I stopped and
got off my motorcycle. I pulled the sleeves
of my jacket up and began to cut at my
wrists. For a moment I watched the life drip
from wrist to the asphalt and I was glad.
When I arrived at Gary's my wrist had
stopped bleeding, because the sleeves to my
jacket had stuck to my wrists. I tried to
reopen the wounds again, but they wouldn't
bleed. For some reason I had thrown the
razor blade away. I tried to find it again,
but couldn't. I tried to get Gary to open
his door, he wouldn't answer. There was

blood all over his door from my pounding on
it with my wrists.

Finally, I gave up and just sat there on
the steps and wondered what to do next. From
somewhere within myself came a voice. I
heard it say that I didn't want to die, I
really wanted to live. It was so clear and,
in that instant, I was changed. I called
Gary from the phone booth and told him that
the blood on the door was mine and that I
was going home now. Gary paid for the doctor
bill the next day. I have not seen him
since, but from that point on I began to
find myself a new path to travel.

..

FATHER CHRIS HAD NO WAY OF KNOWING WHO HAD LOVED
Midge or the other 1,456 people buried alongside her. He needed to
know only that the people being buried were human and therefore
worthy of being loved. And since their families weren't there now,
the strangers gathered at their grave could mark their passing.

The importance of treating the dead with dignity was deeply
rooted in him. His father had died when he was four, and his mother
had taken him as a child for weekly visits to the grave in East Los
Angeles. Later, one of his brothers died after returning from Vietnam, and a younger sister soon followed after a series of health
problems. Father Chris's mother passed away when he was only
thirty-seven. Yet they had all shaped him, and in this way, they lived
on. By having his loved ones interred in a cemetery, where he and
other Ponnet descendants could visit, their memory could be kept
alive.

Father Chris's uncle Charlie, his mother's brother, had died at a
young age. Typical of infant deaths in the early twentieth century,
his grave had been marked in the Calvary Cemetery in Los Angeles

with a simple rock. Father Chris and his mother had scoured the overgrown cemetery to locate Charlie's rock. But they weren't successful. When Father Chris's mother passed away, he became even more determined to locate Charlie's marker. He recruited a local gardener to join him at the cemetery. After some digging, they found the rock. It had sunk two feet into the ground. Father Chris ordered a new tombstone to mark the short existence of an uncle he never met.

Gone, he thought, *but not forgotten.*

FATHER CHRIS BECKONED A young man to his side. Josh Andujo from the Gabrieleno Tongva San Gabriel Band of Mission Indians, the only government-recognized tribe in Los Angeles and the original inhabitants of the land they were now standing on, took the microphone next. He sang in Tongva, filling the air with the melancholic sound of this Uto-Aztecan language that dated back thousands of years. Nearly one hundred Tongva villages once dotted the basin between the San Gabriel Mountains and the ocean bluffs of the Palos Verdes Peninsula, until they were demolished and their inhabitants enslaved, imprisoned, converted, or killed by Spanish missionaries as they established the Mission San Gabriel in 1771. As if physical erasure wasn't enough, the missionaries banned tribal dances and mourning ceremonies. Few traces of the Tongva language survived, save for a translation of the Lord's Prayer, an eleven-word story about a dead body, and a few songs, including the one Andujo was now singing. Yet, the legacy of the Tongva was inscribed in the land: Topanga, Cahuenga, Cucamonga, and Azusa—all landmarks in Los Angeles—are words with Tongva roots.

Andujo only accidentally discovered his own Tongva ancestry. He had always identified as American but some family members spoke of Mexican or Chicano roots. He was in his early twenties when his dying grandmother lost the ability to speak English and Spanish and started making a strange combination of sounds. An aunt whispered that she was speaking a Native American language, which her husband had forbidden. Andujo started digging into his family's history. Baptism records at the San Gabriel Mission archives confirmed Tongva heritage on Andujo's mother's side. He had a Tongva naming ceremony in the mountains, the first since the Spanish forced the tribe to end the ritual in the 1700s. He was given the name Strong Standing Oak. His people had once loved Los Angeles into being, even if now their descendants were unknown to most of the city.

Andujo followed his song with a sage blessing, circling each corner of the grave. Smoke, resilient against the rain, wafted through the air. This was now sacred ground.

Offering a ceremony that mixed traditions created a space for mourners to grieve in their own way—to reflect, without being told what form that reflection should take. Each individual could mold the experience to their life's challenges and reckon with the deepest sorrows in their lives.

A year earlier, Susan Rorke—the woman who had claimed the ashes of her sister Karen just months before they were to be interred alongside Lena Brown—had attended the ceremony. She'd stood close to the grave, a frail sixty-two-year-old woman in an oversized fuchsia parka. Her face was puckered with grief and her cheeks wet with tears.

Susan was an L.A. native, born in the 1950s in a hospital ward for unwed mothers. She later discovered that the staff in such wards were instructed not to touch the babies, believing that the adoptive parents needed to be the first to bond with them. Susan was adopted, but, like Midge, did not end up in a happy family. She clashed repeatedly with her mother. Her sister was no help. Karen beat up Susan's school bullies but then beat up Susan for not defending herself.

Susan married young to escape home, but her marriage disintegrated after her daughters were born. She lost custody in the divorce and later fell out of touch when the girls became adults. She did not know where her oldest daughter lived—maybe in Florida—

and her youngest reached out only sporadically. Susan kept a text on her phone that she had sent the youngest daughter two weeks earlier, wishing her a happy Thanksgiving. The daughter did not reply.

Susan hadn't fully come to terms with her own role in this cycle of rejection and estrangement. In the end, she said, it didn't matter how much she was to blame: *She* was the one who was hurt. She identified with the pitcher in a line from the musical *Man of La Mancha.* "Well, you know how it is Master, whether the stone hits the pitcher, or the pitcher hits the stone, you know it's going to be bad for the pitcher." Her growing isolation was difficult to face: "There's some part of me that can't quite accept that it keeps happening. [That part] keeps striving for something else, it keeps striving for acceptance and connection." But the odds were stacked against her, and she was at a stage in her life when she had no choice but to admit that most of her dreams would never come true.

Instead of looking forward with hope, Susan dreaded the loneliness that seemed to lie in wait for her. Physical problems exacerbated her depression, which, in turn, caused problems at her county clerical job. She frequently called in sick, drawing on unpaid leave provided by the Family and Medical Leave Act. After her last roommate moved out, she confessed that her house could have been a candidate for the *Hoarders* TV show. She could hear rats scurry at night among the piles of paper in the house, but she was too tired to fix the problem. She had stopped inviting anyone inside. Her heater had stopped working and she was too afraid of being evicted to ask her landlady to fix it. Susan was convinced that she would join the growing population of homeless in L.A., destined to live in the green-and-white Dodge van she had inherited from Karen.

Attending the Boyle Heights ceremony and feeling isolation closing in around her, Susan realized that she might be looking at her own funeral. She knew it was unlikely that her daughters, her legal next of kin, would claim her, and the reality of what would happen to her body after that horrified her. She was deeply touched by the ceremony, but she experienced the lack of family as a deep failure. "There's probably going to be just total fucking strangers there for me."

..

> I stopped drinking on my own for two
> years. I went to school to learn how to be a
> cabinetmaker. I got a job and kept it for two
> years. But I wasn't good at coping with the
> pressures that came with trying to be respon-
> sible. I began drinking again. At 31, A.A.
> found me. For over 11½ years I've been clean
> and sober. . . . I cleaned up the wreckage of
> my past. I learned to stay sober one day at a
> time and how to be of service to others. I
> did not learn how to be of service to myself
> though. I became a human doing instead of a
> human being. I believed that I did not have
> any rights to my own life.

After ten years of sobriety, Midge became a senior counselor at a drug and alcohol center for young adults.

> We confronted our problems with each other
> out in the open. I watched them grow and
> change and I grew and changed as a result.
> I allowed them to be who they were and in
> turn I became the person I had always been.
> It took a courage and patience I did not know
> that I had. This community was temporary and
> I hold the memory of these young people fresh
> in my mind. It reminds me of what I [am]
> capable of achieving.

· ·

AFTER THE BURNING OF SAGE, A CHOIR FROM THE L.A. STREET
Symphony, a nonprofit founded by Los Angeles Philharmonic violinist Vijay Gupta, sang French composer Maurice Duruflé's rendi-
tion of "Ubi Caritas." *Et ex corde diligamus nos sincero.* "And from a
sincere heart let us love each other." The Gregorian chant, written
more than one thousand years ago, transformed the cluster of
soaked canopies into a sixth-century monastery.

Father Chris had first invited Gupta, whose then partner was in
the chaplain training program, to participate in the 2015 ceremony.
That same year, Gupta's team had started the Messiah Project, performing excerpts of Handel's *Messiah* at the Midnight Mission, one
of the largest shelters on Skid Row in downtown Los Angeles. The
piece had first been performed in Dublin, in 1742, with the proceeds
donated to two charitable hospitals and a relief fund for indebted
prisoners. Gupta, a scholar of classical music, found the piece's history deeply fitting for the Skid Row setting. Then, after he attended
the Boyle Heights ceremony in 2015, Gupta realized that, at the
Mission, he had been looking into the eyes of the living who were
at risk of going unclaimed. The realization changed him. "There's so
many people for whom I have wondered, my God, am I going to be
playing at your funeral? Am I going to be playing when *you* pass?"
He considered how to live more deliberately with kindness, to treat
the living more charitably.

Soon, Gupta began sharing with audiences how profoundly
moved he was by the Boyle Heights ceremony, which inspired others to attend. That was how a woman named Nicole came to be at
Midge's ceremony. She stood alone, pensive, draped in an elegant
off-white coat and tightly clutching a bouquet of blooming white
roses. She had lost a brother to suicide four years earlier, and she
was still haunted by the memory of the medical examiner's van,
with its telltale blue stripe on the side, as the staff loaded her brother's body. That same year, she had started to attend the ceremony in
Boyle Heights, and had been there every year since. She saw it as a

way to honor the millions of people around the world, who, like her brother, felt lonely in their final moments. Even though her brother was claimed, the Boyle Heights ceremony offered her a chance to connect with others, if only for a moment. "If we didn't give people dignity in life," she said, "then we owe it to them now. I like being around people that feel the same way."

Jon Schleuss, the L.A. *Times* journalist, was at the ceremony, too, but not to cover the event. He wanted to attend one last time before he moved to Washington, D.C. He was on the cusp of winning a heated election to become president of the NewsGuild, America's largest labor union for journalists, unseating a twelve-year incumbent. In his candidate bio, Jon had referred to his reporting on the unclaimed, and he had attended the ceremony regularly, saying on Facebook how proud he was of the work.

At the ceremony four years earlier, a woman had walked up to Jon and reached out her hands to cup his face. It was Cherry Williamson, the woman whose brother had vanished in 1980. Jon's reporting in the *Los Angeles Times* had made her realize she could check the county cemetery. Cherry had driven from her home in San Diego to pay tribute to her brother, Wesley, and to thank Jon in person. She told him that Albert Gaskin had located her brother's name in the cremation register and she finally knew what had happened. Wesley had died in 2005 and was buried in a common grave at the cemetery.

That moment with Cherry would stick with Jon for years. She was one of dozens of people who had seen his articles and called to share their stories of lost loved ones. For many, like Cherry, it was too late to claim the ashes of a disappeared family member who had gone unclaimed. But at least ten people had been able to retrieve the ashes of loved ones before they were interred, including two domestic partners who were cut out of the claiming process because they were not the legal next of kin. One woman told Jon that her late partner, Jermaine, had come to her in a dream, saying, "Nobody wants me." They had been together ten years and had a son. Three years later, she called the crematorium and learned that Jermaine's mother had still not claimed his ashes. The woman filed a court order, secured a burial permit, and picked up her late partner's cremains. The woman told Jon that she felt chills when she finally held the box in her hands. "He's wanted," she said.

. .

```
I have learned how to blend in and be
with others, when once I could only tolerate
others. I speak up for myself, when once I
would hold everything inside and I would
wither and shrink away from the world.
Self-pity has become self-care. I am a strong
presence in a room of people, where once
there was a pitiful excuse for a human being.
I have a loving toughness about me, where
once I thought I could not love. . . .
     Most of my life I took. I looked to see
what was in it for me. I look now to find
what and where I can give. This is my
personal calling.
```

. .

THE CEREMONY CONTINUED WITH A RABBI RECITING PSALM 23 in English and Hebrew. One of the mourners, a writer and artist, wrote later that she saw a "metaphorical table set before" her, just as the Psalm described. Three hospital chaplains took turns reading the Lord's Prayer, in Spanish, English, and Tagalog. The familiar prayer drew the mourners into the ceremony—nearly half the crowd knew the Spanish words.

The ringing of a brass bell signaled a shift from shared grief to inner reflection. Members from the Zen Center of Los Angeles, a Buddhist temple founded in 1967, gathered around Roshi Wendy Egyoku Nakao to chant a dharani of "love and protection" in Sino-Japanese. Many religions make a point of bearing witness. In Christianity, it can mean making oneself aware of the experiences of others and of Christ, and to pay that forward through proselytization. In Judaism, an emphasis on listening is matched by a call to testify when human travails are observed. While this act is woven into Jewish theology and ritual, exemplified by Passover, it became even more integral after the Holocaust. Elie Wiesel waited ten years before he wrote *Night,* needing to sit in silence with the horror he had experienced in Auschwitz and Buchenwald. When he was ready to write, he said his call was to enshrine into collective memory the millions who had died. "To forget the dead," Wiesel wrote, "would be akin to killing them a second time."

For Zen Buddhists, bearing witness is a core tenet, popularized by the Los Angeles Zen Peacemaker Order. Combined with not-knowing (letting go of fixed ideas) and compassionate action, the tenets provide a pathway to an enlightened world. For members of the Zen Center of L.A., to be present at the gravesite of the unclaimed was to acknowledge the joy and pain these dead had experienced, without attachment or judgment. The roshi ended the group's chant by asking, in English, that the unclaimed dead in Los Angeles and throughout the world be liberated from suffering.

Because Father Chris tended to a majority Spanish-speaking population, in the hospital and at his parish, he invited one of his protégés at LAC+USC, Presbyterian Reverend Elizabeth Gibbs Zehnder, to perform a call-and-response prayer, of mixed English and Spanish, that echoed a popular Latin American act of resistance. Throughout Central and South America in the 1980s, hundreds of thousands went missing, disappeared by government or military juntas. The millions of loved ones left behind came to inhabit spaces of "eternal instability," grieving for losses that have never been officially acknowledged—a deliberate tactic of dictators who ruled through fear. Churches embracing liberation theology responded in defiance. During liturgies, priests would read aloud the names of people who had gone missing or were killed; after each name someone would shout from the pews *"Presente!"* Through that word, which means "presence" or "to be present," mourners invoked the disappeared, and affirmed that the missing were still with them, if only in spirit.

"This morning, we have gathered together to offer each of the 1,457 people our blessing," Rev. Gibbs Zehnder addressed the crowd. "And now, as we make our way from this rain-soaked graveside back to the rest of our day, we carry them with us and we say *presente.*"

The crowded repeated, "*Presente.*"

"We carry each child."

"*Presente.*"

"Each teenager."

"*Presente.*"

"Each adult."

"*Presente.*"

"Each immigrant far from home."

"*Presente.*"

"Each person without a home."

"*Presente.*"

"Each one who suffered violence, sickness, abuse."

"*Presente.*"

"Each one who lived with joy, who danced, who loved, who lived."

"*Presente.*"

"We lived together in this place, each one of us members of the human family."

"*Presente.*"

AFTER THE CALL-AND-RESPONSE PRAYER, the ceremony came to an end. Father Chris invited the attendees at the graveside to take sage from a bowl and sprinkle it on the smoldering coals. The rain had lightened enough to make the invitation a welcome one. Several people lined up. A handful of others moved toward the grave. One woman, her hair dyed purple and her right ear covered in piercings, nearly slipped in the mud in her black Converse sneakers as she bent down to place a small rubber unicorn on the gravestone, a stone marker the size of a postcard, engraved with the year 2016. Midge Gonzales was now one of more than a thousand buried underneath.

EPILOGUE

THE KINDNESS OF CLAY

..

They say we die twice;
once when the last breath leaves our body,
and once when the last person we know
says our name.

THE IDEA THAT WE ARE TRULY DEAD WHEN WE NO LONGER
exist in anyone's memory has its roots in many cultures and time
periods, from traditional Mexican folklore to the artist Banksy's re-
flections on the ephemeral nature of his graffiti: Here today, scrubbed
off tomorrow. Forgetting is inevitable, as descendants pass and
physical markers fade. Over centuries, some notable lives remain
etched in our memories, though their ranks dwindle as time passes.
Many others are recalled for a shorter time—years, decades, a lifetime or two. But what of those who are spoken of a final time mere
moments after they leave the earth—or worse, before they even die?

The unclaimed provoke us to ask whether our lives matter. To
claim, which originates from the Latin word *clamare* or to call out,
is an act of connection: When you claim, you are asserting a bond
between yourself and something or someone else. To go unclaimed,
then, is to be disconnected; it is an acknowledgment of severed
bonds. If you die and no one calls out for you, did your life have
meaning?

This question not only hangs as a shadow over individual lives but increasingly haunts American society. The disgrace of Americans going unclaimed, when it makes national headlines, is most often in the aftermath of natural disaster. After Hurricane Katrina devastated New Orleans, authorities buried eighty-three abandoned and unclaimed victims in a granite mausoleum. What does it say about contemporary America that every year, without the exigency of natural disaster, Los Angeles County buries 1,600 unclaimed bodies in a mass grave? Or that all across the country, communities are struggling to dispose of growing numbers of unclaimed bodies with barely a whisper from elected leaders?

The United States is not the only country to face this question. The scandal of ordinary citizens going unclaimed has sparked public debate across Asia, Africa, and Europe. In September 2022, for instance, Nigerian officials from the Kogi State Sanitation and Waste Management Board, facing jam-packed morgues, buried 130 abandoned bodies en masse, most of them victims of road accidents, kidnappings, and robberies. South Korea has seen its numbers of lonely deaths climb to an average annual rate of 8.8 percent over a five-year period; in 2021, its government enacted the Lonely Death Prevention and Management Act, which mandates that local officials provide dignified burials to people who die without relatives. News coverage of the Russian invasion of Ukraine highlights the ways that war leads to unclaimed bodies. Ukrainian officials have struggled to identify bodies, locate families, and convince shell-shocked relatives to claim the fallen.

The country most engaged in public soul-searching over these deaths is Japan. An estimated 32,000 people die unattended every year in Japan, their corpses often lingering undiscovered for days, months, and sometimes years. Most will depend on the government for cremation and burial. The phenomenon is so prevalent that it has its own term: *kodokushi,* which loosely translated means a "lonely death."

The ubiquity of *kodokushi* has come to stand as evidence of a country in decline, where an unrelenting focus on economic growth has undone families and communities. In this way, a *kodokushi* is the worst kind of death, because it reflects all that a postwar industrialized Japan has lost. A recent government survey found that 40 percent of older people in Japan worry that they will meet life's end alone. This has sparked a nationwide discussion about the decline of traditional family, community, and company bonds, which were vital to Japanese identity for generations. Even skeptics who question whether a lonely death means a lonely life admit that every *kodokushi* carries economic and social costs, from the material expense of cleaning up the death scenes—one decedent was discovered three years after death, his bones picked clean by beetles and bugs—to the stigma of abandonment that relatives must navigate. The government is trying to respond to the "era of dying alone" by restoring community ties through local welfare programs that target those most at risk of *kodokushi*, such as neighborhood checks on older residents.

As in Japan, the rise in unclaimed deaths here in the United States reflects the health of our society. But we tend to either look away or fail to grasp the root cause. Economists hypothesize, for example, that the number of unclaimed rises and falls with the price of funerals. It is true that caskets, vaults, and grave plots are outrageously expensive, and the funeral industry, as Jessica Mitford exposed in *The American Way of Death* in 1963, takes advantage of people in their most vulnerable moments. The industry's consolidation— six operators command nearly 30 percent of all funerals in the United States—further drives up costs. It is also true that the number of unclaimed increases during economic recessions and periods of unemployment when people are hard-pressed for cash. But if holding a funeral is mostly about making a rational spending decision, thousands more should go unclaimed—especially in a city like Los Angeles, where 14 percent of the population lives below the federal poverty line. And over a forty-year period, the likelihood of people ending up unclaimed did not fluctuate with poverty levels in L.A. Instead, as in centuries past, the poor go to great lengths to receive a decent funeral, "for they know," sociologist Tony Walter wrote, "there is something appalling about a human life ending, and no one noticing, no one marking it."

Scene investigator Kristina McGuire, who picked up David's body, agrees that money can be a barrier to claiming relatives. "But when you need money, you find it," she said. She has seen families organize car washes and GoFundMe campaigns to provide a basic memorial. Low-cost funeral and cremation options are more readily available now (budget caskets can be ordered online), rendering many traditional cemetery expenses obsolete. The fact that the middle class and wealthy increasingly run the risk of going unclaimed is further proof that money alone is not driving the increase.

If it's not a family's finances, what is it? Some view unclaimed deaths as one more sad casualty of a country in the grips of drug dependency, mental illness, and homelessness. After all, those struggling with these entwined epidemics appear often among the registers of the unclaimed.

But do these social maladies actually increase a person's risk of going unclaimed? Or is something deeper going on? We wanted to understand this puzzle. We started by picking a random week from 2016 and examining all deaths reported to the medical examiner's department. Out of the 181 deaths the department investigated that week, twelve ended up with a county cremation and one was referred for indigent veteran burial at Riverside National Cemetery. Three of the thirteen unclaimed were unhoused. But five other unhoused decedents were claimed by relatives. Coincidentally, two transient men died that week in train accidents, one while sleeping on the tracks and the other while walking in a tunnel. Joyce Kato in the medical examiner's notifications unit located family in both cases. One man was claimed, the other wasn't. At least thirty-one deaths that week were attributed to alcoholism and substance abuse; the majority of them were claimed. Even deaths of despair do not necessarily lead to a common grave.

We then turned to the cremation registers at the county cemetery in Boyle Heights, the thousands of pages in leather-bound books that list the names, dates of birth, sexes, races, and dates of death of the unclaimed. We worked with a demographer to examine forty years of these records. We found that men are 70 percent more likely than women to end up in the county cemetery in Boyle Heights. White Angelenos make up the largest group of L.A.'s unclaimed in terms of overall numbers, but Black Angelenos go unclaimed at higher rates. People who died in middle age (thirty-five to fifty-four) were more likely to end up unclaimed than other age groups.

The next question was why. Why *these* Angelenos?

We found that the demographic patterns point to a common risk factor: social isolation caused by eroding family ties. Take the gender differences we found. The men most at risk for ending up unclaimed are unmarried or divorced, like David Spencer. Women have their own risks; never getting married is riskier than divorce when it comes to having someone to claim them. Women are also likely to outlive their spouses, leaving fewer people to claim them. The racial differences in going unclaimed can also be explained by shifting family ties. Although households of all racial compositions are fragmenting, the decline of traditional families is most common among white Americans, and the association between family isolation and going unclaimed is significantly stronger for white than for Black L.A. residents. The risk of social isolation also accounts for the age differences. As if people in middle age don't face enough existential angst, demographic research shows that they are one of the fastest-growing segments of the population without nuclear family ties. What the spike in unclaimed really reflects, then, is the transformation of the American family.

For much of our history, government officials defined the standard family as a husband and wife in their first marriage, raising biological children in a shared household, albeit with critical exclusions (for example, enslaved people could not form family units). This definition—which is both ideological and legal—grew out of biblical traditionalism, which treated marriage as "natural" and morally superior. The result was that Americans came to see the family unit as the primary institution to nurture social ties.

This was combined with a philosophy of liberal individualism, which arose during the Enlightenment and argued for prioritizing individual autonomy and self-determination, allowing American society to grow without any of the institutions of a mature welfare system—no guaranteed paid leave for new parents, no universal health insurance, little financial security for when people grow old. Instead, families were expected to absorb life's blows.

But the pressure on families to parry all kinds of calamity is out of touch with demographic realities. The number of Americans who live in a "standard" family is falling. The share of households made up of married couples with children under eighteen dropped from 44 to 19 percent between 1960 and 2017. In short, we marry less and later in life, and we have fewer children than the generations before us. We're also "going solo" more often. The proportion of American adults living alone has almost doubled in the past fifty years to nearly 15 percent. Cohabitation is more common, especially among older adults. These bonds often exist without legal protection (and thus without obligation to claim). Kin disconnection will likely increase as baby boomers age, given that more than one in four boomers is divorced or never married and more than one in six live alone. Demographers predict a generation of "kinless seniors," a million strong, without partners or spouses, children or siblings.

Hidden within these profound changes in American family life is widespread fracturing. One in four adult Americans report being estranged from close relatives. Some drift away, others escape abusive intimate relationships. Many people who cut ties try starting over in a different city, as Midge did when she took off on a stolen motorcycle headed for L.A. In an era of growing polarization over politics, faith, and sexuality, parents and children often feel as if they have no choice but to cut off contact. What once were disagreements between kin over money can now turn into unbridgeable rifts. On paper these families are still a unit, but they no longer support one another. In many cases, families are sundered by the government, through incarceration or the foster care system. When the state permanently severs parent-child relationships, the law renders estrangement legally binding.

The COVID-19 pandemic has only exacerbated these trends toward disconnection. Surveys taken before and after the pandemic showed that social distancing and lockdowns led to community distrust and isolation even after lockdowns ended, especially for the middle-aged and elderly, who were already vulnerable. At precisely the moment when we could have collectively benefited the most from social support, the number of social interactions plummeted. Unsurprisingly, Americans felt more alone than ever. "When adult children don't contact you during a pandemic," one respondent said, "it certainly feels [like] they don't care whether you live or die." Just as policymakers use life expectancy to assess the overall health of a population—allowing comparisons between countries and over time—the number of unclaimed deaths offers a sensitive barometer of the weakening of kin support over time.

The uncomfortable truth is that the unclaimed are not marginal outliers. All signs suggest that their numbers will continue to rise if nothing changes, and those at risk already dwell among us. They are the resident of the house on the block with the overgrown front yard and disintegrating cardboard boxes piled next to the front door. The man shuffling bent over on his daily walk, always by himself. The trans teenager hitting the streets after an ugly fight with their parents. The quiet nursing home resident, fighting tears after yet another Mother's Day without a phone call. The unclaimed-in-waiting are everywhere.

HOW CAN WE RESIST this trend? One strategy is to urge people to make their wishes about disposition known. Staff in L.A. County's medical examiner's office, the Office of Decedent Affairs, and the public administrator give talks to civic and church groups to en-courage individuals to decide what they want to do with their bodies and take steps to make sure their wishes are followed. Wills and trusts allow people to leave instructions for their final arrangements, while preneed funeral insurance helps people pay in advance for services with a specific funeral home, burial plot, or both—allowing individuals to maintain control over their own disposition, and avoid saddling relatives with uncomfortable decisions and unexpected costs.

These efforts are laudable, but it's hard not to see them as part of a larger conservative agenda that emphasizes self-sufficiency and denigrates government intervention. As with bootstrap approaches to poverty, the approach has had little success. A review of twenty years of advance directives—documents specifying what a patient would like to have happen at the end of life—concludes that Americans still refuse to plan ahead. And an online survey showed that while 69 percent of respondents over the age of forty were interested in prearranging their own funeral service, only 17 percent had made these arrangements. Americans have trouble prioritizing the end of life and its aftermath.

A more promising way to reduce the numbers of unclaimed bodies is to nurture social ties that fight loneliness and isolation, both by expanding programs for vulnerable individuals and by widening notions of kinship beyond the nuclear family. While it's tempting to romanticize the idea of the close-knit family, where siblings, spouses, and children stand shoulder to shoulder in life and death, demographic trends, as we've seen, paint a different picture. Government burial incentives can help, but they're destined to be less effective when a strict next-of-kin hierarchy is enforced. Even with FEMA burial reimbursement for families of victims of Hurricane Katrina, Superstorm Sandy, and the COVID-19 pandemic, people continued to go unclaimed. David's estate paid for his funeral, and still Tiffany and Mikel refused to be involved. It seems unlikely that stronger incentives could have persuaded Marjorie or Rudy to bury Lena; they simply did not value their relationship with their aunt.

Social programs that foster family ties can make a difference if they bring relatives together *during life*. Every sign indicated that Bobby Hanna was on the road to going unclaimed until New Directions' comprehensive treatment program for homeless veterans provided him professional help for his drug use and a support system that encouraged family reunification. New Directions prompted Bobby to reach out to Donnell, not at the end of his life but years earlier. Because the relationship had been restored, Donnell made personal sacrifices to get his father cremated.

In one sense, Donnell was lucky. Despite financial and emotional turmoil, as the recognized next of kin he was able to claim his father and posthumously strengthen their connection. But an untold number of loved ones aren't as fortunate. The government's strict definition of "family" greatly limits who is allowed to claim.

It doesn't have to be this way. End-of-life care shows what it might look like to allow greater flexibility in who counts as family. Through an advance directive, a terminal patient can appoint a proxy decision-maker. For those lacking documentation, each U.S. state permits a relative to step in as a surrogate decision-maker. Forty-six U.S. states have established a surrogate hierarchy that includes spouse, child, and parent while at least eight states allow for a "partner" or "common-law spouse" to also be the decision-maker. At a person's deathbed, end-of-life decision-making remains inclusive, with medical staff often looking for a consensus among *all* relatives involved and even close friends. In spite of legal requirements, healthcare providers use their discretion to defer to those closest to the dying patient.

The fate of Midge Gonzales reveals how antiquated our legal understandings of family have become, and how they fail to capture the ways people build close, alternative kinships. Had Midge's chosen family from the Westchester Church been recognized as next of kin by the county, she might not have been buried at Boyle Heights, but in a private ceremony organized by the people who knew her best. Instead, her deeply meaningful relationships with the church community were rendered illegitimate by the county system. Midge's story shows that we need a new blueprint, both to foster deeper social ties and to legally recognize and encourage new surrogate kinship networks.

As we watched gloved investigators at the death scene rummage through underwear drawers in search of clues to contacts and assets, we couldn't help but wonder if Americans understand how deeply involved the state is in our afterlives. Once the legal family is no longer in the picture, county officials don the role of benefactor, taking on a responsibility to provide at least a minimum level of social recognition of the unclaimed.

If the government is in our business after death anyway, why not provide as humane a touch as possible? We're not convinced the unclaimed should be stratified in indigent and wealthier tiers, but if a county bureaucrat is going to authorize $10,000 from a decedent's estate for a funeral, as in David's case, could they not give the ritual some heart by tailoring the service to the individual and inviting friends and neighbors to attend? At a bare minimum, can we ensure that *someone,* besides the funeral director and cemetery personnel, is present?

In the United Kingdom, where the National Health Service was designed to provide care from "cradle to grave," some local districts have taken it upon themselves to organize deeply meaningful public health funerals, working with families, friends, and civic organizations to create a service that reflects the individual. In Amsterdam, when the municipality can find no one willing to attend a burial for an unclaimed person, the government hires a foundation that organizes a funeral and writes a poem exclusively for the decedent. South Korea outsources funerals for the unclaimed to a volunteer organization that displays a portrait of the deceased beside their favorite drinks and snacks in line with Korean tradition. What can *we* do differently to not just dispose of unclaimed bodies but honor them?

After all, the support of relatives is no longer guaranteed. Branches of family trees are snapping off. Our social safety net is shot through with holes, and some of the country's most vulnerable individuals are slipping quietly through, drifting into extreme isolation, headed toward a lonely death. We are at an inflection point. It's time to reexamine what we *all* owe one another at the end of life.

· ·

REVERSING THE TOLL OF FAMILY DISCONNECTION AND SOCIAL isolation will take time. In the interim, we will always end up with some people going unclaimed. In this way, every unclaimed death is both a challenge and an opportunity—*their* deaths are *our* losses to feel and process.

The dead body perplexes and enchants us, says historian Thomas Laqueur. It is "powerful, dangerous, preserved, revered, feared, an object of ritual, a thing to be reckoned with." Over millennia, we have felt compelled to engage in ceremonial rites—to ensure passage to the afterlife, to honor loved ones, to gain solace in their absence, to strengthen communal bonds. Even now, when most of us no longer fear haunting by a restless soul, death rituals remain a deeply felt human need.

The nineteenth-century sociologist Émile Durkheim argued that our most basic ability to relate to one another depends on ritualized moments of shared experience. These moments create a sense of solidarity and rally us to action. "If we are all angry, or sad together, we nevertheless feel better and *stronger.*" Think about attending a concert—music that moves you even when you're alone can take on a heightened emotional resonance when you experience it among other adoring fans. In these moments, Durkheim said, we repair the disconnect and anomie we feel in everyday life. Rituals around death are particularly important, he added, because they address existential questions about who we are as a society, what binds us together, and what our collective purpose is.

When a funeral is impossible for loved ones, the trauma that develops, what psychiatrists call "ambiguous loss," haunts for gen-

erations. Governments, their adversaries, and drug cartels exploit
deaths by rendering people unclaimable. Relatives of migrants
swallowed in the killing wasteland of the Sonoran Desert or of
those "disappeared" by authoritarian regimes, like the Mothers of
the Plaza de Mayo in Buenos Aires, ache for the chance to claim
the remains of their loved ones but are denied burial rites. The U.S.
military still spends millions of dollars every year to retrieve the
remains of soldiers killed in foreign wars so families have something tangible to mourn. During pandemic lockdowns, social distancing rules restricted funeral size and practices. Americans unable
to bury their loved ones were suspended in a liminal space of grief.

If denying families a burial causes deep personal pain, denying a
funeral to those without family exacts its own social cost. When we
dispose of the unclaimed out of the public eye, locate their gravesites
in inaccessible areas, or either fail or refuse to mark a mass burial
with a ceremony—the default in most cities in the United States—
we erase these deaths and lives and the vital lessons they offer. It
doesn't matter whether we forget intentionally or not. Hiding the
unclaimed is a way of hiding who we are—and prevents us from
reckoning with what we need to do to become better.

Those who create rituals for the unclaimed understand that living in a society where people routinely go abandoned after death
diminishes us all; their actions point to the power of radical compassion to draw attention to structural inequalities: a kindness
toward others that comes with personal sacrifice. The members of
Veterans Without Family see their efforts to call out for their unclaimed military brothers and sisters as an extension of their service
to the nation. The Garden of Innocence attendants forge a community to send off abandoned babies, even if every funeral remains
heartbreaking. When people's deaths in a global metropolis are as
invisible as their lives, the Boyle Heights ceremony brings people
from every walk of life together—affirmation that all our fates are
linked.

At the same time, these actions aren't completely selfless. Attending a stranger's funeral allows us to confront our own mortality,

opening a space for us to reimagine how we want to live. We may feel compelled to take stock of our life choices, mourn our lingering losses, and mend our strained relationships. Such funerals may vaccinate against the epidemic of loneliness and isolation. They also serve as a prompt for reflecting on the inequities that put so many of us at risk of going unclaimed in contemporary America.

Los Angeles has one of the most elaborate ceremonies in the country to honor the unclaimed (even though the annual service's continuation remains precarious). But Los Angeles County is not alone in its quest to bestow honor. From Florida to Washington State, communities have come together to bury the unclaimed. These efforts are often spearheaded by coroner and medical examiner's offices but also by local politicians, law enforcement, emergency personnel, cemeteries, funeral homes, business groups, and faith communities.

Across the country, mourners are eager to show up and pay respects to unclaimed veterans, the group of unclaimed most likely to receive public attention. The homeless, poor, and forgotten of Lafayette Parish in Louisiana are buried during an annual All Souls Day Mass, with public volunteers as pallbearers. One hundred twenty-five miles west, in the parish of Covington, a community leadership group raised funds for a crypt to bury the unclaimed. In Seattle, the fire department and homeless advocates participated in a ceremony where the unclaimed were interred in a common grave marked with the inscription "Gone But Not Forgotten." In Fort Walton Beach, Florida, the local faith community came together not just to bury the unclaimed but also to build marble benches next to their Lazarus Field, inviting visitors to reflect on these deaths. In Erie County, New York, volunteers at an unclaimed ceremony each received a bag of cremains to spread in a straight line between imposing pines. High school seniors at the all-boys Roxbury Latin School participate as pallbearers in the burial of unclaimed Boston residents and bear witness to those who died alone. At the funeral of one lonely man, the seniors read as a group: "He died alone with no family to comfort him. Today we are his family, we are here as his sons."

There is no universal template for burying the unclaimed. What works in L.A. may not work in Grinnell, Iowa, where "Stranger's Rest," the local potter's field, can go for years without receiving a new resident. The point is simply to bestow honor in whatever way a local community feels is most appropriate.

Burying the unclaimed is an incubator for what sociologist Ruha Benjamin calls *viral justice,* small acts of justice based on care, democratic participation, and solidarity, which inspire larger community movements. She offers the example of Ron Finley, an artist-activist in South Central L.A. When Finley became frustrated with how difficult it was to purchase fresh vegetables in his neighborhood, he decided to plant pumpkins, peppers, corn, and sunflowers in the dirt spaces between the street and the sidewalk. Residents in other depressed urban areas in L.A. followed suit, and soon small-scale urban gardens spread across the city. Finley's goal was not just to provide food but to teach residents how to farm and to empower residents to take control of their environments. On its own, this is an act of justice; as it spreads, it becomes viral justice. Benjamin's core message is that these acts can spark other forms of social change—"a guiding ethos for regenerating life" that recognizes our interdependence. Similarly, we have seen how attending funerals of the unclaimed spreads awareness about the high suicide rate among veterans, the desolation of recent migrants, and the power of acts of kindness.

Respect in death can be a rallying call for respect in life. Holding hands with strangers around the gravesite of the unclaimed as surrogate family members is an act of forgiveness and hope, seeding new viral justice opportunities. These funerals turn anger, sadness, and sorrow into awareness, healing, and connection, feeding the soul of the city like the gardener who cultivates food that nourishes the body. Through ritualized moments of collective effervescence, we transcend our differences and create local change worth fighting for. Even if it may seem there are other social problems more pressing and worthy of our limited time, the unclaimed remind us that unless every body counts, nobody counts.

The fact that many of us are at greater risk of winding up without kin and going unclaimed means it's not a movement to benefit a small sliver of society but one that lifts us all. Attending ceremonies for the unclaimed is a way of affirming that, indeed, "We are their family." It helps mend the fraying of connection caused by misplaced priorities that have untethered and divided us. Remembering the unclaimed confirms that what matters most is not the stuff we squirrel away but the rich connections that make people want to mourn us when we pass.

AFTERWORD

..

MEMENTO MORI

As we leafed through court records summarizing a life as a list of assets and spoke with relatives and friends of the unclaimed who were struggling to let go, it became clear that we had underestimated the grip that the unclaimed have on the living, even on those who had abandoned the dead. We realized that the distance between life and death was not a wide chasm but a narrow traverse. The possibility of ending up unclaimed holds up a mirror and asks: What should *we* do differently in our lives?

Susan

We witnessed Susan Rorke's anguish at the 2018 ceremony in Boyle Heights, where she had stood in front of the gravesite, her head bowed in prayer as cameras snapped. We didn't approach her then. We waited a few days, then used an online search to find her home address and left a handwritten note with our phone numbers. She called the next day, eager to share her story. We volunteered to pick her up at her office in downtown L.A. and drive her to a Metro park-and-ride lot in the San Fernando Valley. Susan's hunger for human contact was palpable—she sat close to us—and her distinctively fresh, floral scent filled the car. Her silver hair was tied neatly into a low ponytail, and she wore a light blue plaid shirt and off-white corduroy pants that hung loosely on her small frame. Her defining piece of jewelry was a necklace of an evil eye talisman. The two bags Susan had carried into the car, a purse and a cloth bag with a used paperback of *Lost Connections: Uncovering the Real Causes of Depression—and the Unexpected Solutions* by Johann Hari, took up more space on the adjacent seat than Susan.

Moments into the drive, Susan admitted she had contemplated suicide, but she found herself unable to go through with it. "I have this kind of belief that I didn't put me here. The Creator did. So it's not my right to take myself out. Yet I sometimes wonder." Without much prompting, a life story of estrangements, arbitrator-mediated conflicts with coworkers, hoarding, mental health struggles, and resentment tumbled out while the three of us progressed slowly through rush hour traffic on the Hollywood Freeway.

After we dropped her off at her van, neither of us spoke until we got back to West L.A., and then it was simply to agree that we both needed time to process what Susan had said. We felt we had been in the presence of someone bound to end up at Boyle Heights, a living version of the unclaimed we had until then only come to know postmortem. Susan's words were an indictment of all of us. "What a horrible, shameful commentary," she said, "that we have evolved to allow this to happen, where people have become pretty much disposable."

Susan was adamant that no human was disposable. She expressed hope that her life could still turn around. "I don't understand why my life worked out this way," she said. "But, God dammit, I don't want to just lay down and die."

The following year we met Susan at a fast-food restaurant near her home for a lunch of veggie burgers and fries. She was off work and dressed in a blue tie-dyed music festival T-shirt and khaki shorts. Her hair was unbrushed, loosely pulled back. The evil eye necklace remained. Her fair skin was a sun-kissed reddish pink, and she looked less frail. It was a noticeably healthier-looking Susan.

As the lunch proceeded, we saw that she wasn't a completely

new woman. Anger and resentments remained. But we were surprised at how far she had come in the seven months since the Boyle Heights ceremony. And the biggest revelation: Susan was talking to her estranged youngest daughter, Emily. That Mother's Day had begun in painful silence; Susan felt it was her daughter's responsibility to reach out. Amid the unexpected silence from her mother, Emily became convinced that something dreadful had happened. At nine-thirty P.M., she rang her mother's doorbell, tears in her eyes. She threw her arms around Susan when the door opened. "You're not dead," Emily sobbed. It proved to be the breakthrough they needed to rekindle their relationship.

Another part of Susan's life had changed for the better—she finally had a close friend; someone she could confide in and cry to. It was Karen's biological sister, Cybil, who had located Susan after Karen's death. Cybil lived in Montana and had started calling Susan every week. Cybil was helping Susan to process the pain of her tortured past and ongoing family issues.

Susan had seemed to exemplify the unstoppable slide from isolation into what would likely be an unclaimed death. The lives of David, Midge, and Lena had sensitized us to the fallout of corroded social connections. Yet Susan had bent her fate—not just because, as described in the book Susan carried around, social connections make us healthier and happier, but because connection is vital to being human. "You need to know that you matter to somebody, you need to know that somebody somewhere knows your name and cares about you," she said. "Because if not, it starts eating at you, and it will fucking kill you." An ungrieved death is heartbreaking. But a life without connection is worse.

Pamela

I'LL ADMIT THAT AT THE START OF THIS PROJECT I APPROACHED next of kin who did not claim with some judgment. How could you not claim someone who had raised you, or whom you had raised, no matter the wrongs committed? To me, it seemed simple: If you have the money to claim, you do. I sympathized with the broken families I met early in my research, in part because my father and I had always struggled to get along. It wasn't unheard of for us to go months without talking. But I never could have imagined either of us letting the other go unclaimed. Surely, I thought, we would step up for each other in the end.

During the writing of this book, however, my father decided that he no longer wanted me in his life. He has not fully explained why. I sense it's a mixture of religious and political differences, combined with decades of strained interactions. What I know for certain is that he stormed out of a lunch in 2021 and has refused to talk to me ever since.

I haven't found a way to explain to people, even my closest friends, how much this hurts. I've had to console a confidante who cried upon hearing the story, saying she didn't understand how any parent could walk away from their only child. People want the unraveling to make sense, and I'm not sure it ever will. But researching the unclaimed has helped me to feel less alone in my family struggles. I have talked to adults in similar situations—estranged from people they loved and perhaps once shared homes with, saddened by the unacknowledged grief that estrangement causes and frustrated by the lack of resolution. Estrangement changes everything. It means rewriting rules you didn't create, while navigating public perceptions and personal pain. It casts doubt where once there was unwavering certainty.

Sixty-seven million Americans—including me—have to plan for a future with family members who are legally connected to us but no longer act like kin. We have no way of knowing if the severing of the relationship is permanent or temporary. Death—like birth, raising children, and marriage—has a way of bringing this uncertainty into sharper focus.

I still plan to claim my father if called upon. Like Donnell, I would see claiming as an opportunity to repair a relationship that I've spent a lifetime hoping would be different. But I have a newfound empathy for next of kin who struggle with what to do amid the larger moral muddling that estrangement creates. We are born into a web of relationships we did not choose but which nonetheless define us. We can denounce familial bonds, but the unclaimed have taught me that we can never fully erase them. Because, as political philosopher Samuel Sheffler has written, "to have repudiated a personal tie is not the same as never having had it."

This reality of foreverness raises questions that don't have easy answers, yet I think deserve wider societal discussion. At the heart of my dilemma—and those of other estranged families: Where do our obligations to family begin and end?

Stefan

IF I DIE . . . TELL MEREL AND JASPER THAT I LOVE THEM VERY *much.* I quickly jotted these words in my phone's notes app while lying on a hospital bed in the Kaiser Permanente West Los Angeles emergency department. An hour earlier, I had barely made it home walking the dogs. My legs had felt leaden. I was gasping for air and had to sit down three separate times to circle one block. For months, I had been noticing that I was increasingly out of breath; routine walks had become a challenge. I even started taking the elevator to my second-floor office because the stairs exhausted me. I thought I had asthma, like my father, and tried an inhaler at my doctor's suggestion, but it didn't seem to help.

Back at the house, I sat down at the kitchen table to catch my breath. I suddenly felt woozy, as if I was about to faint. Terrified, and with no one else around, I drove myself to the emergency room (not recommended) and parked my Jeep in a twenty-minute space because I didn't think I'd be able to handle the stairs in the regular lot. I showed up at triage panting heavily and was rushed past a full waiting area into a small room. Dr. Jain, the ER doctor, listened to my lungs. He looked up and said that I didn't have asthma. My lungs were clear. I worried that I had come in for no reason, but I still felt like something was terribly wrong.

A nurse did an EKG and took blood. A technician wheeled me

to a bed in the back unit. A while later, Dr. Jain opened the curtain and announced that based on the bloodwork, I was either having a heart attack or had a blood clot in my lungs. The EKG showed an irregular heartbeat, but he needed more tests. He handed me three aspirin and sent me off for an MRI.

I was fifty-three, the same age my mother had been when she'd had her first stroke. She died from a second one the following year. My entire adult life I had been terrified that I would end up like her. I bargained with an invisible life force: Maybe if I biked regularly and ate vegetarian, I could live past my midfifties?

After Dr. Jain left, I picked up my phone and added to the note: *If my brain is gone, please let me die. Can you cremate me and spread some of my ashes on Catalina Island?*

The note was for Ruth, my wife. She was in the British Midlands, visiting her ailing father. The physician said I would need to spend several days in the hospital. Even if Ruth took a plane in the morning, I needed someone to feed our dogs that night.

And then it hit me hard. I wasn't just dying. I was utterly alone. My kids, Merel and Jasper, were at their universities, hours away. The nearby friends that I had been close to before the pandemic had gone separate ways—literally. Two of the four couples in our dinner club had split up, making the group defunct. My other friendships had withered during the pandemic. It wasn't always this way. I'd had close friends throughout my childhood, in the early years of my career, and when the kids were younger. At some point, though, it had become just Ruth and me, empty nesters. Busy with work, I had barely noticed.

By this point, Pamela and I had been working on this book for six years, charting the toll that social isolation took on loners. We had observed how remarkable it was that when David Spencer was forced to give up his Jeep, bike, and then long walks, his friendship circle had shrunk to three people, one of whom was his ex-wife. And here I was, in a blue hospital gown covered by a thin blanket, scrolling through my contact list to figure out who to ask to take care of the dogs, and coming up with no one. I made a new bargain: If I walk out of here, I am going to organize my life around making friends, mentoring students, and volunteering. As for those already in my life, I vowed to tell them I loved them and not count on someone finding a note on my phone after I was gone.

You

WE HOPE THAT YOU ARE NOT ESTRANGED FROM LOVED ONES and that you've never had a near-death experience. But at some point, all of us will be forced to confront our own mortality. "If we kept in mind that we will soon inevitably die," Tolstoy wrote, "our lives would be completely different." He admonished us all: "*Memento mori*—remember death!"

Since the Middle Ages, symbols of death, often a skull with bones or a skeleton with a scythe, have reminded people of the fleeting nature of life. In early Christianity, *memento mori* impressed that death was not a threat but a gateway to salvation, dovetailing with similar ideas in other religions such as the cycle of reincarnation in Hinduism. The moral lesson was to turn away from earthly pleasures and prepare for an afterlife. In our death-denying and secular world, what can Tolstoy's warning teach us? What might it look like to remember death?

Some of the people we met over the course of writing this book deal with death every day, often in the aftermath of the worst scenarios. Coroner investigators pull slumped teenage drivers from smashed-up cars. They gather dead babies from the arms of mothers paralyzed by grief. They witness the results of senseless drug overdoses, observe the bloody human toll of gang warfare, and clean up the physical mess of countless suicides. As we crisscrossed the city with them, we asked them what they had learned.

"I had a case recently," coroner investigator Aimee Earl said, "where this kid was just driving on the freeway and there was some metal debris that was rolling on the ground, and no one had seen it fall off of a truck." Another car kicked up the metal when driving over it and it came up through the windshield, hitting the young passenger "straight in the head," killing him.

Death is sneaky. "I'm just trying to tell you, there are literally millions of ways that you can die," said Kristina McGuire. "People can say, 'Oh I realize how precious life is.' But *do you really*? Do you truly understand that in a millisecond it can be taken away? Because we see that every day."

"You learn over time not to be so cavalier with life," Lieutenant David Smith said. He and his fellow investigators gave us several practical tips: Stand away from the curb while waiting for the WALK sign to turn green. Don't rush an intersection when the lights are about to change. And they all warned: *Do not ride a motorcycle.* Images of detached arms and legs haunted them. Seriously, "Don't do it," they said.

At the same time, they told us, have fun. Measure your risks and rewards. It makes no sense to live in a bubble.

"Honestly, if something's gonna happen then it's gonna happen and it's beyond my control," Aimee said. "I think a few of us, we're going skydiving in a few weeks." Who was leading the skydiving trip? we asked. It was Kristina.

Three years into her dream job, thirty-year-old Kristina says she has seen enough to know that she's lived a good life. "My family knows I love them. If I were to die right now, I'd be perfectly fine with it." We're all going to die, the death care workers liked to remind us, so focus on what matters: Keep your friends and relatives close. Kristina jokes that she made a deal with her sister that when they reach their seventies, they'll live together. "Then I won't be a decomp," she said, referring to people like David Spencer, who are found after the decomposition process sets in.

Make sure your loved ones know you care. And then go skydiving.

ABOUT THIS PROJECT

. .

For the past eight years, Stefan and I have been on a journey to understand the unclaimed—who they are, why they are abandoned, and what the phenomenon says about America in the twenty-first century. Our approach followed the principles of the social autopsy. Rather than locating the cause of death inside the deceased's bodily remains as happens in a medical autopsy, we turned outward and searched for common causes for the deaths and probed the mark these deaths left on communities. This quest demanded that we retrace the unclaimed across L.A.'s sprawl, wherever they had lived, died, and had people care for them.

Like many books, our journey began long before the recorder was first turned on. It started with an encounter I had at a mosque in South Central L.A. I was conducting research there for my Ph.D. dissertation in 2008 when I met Sherri, one of the mosque's long-time members. Sister Sherri was witty and charming. She was also burdened by severe mental health problems that prompted uncontrollable outbursts. Community lore held that Sherri once stripped off her clothes at the mosque and fought police officers when they came to arrest her, earning her the unfortunate nickname "Crazy Sherri." Still, she had been a fixture at the mosque for decades and, knowing she was estranged from her biological family, her fellow

Muslims were determined to help care for her. When Sherri's health took a turn for the worse in 2011, a couple from the mosque took her into their small apartment, providing shelter, food, and clothes. Later that year, she died. Her body was being stored at the county morgue. The imam explained that if the community did not act soon, Sherri would be cremated. In Islam, burial is considered a community obligation, and cremation is prohibited.

Members organized a fundraiser, first to hire a lawyer to help mosque leaders claim Sherri, and then to pay for her funeral. The head imam told me that Sherri was the only person they had to go to court to claim; otherwise, they had been able to work with families to secure members' bodies for burial. (In theory, Midge's church family could have done the same. I think mosque members were willing to challenge legal norms because, as a former Nation of Islam community, they were accustomed to fighting for their beliefs while facing hostile government bureaucracies.) The exorbitantly high cost of burial plots in Los Angeles meant that the mosque could afford a grave for Sherri only far out of the city center, in a cemetery nearly ninety miles away. But she was saved from cremation and the mass grave in Boyle Heights.

Years later, as I wrote up Sherri's story, I realized that I had never considered what happened when someone died without people to claim them. A quick internet search on unclaimed bodies in the United States revealed only a modest selection of news stories, including a handful of Los Angeles Times features about the crematorium and annual burial in Boyle Heights. Once I read about the mass burial, I couldn't get it out of my mind. How had I lived in Los Angeles for more than ten years, part of that time only five miles from the public cemetery in Boyle Heights, and not known there was a new mass grave in the city every year?

I reached out to Stefan, whom I had worked with at UCLA (I had since moved to Houston). Stefan had written two books on death and dying, including a behind-the-scenes look at how medical examiners distinguish among suicide, homicide, natural, accidental, and undetermined deaths. He told me he was mulling over the idea of new research on the social hierarchy of mourning. He was inspired by cultural theorist Judith Butler's observation that enemy casualties in war are often deemed less "grievable" because their lives were considered disposable, while the elaborate funeral of a head of state can unite a fractured nation. With this in mind, Stefan told me he, too, was intrigued by what the county's unclaimed meant for how some human deaths are valued less than others.

We agreed to embark on what we thought would be a simple and straightforward project—one that played to our complementary strengths. A former journalist, I had experience cold-calling and knocking on doors to ask people difficult questions. Stefan was well versed in dealing with death professionals. We could work different beats of the same story.

WE QUICKLY REALIZED THAT what makes the unclaimed important for study also makes them exceptionally difficult to research. After we started this project in 2015, we spent years seeking answers to basic questions: How many unclaimed are there annually? Who are the unclaimed? Partly it was because no one had ever really counted the unclaimed dead. There are no federal statistics, nor does Los Angeles County keep a comprehensive tally. The various agencies that dealt with the unclaimed in L.A. had their own records, but, as we discovered, they underestimated the number.

We set out, first, to piece together exactly how many Angelenos went unclaimed each year. Even this was unexpectedly difficult: Estela Inouye in the Office of Decedent Affairs initially denied us access to the ledgers containing the names of 125 years of indigent unclaimed dead. She insisted that there was "no story" when it came to the unclaimed dead, and she dismissed the ceremony as being not worth our time. We spent five months making calls and sending follow-up emails to her and her supervisor. In the meantime, we attended our first Boyle Heights ceremony in December 2015— along with more than one hundred attendees. We were struck by how little was said about the unclaimed during the ceremony, including who they were or where they had come from. The mystery deepened.

Other county officials' reports were confounding. A former division chief at the public administrator's office insisted that his office organized about six hundred individual funerals for the unclaimed dead each year. That figure was stunning (and, we would verify later, wildly inflated). We filed a request with the public administrator's office under the California Public Records Act (CPRA) to figure out how many individual funerals they organized. It took eight months for the request to be processed because the office did not track the unclaimed.

The medical examiner's office was more forthcoming, but their numbers also held surprises. When Captain John Kades told us in an early interview how much pride he took in a program to bury unclaimed veterans directly at Riverside National Cemetery, we realized that these bodies had been siphoned off the annual official total of unclaimed simply because they were not being buried in Boyle Heights. Since we were interested in the phenomenon of going unclaimed rather than each bureaucracy's inclusion criteria, we put our own figures together, which included the Boyle Heights cremains, the unclaimed veterans, and the public administrator funerals. That's when it became clear that the rates were higher than anyone had realized.

WE THEN PULLED BACK to ask what these numbers meant. An unclaimed body is, for many people, a disturbing symbol of personal failure or social collapse—and it is often both. We pondered the source of this quietude, wondering what the refusal to arrange or pay for a relative's disposition really showed. Did it matter if a loved one was tossed in a mass grave? Why did many people assume that the state has a moral duty to provide healthcare, but feel shocked, or at least disapproving, when people relied on it for death care? And why did the homeless dead seem to disturb us in ways that the homeless living among us every day did not? We understood that there were deeper societal puzzles hidden in the stories of the unclaimed.

We spoke to anyone and everyone we thought might have relevant insights into the unclaimed. We interviewed hospital and prison chaplains, social workers, mortuary directors, journalists, and—to understand what makes L.A. unique—government employees in other counties. In an attempt to talk to unhoused people at risk of going unclaimed, we volunteered in the L.A. Catholic Worker Hospitality Kitchen, better known as the "Hippie Kitchen," in downtown L.A. (we spent more time chopping onions than talking to those at risk). We traveled to the U.S.-Mexico border to meet activists advocating on behalf of disappeared migrant bodies. We learned about the Garden of Innocence and Veterans Without Family through local news reports, and soon after drove to both San Diego and Riverside to meet their founders and volunteers. We met up with a sheriff deputy from Imperial County on his family vacation at an RV park in San Diego; it was the only time he was available to talk, and we needed to verify that his office dumped unclaimed cremains at sea. We attended an auction where the public administrator's staff sold off the assets of the unclaimed. And, of course, we participated in ceremonies for the unclaimed. Between us, we participated in twelve Garden of Innocence ceremonies in San Diego, Ventura, and Fresno, California, and fourteen services for unclaimed veterans at Riverside National Cemetery. We attended all annual Boyle Heights ceremonies between 2015 and 2022 (the last three years were online), and we visited the Garden of Angels cemetery in Calimesa.

THIS REPORTING REVEALED THE hidden world of the death care workers tasked with processing unclaimed bodies, as well as the volunteers touched by the phenomenon, but the unclaimed themselves remained an enigma.

To locate their relatives and friends, I trained myself to become an amateur genealogist. The Mormon church has invested millions of dollars into creating a digital ancestry database of U.S. citizens regardless of their religious affiliation (familysearch.org). I visited a local library branch in L.A. with Stefan and learned how to use their online records systems. We also relied on library databases, public records websites, virtual memorials (findagrave.com), and other online tools. I triangulated our list of unclaimed names with dates of birth and dates of death to identify last known addresses. From there I tried to track down family members who would be willing to talk with us. It was delicate work; I didn't want to upset people (though it was often inevitable with a subject like this). When I found reliable addresses but no phone numbers, I knocked on doors—residences and places of death for the unclaimed, as well as the homes of friends, families, and neighbors.

We wanted to see for ourselves how the unclaimed had lived and the circumstances of their deaths. With the blessing of Captain Kades, we tagged along with the coroner investigators as they retrieved bodies and gathered clues about possible causes of death. On these ride-alongs we didn't yet know whether the deceased would end up unclaimed. Some we thought likely would, like a man who died in a messy stately home in one of the city's old-money neighborhoods, his second floor eerily untouched since his mother's death years earlier. The decedent ended up being buried by distant relatives.

Dead bodies at home or on the street gave faces to the numbers and pulled us into individual stories. We were with Kristina McGuire for David Spencer's investigation and body retrieval; we each covered different rooms and wrote separate notes. We decided to include his story because he struck us as the archetype of the isolated elderly man we had found over and over in our database of the unclaimed, but he had money to secure a funeral (Kristina found a statement with his retirement savings at the death scene). We thought that David would almost certainly be claimed when notifications officer Joyce Kato located his brother and sister.

When we were not on a ride-along, we sat in the fluorescent-lit cubicles where notifications officers searched for relatives and tried to persuade them to claim. One woman had a name as unforgetta-ble as her tragic past. She had legally changed her name to Pussycat because of her almond eyes. Her mother committed suicide in front of her when she was three; then, at forty-five, Pussycat overdosed and died in her car. I spoke to Pussycat's ex-husband and tried to track down her friend who went by the name of Troll. We also looked closely at Curley Sloss III, who died from sudden cardiac arrest and "extreme physiological stress" after a man pushed a ham-burger in his face during an altercation outside a fast-food restau-rant (the medical examiner ruled it a homicide; the police disagreed and didn't pursue charges).

Midge became our focal point because everyone who knew her seemed deeply affected by her death. Even the coolheaded Mike Patti wept at her memory. Kids and adults had adored her, even if they bristled at her directness. She had an adoptive family in Albu-querque *and* an unofficial church family in Los Angeles. She wasn't isolated, and she seemed an unlikely candidate for going unclaimed (until we better understood the county's narrow legal definition of family). Midge taught us that unclaimed does not mean unmourned.

Later, Stefan sat next to Maria Diaz in the public administra-tor's office as she picked up Bobby Hanna's file and spent days chas-ing Donnell. Every phone call peeled back a layer of the dead man's life. On paper, Bobby seemed most likely to end up unclaimed: He was an intermittently unhoused veteran, struggling with addictions. He was also divorced, with sons he had ignored for most of their lives. Against the odds and at the last possible moment, Donnell snatched Bobby from an indigent veteran's funeral. Bobby showed us that estranged relatives can claim, exactly because it is the last opportunity to do what families have been expected to do for cen-turies. Later, we both visited Donnell in Gary, Indiana, and spent the better part of a day touring the places where both he and Bobby had grown up, including a stop at Michael Jackson's family home.

Conservator records pointed us to Lena Brown. She could have been anyone's stubborn elderly aunt, hell-bent on living out her days on her own terms. Survival into old age came with a cost. Scrutinizing her extensive court records, we realized that depending on when we would have met her, we would have made wildly different predictions on whether she would go unclaimed: We would have said yes when she was scurrying in the dark by herself in her Hawthorne home, heating up beans in the old percolator. No when Rudy and Marjorie fought in court to remain in her life. And then probably yes again when she entered the nursing home and her family stopped visiting her.

WHEN ALL WAS SAID and done, we conducted 234 interviews, directly observed 15 death investigations, reviewed in detail more than 600 additional deaths between the medical examiner's files and court records of public administrator cases, examined lengthy conservatorship cases for another 26 people, logged more than 20 visits to the county crematorium, attended 37 funerals and ceremonies for unclaimed dead, recorded more than 200 hours of video and audio, including nearly 40 hours of ceremonies, consulted more than 8,500 pages of official records, and quantitatively analyzed more than 16,000 unclaimed deaths.

Our social autopsy searched for what puts people most at risk for going unclaimed at the current historical moment. Early in the project I met with Jon Schleuss, the *Los Angeles Times* data journalist who had digitized a year of cremation records. Jon not only shared his Excel files of unclaimed decedents, he also gave us a map that he had constructed pinpointing where in the city the unclaimed had died. We looked closely at the residential and hospital deaths. Jon had found no obvious spatial clustering; this was a phenomenon that crossed the county and affected poor and wealthy.

A convincing explanation should account for not only why some dead ended up unclaimed but also why those who could have become unclaimed didn't. Working backward from those who ended up unclaimed, we found a number of recurring risk factors (unhoused, mental illness, and poverty, among others), but perhaps most deaths under care of the medical examiner's office and the

Office of Decedent Affairs shared those risk factors. Indeed, when we compared all deaths of one week in 2016 that came to the attention of the medical examiner's office, we saw people with these same vulnerabilities who were claimed. The medical examiner files, however, clued us in on what put people most at risk of going unclaimed: a deep estrangement from the people who would be tasked with burying them. This estrangement and often accompanying social isolation did not occur randomly but was itself the consequence of downstream policy decisions such as antiquated rules regarding who constitutes family, weakened infrastructure for helping people with mental illness and addictions, gaps in long-term care for a growing elderly population, gender and racial disparities in isolation, and lack of services for veterans.

The four people we traced in this book cannot stand for the thousands of people who end up unclaimed across the country every year, but each case captures important risk factors as well as the qualitative turning points that determine whether someone, in the end, winds up unclaimed. The personal narratives demonstrate that going unclaimed is not inevitable: Policies that fight social isolation and estrangement and expand who counts as family are likely to reduce the overall number of unclaimed.

IN THIS BOOK, we have tried to create a permanent record of people too often misunderstood by society and even their families. Because we felt a tremendous responsibility to accurately portray the lives of Midge, Bobby, David, and Lena, we aimed to fact-check every claim. We did this as we wrote, questioning each other's words, and made sure we could source every detail. We know that the temperature in Anaheim was 71 degrees the day Midge went to Disneyland with Nora and Howard, because we looked it up in an online weather almanac. We know that David's apartment was a five-to-ten-minute walk to the nature trail, because we drove to Monrovia to time the walk, accounting for the older man's slower pace. We know that Susan Rorke signed the handwritten cremation register, because we have a photo of her signature as evidence. We know the bench where Bobby spent his final months playing piano and strumming a guitar because we toured the New Directions facility. We reconstructed dialogue based on audio-recorded conversations and interviews and, where possible, by triangulating multiple interviews or records. We also hired a professional fact-checker, sharing our primary and secondary sources so that she, too, could double-check. Inevitably there will be details we missed, but we brought to the project a sense of duty to the dead, who cannot speak for themselves.

EVEN IF MOST OF the names in this book are publicly available, we wrestled with our place in telling their stories. Would the dead want their lives on display? Would those they left behind take offense at our probing?

In 2015, *The New York Times* published an account of one unclaimed man in a front-page piece, "The Lonely Death of George Bell." It described a seventy-two-year-old man who had died alone in his cluttered Queens, New York, apartment. "Clearly the man had not died on July 12, the Saturday last year when he was discovered, nor the day before nor the day before that," the journalist wrote.

The feature on the dead man and the aftermath of his death, including the laborious settling of his estate, generated more than 1,700 comments, plus thousands more across social media. Readers of George Bell's story expressed their own fears of dying alone. Some also pointed out how "ironic" and "disturbing" it seemed that the man featured in the story preferred to live his life quietly only to have his death then splashed across the front page of a newspaper. "I wonder what he would have felt about it," one reader commented.

It's a fair point and raises questions about the ethics of telling the stories of the unclaimed. Whose story should matter more, that of the departed or the living? The natural course of the unclaimed is to fade out of memory, by choice or circumstances, often even while still alive. But to leave the story there is to ignore entire chapters of people's lives, as if going unclaimed is the defining event. Instead, we saw it as an opportunity—a way to get to know people we would otherwise forget too soon.

As Stefan and I set out to catalogue the lives of our subjects, we worried that relatives would be unwilling to talk. We expected slammed doors and phone calls directed to voicemail. Many calls went unanswered or unreturned, but more often doors opened. We found relatives eager to share memories and justify unfortunate endings, even if it was by listing how the deceased had wronged them. Friends of the unclaimed and nearly unclaimed wanted their loved ones humanized, too. Midge's friend and fellow church member Denise Norton wanted us to let the world know about Midge: "She was just one of those people where she could just put a smile on your face." Relatives' and friends' willingness to talk with us was confirmation that, as complicated as the stories of the unclaimed are, they need telling.

ACKNOWLEDGMENTS

· ·

OUR DEEPEST GRATITUDE GOES TO THE PEOPLE WHO knew the unclaimed and shared their memories with us. It was an immense privilege to hold their stories and to translate them into the narratives in this book. And to all the death care workers. We stand in awe of the quiet work they do to bring dignity and respect to the unclaimed. This book would not have been possible without them, particularly staff in the Los Angeles County Medical Examiner–Coroner, Public Administrator, Office of Decedent Affairs, and LAC+USC hospital.

We owe deep thanks for the openness and aid of the Veterans Without Family and Garden of Innocence communities. We feel enriched as human beings having had an opportunity to watch the devotion they have to the unclaimed. Thank you to the advocates working tirelessly on behalf of migrants made unclaimable by U.S. immigration policies, and to all who volunteer their time to care for the forgotten and hidden dead in the United States and around the world.

Our book benefited from its own special-missions A-team. When we shopped the proposal for this book, seven editors thought the book ready to go. The eighth told us that we were "in a great place to start." Naturally, we chose to work with her, and we have cherished every moment since. Authors fortunate to have Amanda Cook as their editor rave about the multiple single-spaced letters they receive with detailed, insightful feedback. Even more than the feedback, we appreciated Amanda's kindness, compassion, intellectual depth, and unwavering vision for what this book could and should be. She also kept us humble by gently suggesting that we should, at times, leave sociologists for the endnotes. Alison MacKeen, our agent, proved the perfect champion to shepherd this book through the publishing world. She showed her continued commitment by sending us news articles and philosophical questions that pushed us to think bigger. Andrea Thompson rounded out the A-team. She became our writing guru, helping us find our joint author voice and pushing us to clarify "from here to there." Their confidence propelled this book.

The team at Crown is marvelous and we feel blessed to work with such an amazingly professional crew. Katie Berry has an impeccable eye and we benefited from her thorough reads. She also has the rare combination of being both patient and responsive. We thank copy editor Michelle Daniel; production editor Nancy Delia; legal reader Matthew Martin; marketing team Chantelle Walker, Melissa Esner, and Julie Cepler; publicity team Gwyneth Stansfield and Dyana Messina; cover designer Anna Kochman; page designer Barbara Bachman; production manager Linnea Knollmueller; deputy publisher Annsley Rosner; publisher Gillian Blake; and Crown president David Drake. We were told Julie Tate is one of the best fact-checkers in the business, and we concur. Thanks, Julie, for your unparalleled precision. We're grateful to the Author's Guild for providing affordable contract advice. Caroline Lester and Campbell Schnebly provided useful feedback on early drafts of our proposal. Thank you to Matt Desmond and Colin Jerolmack for tips on the transition to trade publishing.

We thank our current and former academic colleagues at UCLA, Rice University, and the University of Amsterdam. Nancy Berns, Héctor Carillo, and Debbie Carr read the entire manuscript, and each from their respective academic corners crystallized points for us. We thank Heeju Sohn, Ruha Benjamin, and Sergio Chávez for providing additional feedback. Jim Elliott advised us on how to sample the overwhelming amount of data in the cremation registers. Rubén Hernández León facilitated a productive meeting with the Los Angeles Mexican consulate. Mirian Martinez-Aranda conducted several interviews in Spanish. A number of UCLA undergraduate assistants contributed to the research for this book, including Christine Botello, Hannah Lim, Shannell Logan, Deven Nadudvari, Hector Osorio, and Kristina Veneciano. We benefited from stimulating conversations with Ulrike Bialas, Jason De León, Elaine Howard Ecklund, Gregorio Gonzales, Eric Klinenberg, Omar Lizardo, Megan Rosenbloom, Iddo Tavory, and Kate Woodthorpe.

We thank the audiences at McGill University, the American Sociological Association Annual Meetings, the Society for the Scientific Study of Religion Annual Meetings, Rice University's Religion and Public Life Program, and the "Dying Alone" conference at the Max Planck Institute for Human Development. These audiences provided helpful feedback. So, too, did the editorial team at *The Immanent Frame,* a website of the Social Science Research Council, including Saarah Jappie and Mona Oraby.

We drew on the generosity of a number of experts outside academia, including Jon Schleuss, Robin Reineke of the Colibrí Center, and Dr. Maurice Carter at New Directions. A special note to Megan Smolenyak, genealogist extraordinaire, who constructed detailed family trees for key characters and offered advice on doing life-history research. We also want to thank the staffs of the Central Library and the Stanley Mosk Courthouse, both in downtown L.A., for their guidance and patience as we navigated numerous archives. Sabiha Chunawala read an earlier manuscript and shared her insights as both a sharp legal mind and a voracious book reader. We benefited from eye-opening and inspiring conversations with Evie King and Joris van Casteren. Other experts and government insiders weighed in with important information who asked to remain anonymous—hopefully you know who you are and feel our gratitude.

We entered this project thinking it would be a relatively short one. Eight years later we are still borrowing family time to write (as we finish the last changes to this book on Memorial Day/Pinkster-dag weekend). With humility and indebtedness, we thank our immediate, extended, and chosen kin for their patience and support. Stefan thanks Ruth, Merel, Jasper, his father, Elizabeth, Mark, Dominiek, Kristin, Elias, and Kobe for indulging this morbid fascination. Pamela thanks Ejaz, Grandma, Jill, her in-laws and nephews, as well as Dona, Prisidha, Jayne, Andrea, Katerina, Helen, and Dil. She wishes Rose were still here to thank. And to Sariya, thank you for being this book's fiercest cheerleader. You make life's hues brighter.

NOTES

..

vii **"On Passing a Graveyard"** John O'Donohue, *To Bless the Space Between Us: A Book of Blessings* (New York: Doubleday, 2008), 96.

PROLOGUE: ASHES

6 **Puffs of ash** We drew on the ending scene of the documentary *A Certain Kind of Death* and interviews. The documentary is available on YouTube.

6 **Over five hours** Susannah Rosenblatt, "Unclaimed and Forgotten Are Laid to Rest," *Los Angeles Times*, December 7, 2006.

7 **roughly $400 claim fee** The fee ranged from $352 to $466, so we've taken the approximate average ($409).

7 **Early anthropologists observed** Robert Hertz, *Death and the Right Hand* (New York: Routledge, 1960).

8 **"*humanitas* in Latin"** Giambattista Vico, *The New Science of Giambattista Vico*, trans. Thomas Goddard Bergin and Max Harold Fisch (1744; Ithaca, N.Y.: Cornell University Press, 1984), 12.

8 **"the fundamental phenomenon"** Hans-Georg Gadamer, *Reason in the Age of Science* (Cambridge, Mass.: MIT Press, 1981), 75.

8 **not all of us receive a decent burial** Thomas Bahde, "The Common Dust of the Potter's Field," *Common-Place* 6 (2006); Michael Sappol, *A Traffic of Dead Bodies: Anatomy and Embodied Social Identity in Nineteenth-Century America* (Princeton, N.J.: Princeton University Press, 2002).

8 **biblical times** In Matthew 27:3–10, the original potter's field was said to be purchased with coins that Judas earned in his betrayal of Jesus and was referred to as "field of blood."

8 **"the most worthless"** Graham Denyer Willis, "The Potter's Field," *Comparative Studies in Society and History* 60 (2018): 539–68.

8 **buried in plots next to churches** Steven W. Hackel, "Digging Up the Remains of Early Los Angeles: The Plaza Church Cemetery," *Southern California Quarterly* 94 (Spring 2012): 1–24.

8 **"drank, whored, brawled, lynched, and murdered"** D. J. Waldie, "Murder in Old Los Angeles," Kcet.org, October 17, 2017.

8 **In 1877, Los Angeles established** The city already had been using the plot as a potter's field since at least 1865, but the public cemetery officially opened in 1877. Charles E. Davis, Jr., "Portion of Cemetery for Indigent May Be Sold," *Los Angeles Times*, March 11, 1962.

8 **Paredón Blanco** Or "white bluff." The name changed in 1899 to Boyle Heights.

8 **The city received nine acres** Hadley Meares, "Evergreen Cemetery: Snapshots of a Forever Changing Boyle Heights," Kcet.org, August 30, 2013. Evergreen was the only L.A. cemetery never to have banned the burial of Black residents. For more on the history of this cemetery, see the 2014 book *Evergreen in the City of Angels: A History of a Los Angeles Cemetery* published by the Studio for Southern California History.

9 **Gour Fong** While the cemetery was established in 1877, the county's oldest records date to 1896. Mr. Fong was number 447, but it is the first record available now for viewing.

9 **Chinese Americans were prevented** David Pierson, "Reminders of Bigotry Unearthed," *Los Angeles Times,* March 15, 2006. This ugly chapter in L.A. history surfaced in 2005 when construction for the MTA's Gold Line extension was halted by the discovery of a Chinese burial site of 108 males with rice bowls, jade bracelets, and opium pipes.

9 **"They were treated like animals"** Lai quoted in Pierson, "Reminders of Bigotry Unearthed."

9 **poor Americans deprived themselves** Vincent DiGirolamo, "Newsboy Funerals: Tales of Sorrow and Solidarity in Urban America," *Journal of Social History* 36 (2002): 5–30.

9 **Freshly landed immigrants joined burial societies** David T. Beito, "'This Enormous Army': The Mutual Aid Tradition of American Fraternal Societies Before the Twentieth Century," *Social Philosophy and Policy* 14 (Summer 1997): 20–38; Michael K. Rosenow, *Death and Dying in the Working Class, 1865–1920* (Urbana: University of Illinois Press, 2015).

9 **"right soil"** Lorena Nunez and Brittany Wheeler, "Chronicles of Death Out of Place: Management of Migrant Death in Johannesburg," *African Studies* 71 (2012): 212–33.

9 **Italian Club Cemetery in Tampa** Maureen J. Patrick, "Death in a Strange Land: Burial Practices and Memorials in *Il Cirnitero l'Unione Italiana,* Tampa's c. 1900 Italian Immigrant Cemetery," Tampa Historical Society (2006).

9 **three thousand Jewish burial societies** Jewish Genealogical Society.

9 **"correlation between the quality"** DiGirolamo, "Newsboy Funerals."

9 **"If it had come to this"** Upton Sinclair, *The Jungle* (New York: Doubleday, 1906), chap. 13.

10 **"natural and fundamental" right** Tanya D. Marsh, "When Dirt and Death Collide: Legal and Property Interests in Burial Places," *Probate and Property Magazine,* American Bar Association, March 1, 2017.

10 **11,809 densely packed bodies** Davis, "Portion of Cemetery for Indigent May Be Sold."

11 **Aurora Mardiganian** Her original name was Arshalouys Mardigan, according to Anthony Slide, *Ravished Armenia and the Story of Aurora Mardiganian* (Jackson: University Press of Mississippi, 2014), 12; see also the 2022 animation film *Aurora's Sunrise* based in part on an interview with Aurora in 1984, by Dr. Rouben Adalian, available at zoryaninstitute.org.

11 **Craig and Albert cremated** Craig first drew our attention to Aurora. He pointed us to a collection of news articles about her story tucked inside the cremation logs.

11 **A reporter and novelist** Slide, *Ravished Armenia,* 8.

11 **Ravished America** Republished the next year as *Auction of Souls.*

12 **an estimated 2 to 4 percent** Mary Jordan and Kevin Sullivan, "Alone in Death: Tens of Thousands Die Each Year in the United States and No One Claims Their Bodies," *The Washington Post,* September 17, 2021. The journalists draw their numbers from interviews with medical examiners and coroners as well as from Heeju Sohn, Stefan Timmermans, and Pamela Prickett, "Loneliness in Life and Death? Social and Demographic Patterns of Unclaimed Deaths," *PLOS ONE* 15 (2020): 1–17.

U.S. mortality rates can be found at:

2019: Melonie Heron, "Deaths: Leading Causes for 2019," *National Vital Statistics Reports* 70, no. 9 (2021).

2020: Farida B. Ahmad et al., "Provisional Mortality Data—United States, 2020," *Morbidity and Mortality Weekly Report* 70 (2021): 519–22.

2021: Farida B. Ahmad, Jodi A. Cisewski, and Robert N. Anderson, "Provisional Mortality Data—United States, 2021," *Morbidity and Mortality Weekly Report* 71 (2022): 597–600.

The number of deaths nationally in 2019 (pre-pandemic) was 2,854,838. Two and 4 percent of this number gives a range of 57,000 to 114,193 deaths. In the first year of the pandemic, 2020, 3,383,729 American deaths were registered. Four percent would be 135,349 unclaimed deaths. In 2021, preliminary data shows that 3,458,697 deaths occurred; 4 percent would be 138,347 unclaimed deaths. When coroners and medical examiners estimate that the numbers increased 30 percent, this would be due to more people dying (18 percent) and the remainder of the increase due to more people going unclaimed. Adding 30 percent to the 2019 figures of unclaimed gives us a range of 74,000 to 148,000.

12   **die annually from diabetes**   Heron, "Deaths: Leading Causes for 2019."

12   **1.2 percent of adult deaths**   Sohn, Timmermans, and Prickett, "Loneliness in Life and Death," 11. At the time of writing, we don't know yet how the COVID-19 epidemic has affected the numbers in L.A. County because the Office of Decedent Affairs has not released the 2021 figures.

12   **In Maryland**   Data provided to authors by Adam Puche, chair, Maryland Department of Health State Anatomy Board. Percentage of deaths for 2021 calculated by adding 282 unclaimed infant deaths to 2,317 adult deaths. Maryland had 70,898 deaths in 2021, giving an overall death rate of 3.6 percent. In 2000, 43,602 Maryland residents died, according to Georges C. Benjamin and Isabelle Horon, "Maryland Vital Statistics, Annual Report 2000." That year, 696 adults and an estimated 200 infants went unclaimed. The unclaimed death rate was 2.1 percent. For 2020, Maryland had 60,075 deaths, according to Dennis R. Schrader and S. Lee Hurt, "Maryland Vital Statistics Report 2020." The state had 2,305 adult and 309 infant unclaimed deaths. The unclaimed death rate was 4.4 percent.

12   **revealed a 30 percent spike**   Jordan and Sullivan, "Alone in Death."

13   **Montcalm County**   Elisabeth Waldon, "Montcalm County Sees Increase in Unclaimed Bodies," *Daily News,* August 26, 2020.

13   **Fulton County**   Yamil Berard, "Pauper Burials on the Rise in Parts of Georgia," *Atlanta Journal-Constitution,* May 11, 2021.

13   **Hinds County**   Jimmie E. Gates, "Number of Unclaimed Bodies Increasing in Hinds County, Officials Say," *Clarion Ledger,* August 3, 2020.

13   **abandoned in private**   Jacey Fortin, "Bodies of 11 Babies Found Hidden in Shuttered Detroit Funeral Home," *The New York Times,* October 13, 2018.

13   **"quiet epidemic"**   Interview with Megan Smolenyak, November 19, 2015. See also Jon Schleuss, "At L.A. County Cemetery, Unclaimed Dead Await a Final Resting Place," *Los Angeles Times,* November 9, 2014.

14   **list of names**   Publicly available at lacounty.gov.

CHAPTER 1. NEW DIRECTIONS

15   **One lives in the hope**   Antonio Porchia, *Voces* (1943), from *Voices,* trans. W. S. Merwin (Port Townsend, Wash.: Copper Canyon Press, 2003), 11.

17   **Clara**   Pseudonym by request.

17   **Michael Jackson**   Jackson was born August 29, 1958. Bobby Hanna was born April 6, 1959.

17   **Michael won every time**   Philip Potempa, "Michael Jackson's Gary Second Grade Teacher Eager for Hard Rock Opening," *Chicago Tribune,* May 13, 2021. Further information from interviews with Clara Hanna, George Hill, and Carleton Griffin.

18   **Bobby wasn't a trained singer**   Interview with George Hill, September 21, 2021.

19 **things were stable** Interview with Clara Hanna, September 22, 2021.

19 **Bobby was sentenced** Bobby was initially sentenced to six months in a San Bernardino County jail facility with an additional thirty-six months of probation (on HS11378-F, or possession of methamphetamine with intent to sell) after a jury trial, but when a second charge was added, his probation was revoked and he was sentenced to serve 730 days with 245 days of credit for time served (163 actual days served and 82 days for conduct). San Bernardino Superior Court Records, case SB5611BH.

19 **She had divorce papers served** Interview with Clara Hanna, September 22, 2021. Clara told us she served him with papers at Tehachapi (according to Bobby's publicly available criminal records, he received a two-year sentence to California Correctional Institution).

19 **She drove to the freeway** This story is reconstructed based on interviews with Clara Hanna, August 10, 2020, August 18, 2020, and September 22, 2021.

20 **"I'm dropping you off"** Interview with Clara Hanna, September 22, 2021.

20 **Bobby tried to persuade her** Interview with Clara Hanna, August 10, 2020. Clara said it was July, but it was June 1, 2010, according to the *America's Got Talent* wiki, agt.fandom.com.

20 **"I know you're disappointed"** Interview with Clara Hanna, August 18, 2020.

20 **a historic playhouse** Downtownla.com.

21 **one of twenty-seven acts** *America's Got Talent* wiki, episode 501.

21 **next round in Las Vegas** *America's Got Talent* wiki, season 5 auditions.

21 **"This is the moment"** This and other quotes from the performance drawn from a video available on YouTube.

21 **In the polished style** Interview with George Hill, September 21, 2021.

22 **magical journey** Ibid.

22 **Piers Morgan last** Interview with Carleton Griffin, August 5, 2021.

CHAPTER 2. AGING IN PLACE

23 **leaving food outside** Los Angeles Superior Court records, case BP081196.

23 **soft foods, like soups, beans, and oatmeal** Interview with Teena Colebrook, August 4, 2021.

23 **beans in an old electric coffeepot** Lena's conservatorship court records detail the use of the coffeepot to heat food; Los Angeles Superior Court records, case BP081196. The detail that she ate beans via interview with Leona Shapiro, January 8, 2021.

23 **cash in her refrigerator** Interview with Donna van Gundy, August 9, 2021.

23 **piling coats on top** Interview with Teena Colebrook, August 4, 2021.

24 **light fixtures were broken or missing** Los Angeles Superior Court records, case BP081196.

24 **white hair was unkempt** Interview with Leona Shapiro, January 8, 2021.

24 **Spanish for witch** Interviews with multiple neighbors, August 9, 2021; interview with Teena Colebrook, August 4, 2021; and interview with Marjorie Ramos, August 10, 2020.

25 **"Get out!"** This scene via an interview with Teena Colebrook, August 4, 2021.

25 **upholsterer in the aircraft industry** Benjamin's death certificate; nickname "Frank" via Donna van Gundy. Donna, who enjoyed genealogy, provided us with the Browns' marriage and death certificates.

25 **allowing his son and Lena** Interview with Marjorie Ramos, August 10, 2020, and interview with Donna van Gundy, August 9, 2021. Additional information secured via Ancestry.com and court records.

26 **barley fields hedged by large eucalyptus** Hadley Meares, "Hawthorne's Deceptively Sunny History," *LA Curbed*, January 30, 2018.

26　**Lena cared for her mother-in-law**　Interviews with Marjorie Ramos, August 10, 2020, and August 3, 2021. Details about people's dates of birth and death from Ancestry .com and public records.

26　**Piersons**　The court records list the spelling incorrectly as Pearson.

26　**a young woman had squatted**　Interview with multiple neighbors, August 9, 2021, and interview with Donna van Gundy, August 9, 2021.

26　**Each year since her husband's death**　This is 2003. Frank Brown died in 1966.

26　**two blocks**　Interview with Jerry Pierson, August 2021. Additional details for this paragraph via interview with Teena Colebrook, August 4, 2021.

27　**white bungalow**　Interview with Teena Colebrook, August 4, 2021.

27　**abstract concrete statues**　Interview with Donna van Gundy, August 5, 2021. Also, the court documents incorrectly spell Lynda's name as Linda.

27　**Lena insisted**　Los Angeles Superior Court records, case BP081196.

27　**they didn't get along**　Interview with Marjorie Ramos, August 3, 2021.

27　**owned a triplex in Hawthorne**　Josh Boaks and Jeff Horwitz, "Trump Voter Lost Home, Blames Incoming Treasury Secretary," AP News, December 2, 2016.

27　**she lived in a shack**　Interview with Teena Colebrook, August 4, 2021.

28　**thirteen-time NCAA Division II All-American**　Cal Poly Athletics Hall of Fame, gopoly.com.

28　**orange-size**　Interview with Teena Colebrook, August 4, 2021. She says in the interview that the hospital appointments were for tumors, but based on Lena's medical history, it could also have been for hernia repair (she later had hernia surgery, and many patients undergoing such procedures face repeat surgeries).

29　**long-term care facility**　Dorota Trybusinksa and Agnieszka Saracen, "Loneliness in the Context of Quality of Life of Nursing Home Residents," *Open Medicine* 14 (2019): 354–61.

30　**she struggled to remember**　Los Angeles Superior Court records, case BP081196.

30　**It was Marlene, not Lynda**　Interview with Marjorie Ramos, August 3, 2021.

30　**rich people's money**　Ibid.

30　**average house price in 2002**　Profile of the City of Hawthorne, Southern California Association of Governments, 2019, scag.ca.gov.

30　**seen very little of her aunt**　Interview with Marjorie Ramos, August 3, 2021.

31　**"Oh, Marjorie, I thought"**　Ibid.

31　**interested only in the property**　Los Angeles Superior Court records, case BP081196.

31　**Rudy alleged the house was worth**　Ibid.

31　**demanded that the court**　Ibid.

31　**Leona Shapiro was appointed**　Los Angeles Superior Court records, case BP081196.

31　**given her mother a sleeping pill**　This and other details of the story from interview with Leona Shapiro, January 8, 2021.

31　**She vowed**　Interview with Leona Shapiro, January 8, 2021.

31　**spent approximately three hours**　She billed for four hours (Los Angeles Superior Court records, case BP081196), but that would include travel time.

32　**did not want Rudy**　Interview with Leona Shapiro, January 8, 2021.

32　**case of elder abuse was quickly dismissed**　Details about the abuse case via interview with Teena Colebrook, August 4, 2021.

32　**Lena sat in the front**　Descriptions of the court scene via interview with Teena Colebrook, August 4, 2021.

32　**She scoffed**　Interview with Teena Colebrook, August 4, 2021.

33　**Courts are hesitant**　The court's preference for family outlined in Judicial Council of California, *The Handbook for Conservators: 2016 Revised Edition,* courts.ca.gov. Conservatorship data is not tracked at the federal level. Erica F. Wood, "State-Level Adult Guardianship Data: An Exploratory Survey," American Bar Association, 2006.

33 **Rudy was appointed conservator**   Los Angeles Superior Court records, case BP081196. Most records point to April 7, 2004, as the date of the appointment, and April 12, 2004, as the date in which the letters of conservatorship were finalized. A later file lists the date as August 23, 2004, but this likely is a clerical error.

33 **"made false representations"**   This and other details of the lawsuit via Los Angeles Superior Court records, case BP081196.

33 **Rudy had no qualms**   Rudy was able to buy these items because Lena had money from the sale of her home plus savings accounts in the amount of $148,726.66. Details of the purchases from accounting that Rudy filed with court. Los Angeles Superior Court records, case BP081196.

34 **new pair of shoes from Sears**   Either Sears or Macy's; Marjorie Ramos changes the store in different interviews from August 10, 2020, and August 3, 2021.

34 **Lena was stubborn**   Interview with Marjorie Ramos, August 10, 2020.

CHAPTER 3. MY WAY

35 **mental retardation**   Edgar A. Doll, "The Nature of Mental Deficiency," *Psychological Review* 47 (1940): 395–415.

35 **beliefs of the time**   Anne Harrington, "Mother Love and Mental Illness: An Emotional History," *Osiris* 31 (2016): 94–115.

35 **"Kid, how come"**   All quotes and details of this story via interview with Susan Spencer, August 17, 2020.

35 **David developed asthma**   Interview with Susan Spencer, August 17, 2020. Susan also shared the story about David moving to his grandfather's.

36 **smog bowl**   Waterandpower.org.

36 **Death Valley National Monument**   The presidential proclamation was established on February 11, 1933, under the 1906 Antiquities Act. The monument was later enlarged and changed to Death Valley National Park in 1994.

37 **top-secret government**   Interview with Susan Spencer, August 17, 2020. She asked her brother, who was in the military, to inquire about the program, but he came up with nothing.

37 **catering to every sin imaginable**   For history on Las Vegas during this time, we drew from Geoff Schumacher, *Sun, Sin, and Suburbia: An Essential History of Modern Las Vegas* (Las Vegas: Stephens Press, 2004).

37 **"No one has any right"**   Hubbard quoted in Lawrence Wright, *Going Clear: Scientology, Hollywood, and the Prison of Belief* (New York: Vintage, 2013), 4.

38 **ethics as a series**   Wright, *Going Clear*, 132–33. Also Janet Reitman, *Inside Scientology: The Story of America's Most Secret Religion* (New York: HarperOne, 2013), 78–79. Reitman argues that the third dynamic, the group, was the most important, and that an ethical person was understood as someone who lived within the organization's set principles.

38 **She was the lucky winner**   The unusual story of how David decided he wanted to marry Susan is via an interview with her on August 5, 2020. Susan says he later admitted to her it was all a "con."

38 **private Scientology center**   In our interviews, she referred to it as a "Scientology Center," "counseling center," "franchise," and "private center."

38 **He gave up smoking**   Interview with Susan Spencer, August 17, 2020.

38 **she found herself calling David**   Interview with Susan Spencer, August 5, 2020.

40 **had a question**   Interviews with Susan Spencer, August 5 and August 17, 2020. She is also the source of all subsequent dialogue for this scene.

40 **at the Sparks Scientology Center**   "They're Married," *Reno Gazette-Journal*, November 24, 1969, 15.

40 **no smashing cake**   Interview with Susan Spencer, August 17, 2020. Descriptions of what they wore and how they looked per a wedding photo courtesy of Susan Spencer. Their ages in this paragraph are deduced from birth dates.

41   **his own parents were dead**   Interview with Susan Spencer, August 17, 2020.

41   **Her husband was kind and easygoing**   Ibid.

42   **contented solitude**   Eric Klinenberg, *Going Solo: The Extraordinary Rise and Surprising Appeal of Living Alone* (New York: Penguin, 2012).

CHAPTER 4. VAN LIFE

43   **sixty-one-year-old**   Midge's age is estimated based on her date of birth and Nora Spring's recollection of events described in this chapter, including the day of Midge's hospitalization and diabetes diagnosis, in multiple interviews with authors.

43   **Dodge passenger van**   Emery Pankratz's memories of Midge shared with authors via email from his daughter, Denise Norden, October 3, 2022.

43   **congregation was between pastors**   Timelines conflict in people's recollections. Year is based on triangulation between Nora interviews, Lynne interviews, Huddle online CV, and registered addresses owned by the Westchester Church of the Nazarene.

44   **two previous evictions**   Culver City Courthouse records, case 94A01471 (*Linden v. Gonzales*) and Santa Monica Courthouse records, case 05L00308 (*Stane v. Gonzales*).

44   **Nora was content to ignore Midge**   Interview with Nora Spring, July 5, 2019.

44   **"Let me go get my keys"**   Dialogue from this scene is based on interviews with Nora Spring, July 5, 2019, January 16, 2021, and September 19, 2021.

46   **God had given them**   Interview with Nora and Howard Spring, September 19, 2021.

47   **she enrolled at nearby Loyola Marymount University**   Per an email with LMU on April 10, 2023, Midge graduated in 1994.

47   **"Many a fight we had"**   Interview with Nora Spring, July 5, 2019.

47   **thought of Midge as an aunt**   Interviews with Nora Spring, July 5, 2019, January 16, 2021, and September 19, 2021. Age estimates of her children based on public records and a 2009 timeline date.

48   **she grabbed a child's tricycle**   Interview with Nora Spring, January 16, 2021. Additional information on Midge's church involvement comes from interviews with Nora Spring, July 5, 2019, and September 19, 2021; also with Lynne Patti, July 1, 2019, July 5, 2019, and August 19, 2020; as well as Midge's Facebook page.

48   **Midge's friends bought groceries**   Interview with Denise Norden, June 13, 2022.

48   **Widow's Two Mites**   Luke 21:1–4.

49   **registered Republican**   Beenverified.com. Denise said her mother and Midge had different political views.

50   **worked for World Vision**   Huddle's Facebook account.

CHAPTER 5. GONE

53   **Our dead are never dead**   George Eliot, *Adam Bede* (Hertfordshire: Wordsworth Editions, 1997), 88.

55   **"Somebody else needs to"**   Interview with Lynne Patti, July 5, 2019.

55   *God doesn't meet you in complacency*   Ibid.

56   **"She's got to figure it out"**   Interview with Lynne Patti, August 19, 2021.

56   **Mouse and Lucy**   Mike and others called one cat "Moose" in their interviews, but Midge referred on Facebook to "Mouse." It is possible Midge meant Moose and misspelled it, but we went with the name as Midge had typed it.

56   **They agreed on twenty dollars**   Interview with Lynne Patti, July 5, 2019.

57   **"Oh my gosh"**   Dialogue and details of the scene are from an interview with Lynne Patti, August 19, 2020.

57   **had to rely on a wheelchair**   Interview with Nora and Howard Spring, September 19, 2021.

58   **Buzz Lightyear Astro Blasters ride**   Scene of Midge's attempts in the game is from an interview with Nora and Howard Spring, September 19, 2021.

59   **Big Thunder Ranch for lunch** Chris Strodder, *The Disneyland Encyclopedia*, 3rd ed. (Solana Beach, Calif.: Santa Monica Press, 2017), 83–84.

59   **Midge filled the bag** Interview with Nora Spring, January 16, 2021. Details about Midge's physical appearance that day are based on pictures posted on her public Facebook page.

60   *We are not family* Interview with Lynne Patti, July 5, 2019.

60   **Tuesday, February 2, 2016** Scene of Midge's last night reconstructed via coroner investigator's report, case 2016–01010, and interviews with Lynne Patti, July 5, 2019, and Barbara Fuller, July 15, 2019.

60   **"What's on my mind"** This was on a private Facebook posting. Barbara dictated it to us in an interview.

61   **help them travel the country** They performed at an L.A. Dodgers game the week after their *America's Got Talent* audition round (video available on YouTube, accessed on May 30, 2023).

61   **Bobby gave everything he had** Interviews with Clara Hanna, August 18, 2020, and September 22, 2021.

61   **"tough love" approach** Interview with Carleton Griffin, August 5, 2021.

61   **comprehensive palette of services** Interview with Dr. Maurice Carter, director of transitional housing programs, New Directions, July 29, 2022.

61   **those who made it through** News release: "Redevelopment of VA Greater Los Angeles West L.A. Campus Represents Proof of Concept for the Nation as a Way Forward in Tackling Homelessness," April 22, 2022.

62   **Bobby a success story** Interview with Dr. Maurice Carter, director of transitional housing programs, New Directions, August 9, 2022.

62   **sobriety plaque** The plaque was still present in August 2022, when we toured the New Directions facilities.

62   **a counselor had asked Clara** Interviews with Clara Hanna, August 10, 2020, and September 22, 2021.

62   **"I realize that it's me"** Interview with Clara Hanna, August 18, 2020. Bobby was also quoted in a New Directions Veterans Choir promotional packet as saying he had changed.

62   **how much he had changed** Quote by Bobby from a New Directions choir promotional packet.

63   **work-study job in the VA** Information from Bobby's LinkedIn page.

63   **He could no longer run** Interview with Clara Hanna, August 18, 2020.

65   **Bobby had gone off the deep end** Interview with Clara Hanna, September 22, 2021.

66   **Facebook fundraiser** Bobby also posted on his Facebook page about a GoFundMe fundraiser. Neither fundraiser generated any money. Bobby spelled "its" as "it's" in the posting.

66   **Bobby was fifty-nine** Bobby posted on Facebook in September 2018 that he'd been in New Directions five months following an eviction.

67   **she stopped in disbelief** Ibid.

67   **She stayed for lunch** Interview with Clara Hanna, September 22, 2021.

68   **"concerned about the state of repair"** Los Angeles Superior Court records, case BP081196.

69   **She handled the surgery well** Interview with Marjorie Ramos, August 3, 2021.

69   **drove a FedEx delivery van** Ibid.

69   **inside a lot of nursing homes** Ibid.

69   **She had always suspected** Ibid.

70   **Rudy's wife died** Information on deaths obtained from an interview with Marjorie Ramos, August 10, 2020, and confirmed via mec.lacounty.gov. For Rudy's wife, the website lists "carisoprodol effects and other undetermined factors" as primary cause of death (case 2008–03857) and for his son, the cause of death is "multiple drug intoxication" and "hypertrophic heart disease; anomalous origin of coronary artery" as other significant conditions (case 2009–01226).

70 **Rudy was too overwhelmed** He's quoted as being bewildered in the court records; confirmed in interview with Marjorie Ramos, August 3, 2021.

70 **petition the court** Judicial Council of California, *The Handbook for Conservators: 2016 Revised Edition,* chap. 8.

70 **Shapiro arrived at the nursing home** Interview with Leona Shapiro, January 8, 2021; Los Angeles Superior Court records, case BP081196.

70 **There were no pictures** Interview with Marjorie Ramos, August 3, 2021.

70 **brown leather purse** Los Angeles Superior Court records, case BP081196.

71 **"No good deed goes unpunished"** Interview with Teena Colebrook, August 4, 2021.

71 **"socially dead"** Erika Borgstrom, "Social Death," *QJM: An International Journal of Medicine* 110 (January 2017): 5–7; Jana Králová, "What Is Social Death?" *Contemporary Social Science* 10 (2015): 235–48; Helen Sweeting and Mary L. M. Gilhooly, "Doctor, Am I Dead? A Review of Social Death in Modern Societies," *Omega-Journal of Death and Dying* 24 (1992): 251–69.

71 **"any chance of resuming"** Interview with Leona Shapiro, January 8, 2021.

71 **wore adult diapers** Los Angeles Superior Court records, case BP081196.

72 **Shapiro brought her findings** Ibid.

72 **"conservator of last resort"** Robin Fields, Evelyn Larrubia, and Jack Leonard, "For Most Vulnerable, a Promise Abandoned," *Los Angeles Times,* November 16, 2005.

72 **rejected 84 percent of them** Amid the shortfall, a shadow private-public system had emerged. Former staff members of the Public Guardian set up shop as for-profit private conservators, petitioning courts to take care of incapacitated people with sizable estates, leaving the truly indigent at the mercy of the county's inadequate guardianship system. Fields, Larrubia, and Leonard, "For Most Vulnerable, a Promise Abandoned"; Pamela B. Teaster, "When the State Takes Over a Life: The Public Guardian as Public Administrator," *Public Administration Review* 63 (July 2003): 394–404.

72 **Lena's transfer of conservatorship was approved** The public guardian's petition as successor conservator was filed December 4, 2009. The public guardian was appointed January 15, 2010. Los Angeles Superior Court records, case BP081196.

72 **July 7, 2012** Place of death from Office of Decedent Affairs cremation records.

72 **she notified** Based on standard protocol in similar care facilities. We visited Le Bleu Chateau, but it had changed owners in the years since Lena lived there and the new owner declined to speak with us or allow a tour.

73 **David spoke of his mother** Interviews with Susan Spencer and Diana Lynn. Both of David's parents were living north of Sacramento before their deaths. It's not clear if David knew they had moved. Orrie died in 2001.

74 **living a life of solitude** Interviews with Susan Spencer, August 5, 2020, and August 17, 2020. Susan said he had another girlfriend at one point, but the woman ended it when David made clear that he would never have children.

74 **working as a security guard** Interviews with Susan Spencer, August 5, 2020, and August 17, 2020. We tried to verify David's employment with JPL, but they refused to confirm or deny.

74 **practiced with an independent scientologist** Interviews with Susan Spencer, August 5, 2020, and August 17, 2020. It was someone who had left the church but still engaged in "processing" (her term to describe what David received). She gave us the man's name, but it was too common to locate him and the number on the business card she shared was disconnected.

74 **were built in 1967** This and other details about the history of Royal Park Apartments via an interview with its manager, Diana Lynn, August 4, 2021.

74 **Some residents installed special lights** Interview with Diana Lynn, August 4, 2021.

75 **keen to avoid newer cars** Interviews with Susan Spencer, August 5, 2020, and August 17, 2020; the detail of his Jeep is via an interview with Diana Lynn, August 5, 2021.

75 **David might have been a charmer** Interview with Diana Lynn, August 4, 2021.

76 **as well as you could know a loner** Ibid.

76   **accepted his fate**   In our interview, Diana said: "I wouldn't say content because that also is probably too mediocre of a word to use, content. Yeah, that's not. You accept, you function, you think, you learn, those are his version of emotions."

76   **his social network was small**   Loneliness does not always lead to social isolation (solitude may be energizing). But both feeling left out and not having someone to turn to in times of need negatively affect physical and mental health. Erin York Cornwell and Linda J. Waite, "Social Disconnectedness, Perceived Isolation, and Health Among Older Adults," *Journal of Health and Social Behavior* 50 (March 2009): 31–48. On how feeling lonely may be worse for mental health: Julianne Holt-Lunstad and Andrew Steptoe, "Social Isolation: An Underappreciated Determinant of Physical Health," *Current Opinion in Psychology* 43 (2022): 232–37.

76   **especially as a man**   Claude S. Fischer and Lauren Beresford, "Changes in Support Networks in Late Middle Age: The Extension of Gender and Educational Differences," *The Journals of Gerontology, Series B: Psychological Sciences and Social Sciences* 70 (2015): 123–31.

76   **higher risk of dying prematurely**   Cornwell and Waite, "Social Disconnectedness."

76   **social connections are essential to health**   This relationship between social isolation and premature mortality was discovered in Northern California in 1979, when two researchers, Lisa Berkman and Leonard Syme, followed seven thousand adults for nine years and found that isolated individuals were twice as likely to die as their socially integrated neighbors. Lisa F. Berkman and S. Leonard Syme, "Social Networks, Host Resistance, and Mortality: A Nine-Year Follow-Up Study of Alameda County Residents," *American Journal of Epidemiology* 109 (1979): 186–204. Over the next decades, these findings have been replicated across the United States, Europe, and the globe. James S. House, Karl R. Landis, and Debra Umberson, "Social Relationships and Health," *Science* 241 (1988): 540–45; James S. House, "Social Isolation Kills, but How and Why?," *Psychosomatic Medicine* 63 (March 2001): 273–74.

A synthesis of these studies calculated that individuals with adequate social relationships have a 50 percent greater likelihood of survival compared with those with poor or insufficient social relationships. Julianne Holt-Lunstad, Timothy B. Smith, and J. Bradley Layton, "Social Relationships and Mortality Risk: A Meta-Analytic Review," *PLOS Medicine* 7 (2010): 1–19.

76   **matter more for longevity**   Julianne Holt-Lunstad, "The Potential Public Health Relevance of Social Isolation and Loneliness: Prevalence, Epidemiology, and Risk Factors," *Public Policy and Aging Report* 27 (2018): 127–30; Julianne Holt-Lunstad et al., "Loneliness and Social Isolation as Risk Factors for Mortality: A Meta-Analytic Review," *Perspectives on Psychological Science* 10 (March 2015): 227–37.

76   **About a quarter of Americans**   Julianne Holt-Lunstad, "Why Social Relationships Are Important for Physical Health: A Systems Approach to Understanding and Modifying Risk and Protection," *Annual Review Psychology* 69 (2018): 437–58; Holt-Lunstad et al., "Loneliness and Social Isolation as Risk Factors for Mortality"; G. O. Anderson and Colette E. Thayer, *Loneliness and Social Connections: A National Survey of Adults 45 and Older* (Washington, D.C.: AARP Foundation, 2018); Thomas K. M. Cudjoe et al., "The Epidemiology of Social Isolation: National Health and Aging Trends Study," *The Journals of Gerontology, Series B* 75 (2020): 107–13; Carla M. Perissinotto, Irena Stijacic Cenzer, and Kenneth E. Covinsky, "Loneliness in Older Persons: A Predictor of Functional Decline and Death," *Archives of Internal Medicine* 172 (2012): 1078–84; Ellen Idler and Yael Benyamini, "Self-Rated Health and Mortality: A Review of 27 Community Studies," *Journal of Health and Social Behavior* 38 (1997): 21–37.

76   **more likely to end up**   Benjamin Cornwell, Edward O. Laumann, and L. Philip Schumm, "The Social Connectedness of Older Adults: A National Profile," *American Sociological Review* 73 (2008): 185–203. This research also suggests that elderly people

can compensate for the loss of close ties with increased participation in religious organizations and volunteering.

76   **radius he was able to travel**   Interview with Susan Spencer, August 17, 2020.

77   **spiritual self would roam free**   Hugh B. Urban, *The Church of Scientology: A History of a New Religion* (Princeton, N.J.: Princeton University Press, 2011).

77   **Hubbard's writings about the thetan**   Ibid., 36.

78   **The goal of religion**   Wright, *Going Clear,* 17–18.

78   **"rise to greater heights"**   Ibid., 11.

78   **conquer their mind**   Ibid.

78   **"awaken individuals"**   Ibid., 17.

78   **"Grand Tour"**   Urban, *Church of Scientology,* 78.

78   **"Be three feet back"**   Ibid.

CHAPTER 6. INVESTIGATION

80   **"California Bucket List" destination**   Christopher Reynolds, "Buy the Body-Outline Beach Towel of Your Nightmares at the LA County Coroner's Gift Shop," *Los Angeles Times,* October 30, 2018. The Los Angeles County Department of Medical Examiner–Coroner's gift shop was called Skeletons in the Closet. It closed permanently in 2019.

81   **Los Angeles County Medical Examiner–Coroner**   The full name of the department is Los Angeles County Medical Examiner–Coroner. We will use the term *medical examiner* to refer to the office because the office follows a medical examiner model. Stefan Timmermans, *Postmortem: How Medical Examiners Explain Suspicious Deaths* (Chicago: University of Chicago Press, 2006).

81   **doctor to sign a death certificate**   "Recently seen a physician" is within twenty days in California. See the question "Why Is the Department of Medical Examiner–Coroner Involved?" for families at mec.lacounty.gov.

81   **In 2019, 64,517 deaths were reported**   Jonathan Lucas, "County of Los Angeles Department of Medical Examiner–Coroner 2019 Annual Report"; "Deaths in LA County: Mortality in Los Angeles County, 2020: Provisional Report," Los Angeles County Department of Public Health, Office of Health Assessment and Epidemiology (May 2022).

81   **more run-of-the-mill deaths**   Sometimes a hospital death was transferred to the medical examiner's office if the death was deemed suspicious, such as a traffic accident or fatal gunshot, but otherwise the Office of Decedent Affairs handled the body and coordinated with the public administrator to find next of kin.

81   **opened during the California gold rush**   Interview with Craig Hendrickson, July 19, 2016. Other states also have a judicial means of appointing an administrator if the estate is intestate (decedent died without a will). Mary Randolph, "How an Estate Is Settled if There's No Will, Intestate Succession," NOLO.com.

82   **protector of people's property**   Public administrator general information at ttc.lacounty .gov.

82   **black L.A. County Coroner jacket**   Even though the office changed its name to Medical Examiner–Coroner, the jacket still had L.A. CORONER monogrammed on it.

83   **left the shoes at the office**   Maria L. La Ganga, "From Health Care Worker to Patient: Death in Room 311," *Los Angeles Times,* December 20, 2020.

83   **Monrovia Police Department**   David Spencer's medical examiner report, case 2017–03835.

84   **eight days ago**   According to David Spencer's medical examiner report, case 2017–03835, David was last seen alive May 15, 2017, at 1800 hours.

84   **worked as an instructor**   LinkedIn profile.

84   **bigger risk was disease**   Horror stories, passed around from insiders to novices, not

NOTES

only reminded investigators to always take precautions at scenes but also reminded listeners that even taking care of the dead can be deadly. Frederic W. Hafferty, "Cadaver Stories and the Emotional Socialization of Medical Students," *Journal of Health and Social Behavior* 29 (1988): 344–56; Charles L. Bosk, *Forgive and Remember: Managing Medical Failure* (Chicago: University of Chicago Press, 1979).

86   **"He was gonna kill anybody"**   Authors' field notes, May 23, 2017.

86   **Scientology's "mind over matter"**   Throughout his book *Dianetics*, Hubbard refers to illness and pain as "psychosomatic" and best resolved by his "technologies" such as exteriorization (see, for example, page 29).

87   **"Okay, when she falls"**   Interview with Kristina McGuire, February 20, 2018.

88   **he crashed the car**   Ibid.

89   **Bobby was taking a nap**   Interview with Clara Hanna, September 22, 2021.

89   **retrieve a medication cart**   Interviews with Donnell Wells, September 6, 2020, and June 17, 2022.

89   **It was July 8, 2019**   Bobby's primary cause of death was cardiopulmonary failure with malignant neoplasm of the lung as secondary cause. His primary physician signed the death certificate, medical examiner report, case 2019–07136.

90   **shopping inside a Sam's Club**   In interviews, Donnell told us repeatedly that he was first contacted by his dad when he was thirty-seven and they knew each other for only four years. However, dated Facebook pictures and posts show that Bobby visited Gary in 2013 and one picture shows Bobby embracing Donnell's two daughters. Also, Donnell posted a picture of Bobby in 2011. We determined that 2011 for first contact makes more sense because that is when Bobby first went into the New Directions program.

90   **"Yeah, this is my dad"**   Interview with Donnell Wells, August 10, 2020.

91   **his two daughters**   The daughters' ages are based on Facebook birthday celebrations and the date of the reunion posts.

91   **live for a year with an uncle**   Interview with Donnell Wells, August 10, 2020.

92   **"I became a whole different man"**   Interview with Donnell Wells, September 6, 2020.

92   **Funeraria Del Angel West Covina**   This funeral home is part of Dignity Memorial, one of the brands of Houston-based conglomerate Service Corporation International. The company operates the largest network of funeral homes and crematoria in the United States.

93   **Donnell knew of a half brother**   Interview with Donnell Wells, September 6, 2020. There may have been a third child, according to Donnell. It's unclear exactly when Bobby or Isaac knew of each other. Bobby posted a picture on Facebook in 2015 saying the man on the left was his son and the picture looks like Isaac, but in interviews with Donnell, Clara, and observations in the public administrator's office, everyone said it was only recently (2018–19) that Isaac learned Bobby was his father. Isaac has not responded to multiple requests for an interview. Out of respect for his privacy, Isaac is a pseudonym.

93   **like most nursing homes**   Interview with Estela Inouye, May 26, 2017.

93   **private mortuaries preferred not to**   Jaber F. Gubrium and James A. Holstein, "The Nursing Home as a Discursive Anchor for the Ageing Body," *Ageing and Society* 19 (1999): 519–38; Heidi H. Ewen, Katherina Nikzad-Terhune, and Jasleen K. Chahal, "The Rote Administrative Approach to Death in Senior Housing: Using the Other Door," *Geriatric Nursing* 37 (2016): 360–64.

94   **LAC+USC**   In May 2023, the county changed the name to Los Angeles General Medical Center (L.A. General), but it remained Los Angeles County Medical Center and more commonly LAC+USC throughout the research for this book.

94   **Only 4.5 percent of their patients**   See data at HCAI Patient Discharge Data, hcai.ca .gov.

94   **eleven bodies per day**   Interview with Estela Inouye, May 26, 2017.

94   **nursing homes didn't always notify**   Ibid.

94   **patient's surprised relatives**   Interview with Albert Gaskin, July 8, 2019. For another

story about a nursing home not notifying relatives, see the Fogarty case in Jo Ciavaglia, "Grave Decisions: Unclaimed Dead a Growing Burden on Counties," http://journalismjo.blogspot.com/2019/10/grave-decisions-unclaimed-dead-growing.html.

94 **metal roll-in storage cabinets** This description is from hospital chaplain Father Chris Ponnet. The public information officer who handles requests for the Office of Decedent Affairs refused our multiple requests for a tour of the space.

95 **Lena Cecilia Berumen** Interview with Marjorie Ramos, August 3, 2021. She said the family had Jewish roots and the original name was Burman; both spellings (as well as *Berman*) are used in newspaper clippings tied to family members.

95 **married in 1889 in Tepetongo, Zacatecas** According to genealogist Megan Smolenyak, Lena's parents had given birth to at least three children, two sons and a daughter. One of the boys died in Mexico in 1904 at the age of twelve. The others stayed in Mexico after their parents' northern migration. More children seem to have been born just before and after the move, though it is unclear which ones survived. Some of the records that emerged on the U.S. side may have been duplicates of births registered in Mexico, repeating names but assigning different birth years. The names *Mary* and *Maria* appear separately, but the latter was often used by default in records. Another boy, Aurelio, appears to have migrated with the family from Mexico but quickly fell into trouble with the law and eventually died in a state prison in San Joaquin. No one in the family spoke of him. Nor of Guadalupe, known in the newspapers as Lupe. Less than a year before Lena was born, Lupe had been roped into custody—literally, a probation officer used a lariat that he carried to "chase runaway boys" to haul the teen boy back to the juvenile hall where he had escaped. "Ropes Runaway Boy," *Los Angeles Times,* August 4, 1914. It hadn't been Lupe's first encounter with the law; he had been arrested a year earlier as a member of a burglary gang.

95 **Catholic Calvary Cemetery** State of California, Department of Public Health Vital Statistics, Certificate of Death.

95 **mother suffered a mental breakdown** This is based on an interview with Marjorie Ramos, August 3, 2021. Smolenyak noted that Lena's mother was no longer listed as a member of the family in the 1930 census. This could mean that she had already died, had not been counted, or was living outside the family.

96 **$148,726.66** Los Angeles Superior Court records, case BP081196.

96 **monthly Social Security check** Ibid. This was the amount in 2010; it was $621 in 2008 and $569 in 2004.

96 **Supplemental Security Income** Los Angeles Superior Court records, case BP081196.

97 **totaling $17,236** Ibid.

97 **70 percent of Americans over sixty-five** Richard W. Johnson, *What Is the Lifetime Risk of Needing and Receiving Long-Term Services and Supports?* (Washington, D. C.: Department of Health and Human Services, 2019).

97 **majority of Americans** Polling information at longtermcarepoll.org.

97 **Lena's monthly bill** Los Angeles Superior Court records, case BP081196.

97 **Rudy paid the facility $2,400** Ibid. Conservator records for Lena indicate the total is $50,757.

97 **Rudy had transferred** He made this payment on October 12, 2008.

98 **court did not pursue** Conservators routinely take fees, and thus the court likely did not consider the amount unreasonable. Judicial Council of California, *The Handbook for Conservators: 2016 Revised Edition.*

98 **Rudy's lawyers submitted bills** Los Angeles Superior Court records, case BP081196. The amount includes preparing and finishing conservatorship documents, telephone calls, appearances in court, conferences with Rudy, letter writing, working on accounting, preparing for a hearing. Attorney time came to 66.56 hours for the conservatorship and an additional 9.81 hours of paralegal time. The lawyers also charged 7.82 hours of paralegal time and 48.89 hours on conveyance of the property (Lena's house).

98 **an unspecified amount** In January 2011, the public guardian petitioned the probate court for Lena's dwindled estate to become a "small asset estate" that would waive

future court accountings, rendering the information unattainable. Until that point, the "conservator" (public guardian) and "petitioner's attorney" (county counsel) had been receiving $100 per month.

98 **$5,192** Los Angeles Superior Court records, case BP081196.

98 **pro bono rate** Interview with Leona Shapiro, January 8, 2021.

98 **$5,502.50** Los Angeles Superior Court records, case BP081196.

98 **stopped communicating with his own lawyers** Los Angeles Superior Court records, case BP081196.

98 **The bulk of the money** Ibid.

98 **automatically entitled to Medicare** Wealthy Americans pay more into Medicare but they also benefit more because they live longer and use more services: Mark McClennan and Jonathan Skinner, "The Incidence of Medicare," *Journal of Public Economics* 90 (2006): 257–76.

98 **first time they qualify** J. Michael McWilliams et al., "Medicare Spending for Previously Uninsured Adults," *Annals of Internal Medicine* 151 (2009): 757–66.

98 **lead to more diagnoses** Deven C. Patel et al., "Cancer Diagnoses and Survival Rise as 65-Year-Olds Become Medicare-Eligible," *Cancer* 127 (July 2021): 2302–10.

98 **doesn't pay for long-term** Medicare does not pay the facility fees for a nursing home stay but the program still covers hospital care (including hospice care), doctor services, and medical supplies while someone is in a nursing home. Kirsten J. Colello et al., *Long-Term Services and Supports: Overview and Financing* (Washington, D.C.: Congressional Research Service, 2012).

99 **national average of $7,908** Genworth Cost of Care survey at genworth.com. The figures are for 2021 and for a semi-private room.

99 **Medicaid** About 16 percent of older adults in California qualify for both Medicaid and Medicare, because they are poor and over sixty-five: *California Health Care Almanac: Medi-Cal Facts and Figures: Essential Source of Coverage for Millions* (Oakland: California Health Care Foundation, 2021).

99 **they use 19 percent** Ibid., 47.

99 **would make Lena ineligible** Los Angeles Superior Court records, case BP081196. Shapiro may have been overly cautious because California allows for larger amounts of assets.

99 **moving their assets** This is allowed if the funds are transferred five years prior to requiring long-term care.

99 **Medicaid pays about 25 percent less** "Medicaid Coverage of Nursing Home Care: When, Where, and How Much They Pay," December 26, 2022, medicaidplanningassistance .org.

99 **Shapiro knew of nursing homes** See also Michael J. Lepore, Patricia K. Yuen, and Samantha Zepeda, "Nursing Home Facility-Initiated Involuntary Discharge," *Journal of Gerontological Nursing* 45 (2019): 23–31.

99 **practice was illegal** Ashvin Gandhi, "Picking Your Patients: Selective Admissions in the Nursing Home Industry," working paper, SSRN 3613950 (2019); Matt Sedensky, "Nursing Homes Turn to Eviction to Drop Difficult Patients," Associated Press, May 5, 2016; Fran Kritz, "Patient Dumping Is Still a Problem," *American Journal of Nursing* 118 (November 2018): 16–17; Ryan M. McKenna et al., "Examining EMTALA in the Era of the Patient Protection and Affordable Care Act," *AIMS Public Health* 5 (2018): 366–77.

100 **purchase burial insurance** Burial insurance, also known as final expense life insurance, is an insurance policy typically in the $5,000–$10,000 range that can be used to pay for final arrangements. Heirs, however, may also use the money to pay down medical debt or credit card balances. California Department of Consumer Affairs, Cemetery and Funeral Bureau. Funeral insurance can also be obtained from a funeral establishment: *Consumer Guide to Funeral and Cemetery Purchases* (Sacramento, Calif.: Cemetery and Funeral Bureau, 2013).

101 **"I don't hear Midge. What do I do?"** Based on interviews with Nora Spring, July 5,

2019, January 16, 2021, and September 19, 2021. We made multiple attempts to interview Huddle.

103   **Only two of the unit's eight**   Based on direct observation over an eight-month period in 2017.

103   **"part detective, part grief counselor"**   Angie Chuang, "Death and Kindness," *Los Angeles Times,* January 6, 2007.

104   **fifty cases at a time**   Interview with Joyce Kato, February 20, 2018.

105   **red and blue folders**   The public administrator disagreed with the medical examiner's office policy of triaging cases in red and blue folders based on scene evidence and claimed they did not know about this practice until we asked about it. Looks could be deceiving, they said. It was not unheard of for a homeless person to accumulate automatically deposited Social Security funds or to have forgotten about an inheritance tucked away in a bank account (interview with Craig Henderson, April 3, 2018). They may have lost access to the account, their belongings thrown, literally, in the trash by police during one of LAPD's notorious homeless encampment sweeps; Forrest Stuart, *Down and Out: Policing and Everyday Life on Skid Row* (Chicago: University of Chicago Press, 2018). Without being notified of the death, the public administrator could not start its own inquiry into possible assets. Triaging helped the medical examiner's staff to speed up the forensic investigation because notifications staff did not need to coordinate their work with the public administrator.
   When we googled Da-Som Pitino's name (see chapter 7), we found that she had unclaimed funds with the state. The funds were insufficient to make a difference in her funeral, but they had been overlooked.

105   **up to four each day**   Isabelle Zavarise, "More than 1,600 People Experiencing Homelessness Died in Los Angeles Last Year," Crosstown LA, February 18, 2020; Ethan Ward, "They Were Homeless, Now They're Dead," Crosstown LA, February 10, 2021.

105   **most important person**   Tom L. Beauchamp and James F. Childress, *Principles of Biomedical Ethics* (Oxford: Oxford University Press, 1979).

105   **few people designate**   Kuldeep N. Yadav et al., "Approximately One in Three US Adults Completes Any Type of Advance Directive for End-of-Life Care," *Health Affairs* 36 (2017): 1244–51; Jaya K. Rao et al., "Completion of Advance Directives Among U.S. Consumers," *American Journal of Preventive Medicine* 46 (2014): 65–70.

105   **registered domestic partner**   Note that equation of the registered domestic partner with a spouse occurred only in 1999 in California, and while the rights of the domestic partner remain limited, from the beginning they included the right to be declared next of kin. Ninez A. Ponce et al., "The Effects of Unequal Access to Health Insurance for Same-Sex Couples in California," *Health Affairs* 29 (August 2010): 1539–48.

106   **The investigators joked**   Interview with Craig Harvey, July 12, 2019.

107   **official confirmation**   New Mexico, at the time, was a sealed adoption record state, meaning its records were restricted from public inspection without a court order.

107   **She had last reached out to him**   This and the details about Ernie's cancer via interviews with Barbara Fuller, July 15, 2019, August 17, 2020, and November 2, 2021.

108   **Each statement**   For more on how close ties can be harmful: Jennifer A. Ailshire and Sarah A. Burgard, "Family Relationships and Troubled Sleep Among US Adults: Examining the Influences of Contact Frequency and Relationship Quality," *Journal of Health and Social Behavior* 53 (2012): 248–62; Shira Offer and Claude S. Fischer, "Difficult People: Who Is Perceived to Be Demanding in Personal Networks and Why Are They There?" *American Sociological Review* 83 (2018): 111–42. Offer and Fisher find that people in their fifties to seventies are more likely to list close kin as difficult.

108   **many relationships had completely unraveled**   Kylie Agllias, "The Gendered Experience of Family Estrangement in Later Life," *Affilia-Journal of Women and Social Work* 28 (August 2013): 309–21; Keith Berry and Tony E. Adams, "Family Bullies," *Journal of Family Communication* 16 (2016): 51–63; Kristina M. Scharp and Lindsey J. Thomas, "Family 'Bonds': Making Meaning of Parent–Child Relationships in Estrangement

Narratives," *Journal of Family Communication* 16 (2016): 32–50; Lucy Blake, "Parents and Children Who Are Estranged in Adulthood: A Review and Discussion of the Literature," *Journal of Family Theory and Review* 9 (2017): 521–36.

108   **more than 40 percent**   Richard P. Conti, "Family Estrangement: Establishing a Prevalence Rate," *Journal of Psychology and Behavioral Science* 3 (2015): 28–35. For more on estrangement: Oliver Arranz Becker and Karsten Hank, "Adult Children's Estrangement from Parents in Germany," *Journal of Marriage and Family* 84 (2022): 347–60; Megan Gilligan, J. Jill Suitor, and Karl Pillemer, "Estrangement Between Mothers and Adult Children: The Role of Norms and Values," *Journal of Marriage and Family* 77 (2015): 908–20.

108   **state law dictated**   California Health and Safety Code, section 7100.

109   **She found reactions like Barbara's gratifying**   In an interview (February 20, 2018), Joyce noted that this kind of gratification is fleeting because she has so many new cases waiting for her.

CHAPTER 7. COUNTY DISPO

110   **Mike needed a death certificate**   Interview with Mike Patti, July 1, 2019.

110   **woman behind the counter**   Interview with Lynne Patti, August 19, 2020.

110   **Mike sold Midge's car**   Because the medical examiner did not forward the case to the public administrator, they did not add the $3,000 for the car to her assets.

111   **"the decedent has no living relatives"**   The form is called an "Ex Parte Petition for Order to Release Remains" and is available at LAcourt.org.

111   **Saturday, March 19, 2016**   Interview with Lynne Patti, July 5, 2019.

111   **Flowers remembered passing Midge**   Interview with Joan Flowers, January 15, 2021.

112   **Midge's favorite song**   Interview with Lynne Patti, August 19, 2020. There are several versions of the song. Lynne said that Midge preferred Cohen's, available at leonardcohen.com.

112   **he reminisced**   Interview with Lynne Patti, July 5, 2019.

112   **Justin's girlfriend**   Ibid.; also interview with Nora and Howard Spring, September 19, 2021.

112   **they had been Midge's actual family**   For more on chosen families and their sociological importance: Dawn O. Braithwaite et al., "Constructing Family: A Typology of Voluntary Kin," *Journal of Social and Personal Relationships* 27 (2010): 388–407; Frank F. Furstenberg et al., "Kinship Practices Among Alternative Family Forms in Western Industrialized Societies," *Journal of Marriage and Family* 82 (2020): 1403–30; Anna Muraco, "Intentional Families: Fictive Kin Ties Between Cross-Gender, Different Sexual Orientation Friends," *Journal of Marriage and Family* 68 (2006): 1313–25; Margaret K. Nelson, "Fictive Kin, Families We Choose, and Voluntary Kin: What Does the Discourse Tell Us?," *Journal of Family Theory and Review* 5 (2013): 259–81; Brian Powell et al., "Implications of Changing Family Forms for Children," *Annual Review of Sociology* 42 (2016): 301–22; Carol Stack, *All Our Kin: Strategies for Survival in a Black Community* (New York: Basic Books, 1975); Kath Weston, *Families We Choose: Lesbians, Gays, Kinship* (New York: Columbia University Press, 1991); Daniel R. Meyer and Marcia J. Carlson, "Family Complexity: Implications for Policy and Research," *Annals of the American Academy of Political and Social Science* 654 (2014): 259–76.

113   **Da-Som Pitino**   Da-Som, Walter, and Daria are all pseudonyms.

114   **obtaining a court order**   State laws also allowed for an ex parte petition that gave non–next of kin, such as friends and unregistered partners, the right to dispose of a body. The form could be filed after all notices required by law had been made and next of kin had been given sufficient time to claim. However, the notifications staff did not advertise the ex parte petition route. It only came up if non–next of kin initiated the conversation by expressing interest in claiming.

In 362 files of unclaimed bodies we reviewed in the medical examiner's office, friends filed an ex parte petition only twice, and even then the legal move did not lead to a body being claimed. Sherry Reed, a fifty-year-old Black woman, died in a hospital. Her fiancé, Cyrill Holmes, told the notifications staff that Sherry was estranged from her two adult daughters and that he wanted to claim. Through extensive database sleuthing, notifications staff located someone who thought Sherry could be the sister he never knew. The county workers asked the potential brother whether he was willing to pick a funeral home but a couple of days later he had second thoughts and questioned whether he was even related to Sherry. Cyrill successfully filed an ex parte petition but indicated that he did not want to make funeral arrangements until he was sure about what caused Sherry's death. A week later he called back to say that he lacked the funds and requested county disposition.

114   **posted a query**   Barbara made similar requests several times. This quote is from September 18, 2018, but she had also asked about information on a Facebook post on March 5, 2016 (which was the day after Midge's birthday).

114   **"I'm not a Mexican"**   Interview with Barbara Fuller, November 2, 2021; interview with Nora Spring, September 19, 2021.

115   **Midge was indeed adopted**   Midge told Nora that she was five when she was adopted. However, census records indicate she was living with the Gonzales family in 1950, at the age of two.

115   **older biological half sister, Vidalia**   The older sister died in 1963 at age forty-seven of cancer, a decade after Midge joined the family.

116   **Midge returned once**   Interview with Barbara Fuller, July 15, 2019. Barbara said that her "grandmother was very mean to" Midge.

116   **Gallup, New Mexico**   Obtained via a confidential source with access to closed records.

117   **long history of *genízaros***   Russell M. Magnaghi, "Plains Indians in New Mexico: The Genízaro Experience," *Great Plains Quarterly* 10, no. 2 (1990): 86–95.

117   **ambiguous ethnic category**   Moises Gonzales, "The Genizaro Land Grant Settlements of New Mexico," *Journal of the Southwest* 56 (2014): 583–602.

117   **less likely to be recognized**   Marc Simmons, "Trail Dust: Class of Indians Once Called 'Genizaros' in New Mexico," *The Santa Fe Mexican,* January 17, 2014.

117   **online paperwork**   The form is available on mec.lacounty.gov.

117   **found out about her aunt's death**   Legally, Virginia was also next of kin. However, the medical examiner's office generally stopped searching after *one* next of kin was found. Health and Safety Code, section 7100, specified only that in cases of "more than one surviving competent adult person of the same degree of kinship" the "majority of those persons" shall have the duty of disposition. Virginia indicated in a phone interview with Pamela that Barbara had called her asking for information on family history, but Virginia was surprised when Pamela mentioned Midge's death. She didn't know her aunt had died.

118   **anything to prevent**   Susan C. Weller et al., "Variation and Persistence in Latin American Beliefs About Evil Eye," *Cross-Cultural Research* 49 (2015): 174–203.

119   **contracted private cemetery**   At the time of the case, it was Forest Lawn Cemetery in Covina.

119   **office organized about sixty**   We pieced this number together with information received from two California Public Records Act (CPRA) requests and court records. After the CPRA requests, the public administrator provided files with thirty-three names of decedents for whom they organized a funeral in 2016. Of those, sixteen had assets between about $13,500 and $50,000. For estates with assets over $50,000, probate court appoints the public administrator as executor of the estate and a court record is created. Checking court records, we found that the public administrator had indeed been appointed in the seventeen cases and that those cases had one of two contracted mortuaries as claimants for burial costs to the estate. However, we found an additional twenty-four estates handled by the public administrator with these mortuaries as claimants in the court records. This brings the total to fifty-eight. If the

public administrator undercounted estates under $50,000 in the same way as they undercounted those over the threshold, they would have organized an additional twenty-three funerals (there are no court records of those, so we cannot verify). Our best guess is that the public administrator organized between fifty-eight and eighty-one funerals in 2016 for decedents whose assets met the minimum financial amount to authorize a funeral. We erred toward a conservative but evidenced number of "about sixty."

119 **called *heir hunters*** Interview with Craig Hendrickson, July 19, 2016; interview with John Hilbert, heir locator company, March 15, 2017.

119 **Hall of Records** The public guardian employees moved to a different building in November 2021.

119 **architect used vertical aluminum louvers** For more on the history of the building, see "Los Angeles County Hall of Records," on laconservancy.org.

122 **total for forwarding remains** Donnell had inconsistent recollections of costs. The director of the funeral home refused to speak to us when we called. We went to the funeral home and posed as potential customers, receiving their funeral rates and package list. The price list includes a flat fee for "Forwarding Remains to Another Funeral Home," and the charge includes "use of preparation room, Basic Professional Service Fee when Forwarding Remains, Embalming, transportation to or from local airport or other place of shipment within a 50 mile radius, Transfer of remains from place of death to funeral home and obtaining necessary authorizations. This charge does not include visitation or ceremonies. This charge applies to shipment within the continental U.S. only."

122 **picked up bodies without signed contracts** Interview with Maria Diaz, September 4, 2019.

122 **have it picked up** According to Estela Inouye, head of the Office of Decedent Affairs, they are the only county entity with legal permission to bury abandoned remains. If a family member orders a cremation but doesn't pick up the cremains, they must be transferred to the county morgue.

122 **right to interment and a grave marker** VA benefits for veterans who were not dishonorably discharged available at VA.gov.

124 **keeping the car** Clara wasn't the rightful heir so, had she tried to keep it, she would have needed to buy it from Donnell and Isaac or receive their permission to take it. She had Donnell's approval to help close out Bobby's estate.

124 **sued by thirty-four state** Ben Eisen and AnnaMaria Andriotis, "Santander Settles Predatory Auto-Lending Claims for $550 Million," *The Wall Street Journal,* May 19, 2020.

125 **inspected the body** David Spencer's medical examiner report, case 2017–03835.

125 **pathologist took fluids** Some medical examiner offices send out every deceased's blood for toxicology while others do so only when the scene investigation suggests that it would provide meaningful information for cause-of-death determination.

125 **default natural cause of death** Stefan Timmermans, *Postmortem: How Medical Examiners Explain Suspicious Deaths* (Chicago: University of Chicago Press, 2006), chap. 1.

125 **case of Yvette Vickers** Valerie J. Nelson, "Yvette Vickers Dies at 82, Former Actress and *Playboy* Playmate," *Los Angeles Times,* May 3, 2011.

127 **few carrots** The Los Angeles County Medical Examiner–Coroner's website states, "If County disposition is authorized, there may be substantial delays in receiving a death certificate and as a consequence, certain benefits."

127 **total of 520** Interview with John Kades, February 20, 2018.

127 **recuperate triple the cost** California Health and Safety Code, section 7103.

128 **be more professional to survive** For more on the emotional detachment common in careers like Joyce's: Renee C. Fox, "Training for Uncertainty," in *The Student Physician,* ed. Robert K. Merton, G. Reader, and P. L. Kendall (Cambridge, Mass.: Harvard University Press, 1957); Kelly Underman and Laura E. Hirshfield, "Detached Concern?: Emotional Socialization in Twenty-first Century Medical Education," *Social Science and Medicine* 160 (2016): 94–101.

128 **made direct deposits** A brochure on ssa.gov explains what is supposed to happen:

"How Social Security Can Help You When a Family Member Dies." But news reports suggest otherwise; for example, Eduardo Medina, "Man Cashed His Dead Mother's Social Security Checks for 26 Years, U.S. Says," *The New York Times*, December 2, 2022. In their final accounting, the public administrator in Los Angeles would determine if funds needed to be paid back to Social Security.

128 **$6,179.26**   Los Angeles Superior Court, case 18STPN00460.

129 **Thomas received a certified check**   Los Angeles Superior Court, case BP142409. Heir hunters did not pursue the case, despite the dollar amount, because the decedent had a will.

129 **be in limbo for months**   The public administrator could not keep an apartment in limbo for years, though. After some time, an apartment could be released, but in those cases the office recommended that property managers store the deceased's stuff for a few months, in case relatives asked for it. Few in the public administrator's office believed this advice was followed.

131 **Fewer than half of Americans**   Jeffrey M. Jones, "How Many Americans Have a Will?" Gallup, June 23, 2021.

131 **an even smaller percentage (32 percent)**   Adrienne Oleck, *Older Americans and Preneed Funeral and Burial Arrangements: Findings from a Five-State Telephone Survey* (Washington, D.C.: AARP, 1999).

131 **county had strict ideas**   Authors' field notes, September 18, 2019.

131 **burial was preferred over cremation**   Interview with Maria Diaz, July 18, 2022.

131 **more Americans were cremated**   See statistics at the Cremation Association of North America, cremationassociation.org.

131 **estate was settled**   Los Angeles Superior Court, case 18STPN00460.

131 **Every workday**   Conversation with Craig Garnette, July 3, 2019.

132 **He counted seven**   We spoke with Craig about the squirrels in July 2019, and he said he'd been feeding the squirrels for years. Lena Brown was cremated on September 19, 2012.

133 **wrapped like an unwieldy parcel**   The description of the cremation is based on multiple conversations with Craig Garnette and Albert Gaskin, as well as the documentary *A Certain Kind of Death* (available on YouTube, the cremation process starts at 53:30 and goes to 58:39 minutes). See also Jon Schleuss, "At L.A. County Cemetery, Unclaimed Dead Await a Final Resting Place," *Los Angeles Times*, November 9, 2014.

133 **thirty years working together**   Conversation with Craig Garnette, July 3, 2019, combined with direct observation.

135 **medical examiner's office outsourced**   The medical examiner's office is allowed by law to cremate within thirty days after they took jurisdiction of a body but in reality they often gave relatives more time to make a decision.

135 **drafting and engineering school**   Conversation with Craig Garnette, July 20, 2022.

136 **neighbors had complained**   Interview with Albert Gaskin, July 6, 2019.

136 **received the letter**   Interview with Marjorie Ramos, August 3, 2021. Court records would show that Lena's already depleted estate was charged $80.62 for the public administrator to telephone Marjorie and leave a voicemail message.

CHAPTER 8. THE DEAD DON'T VOTE

137 **Margaret Mead**   Margaret Mead, "Remember Me," Poemist.com.

139 **joined LAC+USC in 2009**   Email from Father Chris to author on February 18, 2023. He said that he joined St. Camillus as pastor and chaplain in 1995. He led the ceremony in 2009.

140 **irked Father Chris**   Interviews with Chris Ponnet, April 16, 2016, July 3, 2019, and July 8, 2022.

140 **Catholicism's seven corporal works of mercy**   Interview with Chris Ponnet, April 16, 2016. Additional information on the works of mercy from United States Conference of Catholic Bishops' website www.usccb.org.

140 **Ethan**   This is a pseudonym.
140 **started while he was incarcerated**   Jennifer Bronson et al., "Drug Use, Dependence, and Abuse Among State Prisoners and Jail Inmates, 2007–2009," Bureau of Justice Statistics, 2017. About the prevalence of drug use in prisons and jails: Beth Schwartzapel and Jimmy Jenkins, "Inside the Nation's Overdose Crisis in Prisons and Jails," Marshall Project, 2021.
141 **squeezed Father Chris's hands**   Direct observation and participation.
142 **welcomed him into their religious order**   This is based on Father Chris's recollection of the story (interview, July 8, 2022). In the 1955 movie version, the boy asks Jesus to take him to his mother and he dies.
142 **became an ordained Catholic priest**   Email from Father Chris to author on February 18, 2023.
142 **established an official ministry**   Mitchell Landsberg, "Much Has Changed for Gay and Lesbian Catholics in Los Angeles," *Los Angeles Times*, October 23, 2011.
143 **spent a couple of days in jail**   Erika Hayasaki, Steve Hymon, and Rebecca Trounson, "Thousands of Students Join Antiwar Rallies," *Los Angeles Times*, March 6, 2003. Most of this story came directly from an interview with Father Chris on July 8, 2022.
143 **If Proposition 62 passed**   "Year of Mercy: Grassroots Catholics Work to End the Use of the Death Penalty," California Catholic Conference, September 30, 2016.
143 **They gathered signatures**   Father Chris also gave pointers on how priests could integrate the death penalty abolition campaign in their homilies at californiapeopleoffaith.org, and he made videos that he posted to Facebook.
143 **bishops issued a statement**   "California Bishops Announce Support for Prop 62," California Catholic Conference, catholicsmobilizing.org.
143 **real challenge for the faithful**   Father Chris Ponnet, 2016 Good Friday Reflection, posted on Facebook, April 4, 2016.
143 **"Who Would Jesus Execute?"**   The coalition included actor Mike Farrell; Ron Briggs, who was instrumental in bringing the death penalty to California; civil rights activist and labor leader Dolores Huerta; county supervisor Hilda Solis; formerly attorney general of California John Van de Kamp; and L.A. County district attorney Gil Garcetti. See kickoff campaign of Proposition 62 at Facebook.
143 **But they lost**   In 2016, two competing propositions regarding the death penalty were put in front of voters. Proposition 62 would have abolished the death penalty. It was rejected 53.16 percent to 46.83 percent. In 2012, a proposition (34) with similar intent had failed as well. Instead, voters in 2016 approved Proposition 66, which reduced the time of legal challenges to the death penalty to a maximum of five years. This proposition passed 51.13 percent to 48.87 percent. The California Supreme Court held that Proposition 66 was constitutional but that provisions requiring the state to speed up the death penalty appeals process were directive, rather than mandatory.
143 **"We're at a time when mercy"**   Kevin Theriault, "Measure to Abolish Death Penalty Falls Short: Californians Vote to Reform Criminal Justice, Legalize Pot," *Angelus*, November 12, 2016.
143 **influx of new activists**   Father Chris welcomed new activists in the YouTube video *Yes on 62-Forward.*
144 **The day after**   Mike Cruz, "DA Urges Denial of More DNA Testing in Brutal 1983 California Murders," *The Mercury News*, May 22, 2018.
144 **consult an iPhone app**   Father Ponnet quoted in Maila Wollan, "How to Eulogize Someone You've Never Met," *The New York Times*, December 18, 2015.
144 **its share of homeless patients**   "Inpatient Hospitalizations and Emergency Department Visits for Persons Experiencing Homelessness in California: Patient Demographics by Facility," hcai.ca.gov. The exact number is 10.3 percent.
144 **four hundred yearly pager calls**   Fundraising email for St. Camillus Center from Father Chris Ponnet, December 28, 2021.
145 **Zoroastrians adopted sky burials**   James R. Russell, "Burial in Zoroastrianism," *Encyclopaedia Iranica* 6 (2000): 561–63.

145 **remains to be thrown over the city walls** Thomas M. Laqueur, *The Work of the Dead: A Cultural History of Mortal Remains* (Princeton, N.J.: Princeton University Press, 2015).

145 **elaborate marble pillar** Robert Drew Hicks, *Diogenes Laertius: Lives of Eminent Philosophers* (Cambridge, Mass.: Harvard University Press, 1925).

145 **buried in a local cemetery** Tatiana Sanchez, "Remains of Hundreds of Unidentified Immigrants Are Buried in Imperial County Cemetery," *Los Angeles Times,* June 8, 2016.

145 **cost-saving measure** Ibid. We also interviewed both the assistant public administrator and coroner-sheriff for Imperial County in 2016.

147 **one of every six** The 17.5 percent figure from Sohn, Timmermans, and Prickett, "Loneliness in Life and Death?", 1–17.

147 **more than 82 percent** These included ashes that came from the medical examiner's office, which were stored alongside the other boxed cremains. Any ashes left abandoned at private mortuaries also ended up in the control of the Office of Decedent Affairs.

147 **someone came in** Cremation records.

148 **earned $57,000** Salaries of California state workers are publicly available at the website Transparent California. Susan Rorke's salary for 2012 is listed as $57,713.12.

148 **"like she was garbage"** Interview with Susan Rorke, December 12, 2018.

148 **paid an administrative fee** Susan Rorke remembered it as "two hundred and something whatever dollars" in an interview on December 12, 2018, but the fee ranged from $352 to $466 according to Office of Decedent Affairs (confirmed via email with Estela Inouye on April 6, 2023).

148 **lost a week's wages** Interview with Susan Rorke, July 5, 2019.

149 **"I don't think I could sleep"** Quoted in Susannah Rosenblatt, "Unclaimed and Forgotten Are Laid to Rest," *Los Angeles Times,* December 7, 2006.

149 **life's work** Interview with Albert Gaskin, July 8, 2019.

150 **backlog of dead bodies** In 2016, the Office of Decedent Affairs had a backlog of 250 bodies. Los Angeles County Civil Grand Jury, *Who Cares for the Dead When the Dead Don't Vote? An Interim Report,* 2015–2016.

150 **checked the morgue's inventory** Estela Inouye used the term *inventory* as a verb in her interview on May 26, 2017.

150 **didn't receive enough resources** The total budget was $400,000 out of a total $7 billion budget for the Department of Health Services. Los Angeles County Civil Grand Jury, *Who Cares for the Dead When the Dead Don't Vote?*

150 **relatives come in person** We witnessed a family from Peru retrieving remains. They told us that this had been the sole purpose of their trip to Los Angeles.

151 **grown up in rural Arkansas** Interview with Jon Schleuss, October 25, 2015. Also Jon Snyder, "South Arkansas Native Voted President of National Journalism Union," *Arkansas-Democrat Gazette,* December 11, 2019.

151 **HIPAA** The Health Insurance Portability and Accountability Act of 1996 includes standards for the electronic exchange, privacy, and security of health information. The rule is known as the Privacy Rule. Jon detailed his reporting steps in Jon Schleuss and Maloy Moore, "L.A. County's Unclaimed Dead: How We Reported the Story," *Los Angeles Times,* November 8, 2014.

151 **Privacy Rule** Health information for the dead is protected for fifty years: 45 CFR 160.103, paragraph (2)(iv) of the definition of "protected health information."

152 **cremate his body** Interview with Jon Schleuss, October 25, 2015. After covering the unclaimed, Jon had learned a cost-saving workaround, that people could be cremated by the county and later have their ashes reclaimed.

152 **"two diamonds in a field of coal"** Interview with Craig Harvey, July 12, 2019.

152 **"It's like if you go"** Quoted in Jon Schleuss, "At L.A. County Cemetery, Unclaimed Dead Await a Final Resting Place," *Los Angeles Times,* November 9, 2014. Jon writes that Albert wanted to be cremated by the county. Albert told us specifically that he'd like to be cremated by Craig.

152   **retired YMCA employee**   Per her LinkedIn profile.
152   **disappeared in 1980**   Jon Schleuss and Maloy Moore, "At a Boyle Heights Cemetery, a Time to Mourn the Unclaimed," *Los Angeles Times,* December 15, 2015. We observed Jon's interaction with Cherry at the 2015 ceremony and acquired additional information by interviewing Cherry.
153   **decades longing to know**   This book is primarily about relatives who refuse to claim their deceased relatives but the opposite situation, people desperately seeking for the fate of their loved ones, occurs as well. This is an issue, for instance, when people go missing during migration journeys: Jason De León, *The Land of Open Graves: Living and Dying on the Migrant Trail* (Berkeley: University of California Press, 2015). It is an issue of the disappeared in Argentina and other war-ravaged countries: Rita Arditti, *Searching for Life: The Grandmothers of the Plaza de Mayo and the Disappeared Children of Argentina* (Berkeley: University of California Press, 1999). Or people going missing: Matthew Wolfe, "Policing the Lost: The Emergence of Missing Persons and the Classification of Deviant Absence," *Theory and Society* 51 (2021).
        The federal government maintains a database of missing persons, NamUS, that includes unclaimed bodies.
153   **searchable database**   The database is available online at dhs.lacounty.gov.
153   **providing bodies for scientific study**   Interview with Albert Gaskin, July 8, 2019. According to our public-records request of August 18, 2022, the Office of Decedent Affairs transferred 598 unclaimed bodies between 2017 and 2022 to Cypress College. The college paid $15 for each body. Some of the bodies were veterans.
        Confirming the use of unclaimed bodies as medical-school cadavers has been harder. Gaskin first clued us in to the practice in an interview. Later we located published medical-research articles implying coordination between the county and USC's departments of surgery and pathology. In 2006, the university set up a Fresh Tissue Dissection Laboratory in what used to be the morgue of the old General Hospital. The lab allowed educators at the University of Southern California to teach students how to place a central intravenous line and led to a handful of published articles. Christina L. Greene et al., "Pressurized Cadaver Model in Cardiothoracic Surgical Simulation," *Annals of Thoracic Surgery* 100 (2015): 1118–20; Stephen Varga et al., "Central Venous Catheterization Using a Perfused Human Cadaveric Model: Application to Surgical Education," *Journal of Surgical Education* 72 (2015): 28–32; Martin Pham et al., "A Perfusion-Based Human Cadaveric Model for Management of Carotid Artery Injury During Endoscopic Endonasal Skull Base Surgery," *Journal of Neurological Surgery Part B: Skull Base* 75 (2014): 309–13.
        In one of those articles, the authors admitted that while working on perfused bodies is the gold standard for surgical simulation, "the greatest limitation to this model is the access to fresh cadavers" (Varga et al., "Central Venous Catheterization," 31). Former county medical examiner/coroner Dr. Thomas Noguchi is listed as a coauthor in the Varga et al. article. The origins of the bodies remained vague: Bodies were simply "acquired in compliance with hospital policy and California law" (Greene et al., "Pressurized Cadaver Model," 1118).
        In the mid-2000s, Dr. Noguchi served as a state curator (an official California position allowed by the Anatomy Act of 1927) for unclaimed bodies. Noguchi had courted international fame, speaking publicly and later writing books about the autopsies he conducted on Marilyn Monroe, Robert F. Kennedy, John Belushi, and more. Noguchi dubbed himself the "coroner to the stars," and in the years after his retirement from the county, he worked in a variety of health-related roles, including as a professor of pathology for USC. We reached him for a short phone interview. When we told him that we were interested in unclaimed bodies, he said, before hanging up the phone, that unclaimed bodies are good only for scientific research. Whether this practice of transferring unclaimed bodies to medical schools for dissection and research in L.A. County continues is unclear. Our August 18, 2022, public records request with the L.A. County medical examiner's office and the Office of Decedent

Affairs did not produce any records of unclaimed bodies being transferred to medical schools between 2017 and 2022. Some other counties in California, including Santa Clara, openly explain that they "offer" unclaimed indigent bodies for such purposes (see medicalexaminer.sccgov.org/indigent-cremation).

153   **California's Health and Safety Code**   Disposal of unclaimed dead is in sections 7200–208.

153   **"willed-body" program**   The Uniform Anatomical Gift Act of 1968 promoted body donation (including giving the wishes of the decedent about body disposition priority over the wishes of relatives). The law embraced an "opt in" principle to donate, meaning that the donor or their agents (which goes beyond relatives to include healthcare officials and "close friends") needed to consent to donation. The act also streamlined the process of donating bodies to medical science.

On who donates in California: Asad L. Asad, Michel Anteby, and Filiz Garip, "Who Donates Their Bodies to Science?: The Combined Role of Gender and Migration Status Among California Whole-Body Donors," *Social Science and Medicine* 106 (2014): 53–58.

153   **first formal anatomy course**   Aaron D. Tward and Hugh A. Patterson, "From Grave Robbing to Gifting: Cadaver Supply in the United States," *JAMA* 287 (2002): 1183; Ruth Richardson, *Death, Dissection and the Destitute* (Chicago: University of Chicago Press, 2001).

154   **add dissection to a death sentence**   Raphael Hulkhower, "From Sacrilege to Privilege: The Tale of Body Procurement for Anatomical Dissection in the United States," *The Einstein Journal of Biology and Medicine* 27 (2011): 23–26.

154   **desecration of the corpse**   Richardson, *Death, Dissection and the Destitute.*

154   **robbing the graves**   Edward C. Halperin, "The Poor, the Black, and the Marginalized as the Source of Cadavers in United States Anatomical Education," *Clinical Anatomy* 20 (2007): 489–95.

154   **six hundred to seven hundred bodies snatched**   David C. Humphrey, "Dissection and Discrimination: The Social Origins of Cadavers in America, 1760–1915," *Bulletin of the New York Academy of Medicine* 59 (1973): 819–27; Frederick C. Waite, "Grave Robbing in New England," *Bulletin of the Medical Library Association* 33 (1945): 272–94.

154   **punished more severely**   Ann Garment et al., "Let the Dead Teach the Living: The Rise of Body Bequeathal in 20th-Century America," *Academic Medicine* 82 (2007): 1000–1005.

154   **mob violence**   Humphrey, "Dissection and Discrimination," 821; Richardson, *Death, Dissection and the Destitute;* Emily Bazelon, "Grave Offense," *Legal Affairs* (July–August 2002).

154   **quasi-property**   Alix Rogers, "Unearthing the Origins of Quasi-property Status," *Hastings Law Journal* 72 (2020): 291–336. Rogers writes: "Judges apply quasi-property broadly, and often do not provide a concise definition beyond that it is intended to effectuate the right of sepulcher, namely the right to bury one's dead. The case law reflects a general sense that quasi-property in human remains entails limited rights of exclusion, control and damages. . . . Often the legal language of quasi-property mirrors that of the tort of emotional distress. The causes of action are, however, crucially different. Quasi-property of human remains focuses on the effect of the defendant's actions on the corpse, not on the effect those actions have on the next of kin," 302–3.

154   **right of sepulcher**   Tanya D. Marsh, "When Dirt and Death Collide: Legal and Property Interests in Burial Places," American Bar Association, 2017.

154   **first state to pass laws**   Garment et al., "Let the Dead Teach the Living," 1001.

154   **California in 1927**   See information about the willed-body program at ucsf.edu.

155   **travelers and soldiers**   Garment et al., "Let the Dead Teach the Living," 1001.

155   **public outcry**   Nina Bernstein, "New York State Bans Use of Unclaimed Dead as Cadavers Without Consent," *The New York Times,* August 19, 2016.

155 **issued a report**   Los Angeles County Civil Grand Jury, *Who Cares for the Dead When the Dead Don't Vote?*, 1–24.

156 **decided he'd had enough**   The scene of Albert's quitting comes from a well-placed anonymous source.

156 **no longer be his burden**   Interview with Albert Gaskin, July 8, 2019.

CHAPTER 9. A CALLING

157 *Someone really hated her*   Doyle quoted in Norma Meyer, "The Garden of Angels: In Death, Discarded Babies Are Adopted by a Stranger," Copley News Service, July 12, 1998.

158 **he was awarded**   U.S. Air Force records.

158 **He spoke often**   Doyle died in January 2020. Before his death, he spoke to a number of news outlets, and over the years the statement that he served "three tours in Vietnam and one in Pakistan" was published repeatedly. For example, Ann M. Simmons, "Bikers Group Escort Fallen Troops," *Los Angeles Times,* October 1, 2007. Doyle's U.S. Air Force records, some of which were redacted, do not list Vietnam under his foreign service. His daughter, Tiffany, told us that Doyle was in Cambodia "without insignias." She recalled that her father spoke fluent Vietnamese and complained of lifelong knee problems caused by jumping out of "a lot" of planes. Interview with Tiffany Tolbert, August 22, 2023.

158 **two decades as a police officer**   Lisa Leff, "The People Who ID the Does," *Los Angeles Times,* May 6, 2001.

158 **married in 1992**   Per Doyle's Facebook page, September 26, 2017.

158 **fourth marriage**   Interview with Tiffany Tolbert, August 22, 2023.

159 **"carefree" society**   Interview with Doyle Tolbert, May 23, 2017.

159 **ex-wives were bitter and vengeful**   Ibid.

159 **it was all a con**   Claudia Puig, "After Being Duped Out of Body, Coroner Revises Rules," *Los Angeles Times,* July 25, 1988.

159 **kept the folders of the babies close**   Diana L. Roemer, "Amanda Laid to Rest: Dozens Attend Burial of Infant Found in Trash," *San Gabriel Valley Tribune,* July 13, 2002.

159 **seen babies cast aside**   Roemer, "Amanda Laid to Rest."

159 **abandoning Doyle**   Al Jazeera, *America Tonight,* May 28, 2005, available on YouTube. According to an obituary we found through genealogy research, Doyle's mother remarried soon after leaving California and had four more children. She died in 2008, the obituary describing her as "the light" of her small-town community.

160 **nothing to go on**   With DNA databases, the outcome could now be different, but these databases were unavailable when Doyle did his research.

160 **babies deserved more**   Bob Pool, "Mourning the Unloved," *Los Angeles Times,* June 15, 1997.

160 **buried half a dozen**   Ibid.

160 **read about in the news**   *Good Morning America* interview, January 20, 2000.

160 **answer to Doyle's prayers**   Laura Mecoy, "Abandoned Babies Rest in Garden of Angels," *The Sacramento Bee,* April 5, 2000.

160 *more love than their parents*   Gilda Tolbert quoted in Erika Hayasaki, "Strangers Say Goodbye to Abandoned Infants," *Los Angeles Times,* July 14, 2000.

161 **"old duffer"**   Doyle quoted in Laura Mecoy, "Abandoned Babies Rest in Garden of Angels."

161 **A story caught her eye**   Interview with Elissa Davey, August 7, 2017.

161 *Whoever did it should be shot*   Interview with Elissa Davey, September 4, 2021.

161 **"Show me you have a dignified"**   Interview with Elissa Davey, August 7, 2016. Elissa also regularly retold the story in news interviews, and it's on the Garden of Innocence's website.

161   **more willing**   Both medical examiners worked within California's legal framework of how to dispose of the unclaimed. Public Health Code 7104.1 specifies, "If, within 30 days after the coroner notifies or diligently attempts to notify the person responsible for the interment of a decedent's remains which are in the possession of the coroner, the person fails, refuses, or neglects to inter the remains, the coroner may inter the remains. The coroner may recover any expenses of the interment from the responsible person."

This statute does not specify how unclaimed dead need to be disposed, just that the coroner may inter the remains. Coroners and medical examiners have thus some discretion in how to fulfill this mandate.

162   **newspaper profile of Debi Faris**   Meyer, "The Garden of Angels."

162   **outside Los Angeles**   Faris buried the babies at Desert Lawn Cemetery in Calimesa, California. Rachael Gustuson, "Garden of Angels Commemorates 20 Years of Love," *News Mirror,* September 2, 2016.

162   **"premier cemetery since 1960"**   Marketing materials, available at their website.

163   **$16,000 in total**   Based on our interviews with her. In some news stories, Elissa remembered that the amount was $14,700; for example, Ernie Grimm, "Garden of Innocents Saves Babies from the Trash," *San Diego Reader,* January 9, 2008.

163   **active volunteer**   Interview with Elissa Davey, September 4, 2021.

163   **store them**   The GOI didn't pay for storage. Elissa made deals with funeral homes willing to store the remains for her until it was time for the burial, which could occasionally be months.

164   **"Ministers know what to do"**   Interview with Elissa Davey, August 10, 2020.

164   **published an article**   Interview with Elissa Davey, August 16, 2016. The article she's referring to is Dong-Phuong Nguyen, "Infant Burial Program in Review; Group Erred on Facts for Miscarried Fetus," *The San Diego Union-Tribune,* June 28, 1999.

165   **lingering smell**   Interview with Clara Hanna, August 18, 2020.

165   **poured his energy**   Bobby played bass and keys, as well as other instruments, according to choirmate Carleton Griffin, August 5, 2021.

167   **"I can't believe you kept this"**   Interviews with Clara Hanna, August 18, 2020, and September 22, 2021.

167   **On a podium**   Reconstruction of Bobby's memorial from interviews with Clara Hanna, George Hill, and Carleton Griffin. Clara also shared a copy of the program with us.

168   **"the wife"**   Interview with Carleton Griffin, August 5, 2021. George Hill referred to Clara as the ex-wife in our interview with him on September 21, 2021.

168   **it felt wrong to perform**   Interview with Carleton Griffin, August 5, 2021. Carleton describes it as a skit that occurred before the main song; a YouTube video of one of the performances suggests it was throughout the song.

168   **"You came here for one thing"**   Interview with Carleton Griffin, August 5, 2021.

170   **how sad**   Field observations of September 5, 2019.

170   **NH04**   Phone call to Maria in January 2020. NH stands for Non Handling, meaning that the office will not handle the funeral.

170   **pile up in the county morgue**   Darrell R. Santschi, "No Burials for Some Veterans: Cause of Backlog Bodies Disputed," *The Orange County Register,* May 29, 2014.

170   **wealthy ZIP codes**   Interview with John Kades, February 20, 2018.

172   **Donnell's mother had listed "unknown"**   In our first interview with Donnell, he said: "Well, the VA had claimed that by him not putting me down as his son when he enlisted into the military, there was nothing they could really do." In the second interview, where the quote is from, he said that it was the birth certificate that didn't contain Bobby's name. The latter seemed more logical.

172   **Kades made one last call**   Donnell didn't remember any names, but Kades was the one who made final calls and authorizations on veterans' burials.

CHAPTER 10. STEEL AND SASSAFRAS

175 **eligible for a military burial**   When we followed up with the public administrator, a staff member acknowledged that the office made a mistake. David should have received a military funeral.

175 **"standard of living"**   California Health and Safety Code, section 7101, states: "When any decedent leaves an estate in this state, the reasonable cost of interment and an interment plot of sufficient size to constitute a family plot and memorial including reasonable sums for either, or both, general and special endowment care of the plot proportionate to the value of the estate and in keeping with the standard of living adopted by the decedent prior to his demise, together with interest thereon from 60 days after the date of death, shall be considered as a part of the funeral expenses of the decedent and shall be paid as a preferred charge against his estate as provided in the Probate Code. Reasonable costs of funeral services, together with interest thereon from 60 days after the date of death, shall be considered as a part of the funeral expenses of the decedent and shall be paid as a preferred charge against his estate as provided in the Probate Code."

175 **package would have cost**   "Master Agreement By and Between County of Los Angeles and Armstrong Family Malloy-Mitten for Mortuary Services," April 2017. Provided by the public administrator.

175 **"Going Home"**   Los Angeles Superior Court, case 18STPN00460.

176 **total charges**   Los Angeles Superior Court, case 18STPN00460.

176 **Vaults are not required**   *Consumer Guide to Funeral and Cemetery Purchases* (Sacramento, Calif.: Cemetery and Funeral Bureau, 2013).

176 **estate was charged**   Charge listed in Odd Fellows' Creditor Claim, Los Angeles Superior Court, case 18STPN00460. We visited the grave, and photographs show a vase holder but no vase.

176 **burial cost just over $10,000**   Los Angeles Superior Court, case 18STPN00460.

176 **"worthless"**   Interview with Susan Spencer, August 5, 2020.

176 **more than 827,000 gallons**   Alexandra Harker, "Landscapes of the Dead: An Argument for Conservation Burial," *Berkeley Planning Journal* 25 (2012): 150–59.

177 **Green burials**   Caitlin Doughty, *Smoke Gets in Your Eyes: And Other Lessons from the Crematory* (New York: W. W. Norton, 2014); Elizabeth Fournier, *The Green Burial Guidebook: Everything You Need to Plan an Affordable, Environmentally Friendly Burial* (Novato, Calif.: New World Library, 2018); Mark Shelvock, Elizabeth A. Kinsella, and Darcy Harris, "Beyond the Corporatization of Death Systems: Towards Green Death Practices," *Illness, Crisis and Loss* 30 (2022): 640–58.

177 **Victor Hugo requested a pauper's grave**   The French author Victor Hugo requested a pauper's grave but the French nation would not have it and gave its favorite poet an extravagant burial that included being displayed under the Arc de Triomphe.

177 **Odd Fellows Cemetery**   This cemetery became the backdrop for a national debate about abortion rights in the early 1980s when 16,433 fetuses were buried in unmarked graves in the cemetery (for instance, Judith Michaelson, "500 Fetuses Found in Storage," *Los Angeles Times*, February 6, 1982). A lab owner, who claimed not to be able to afford to properly dispose of the terminated remains, had stored the formaldehyde-suspended fetuses in a shipping container in his Woodland Hills backyard. When the check he used to buy the container bounced, the container was repossessed and the fetal remains found. Then president Ronald Reagan called the discovery a "national tragedy," and a three-year legal battle ensued, making its way to the Supreme Court. The court ruled that the remains could be buried in a nonreligious ceremony, which took place in October 1985 and included a eulogy written by the president and read by a local official to the hundreds of anti-abortion activists in attendance. David was interred close to the fetal remains.

177 **"looney bin"**   Interview with Ana Cornejo (Carmine's neighbor and friend), July 5, 2019.

178   **Carmine's belongings**   Los Angeles Superior Court, case 1857PB03407.

178   **weren't notified**   Interview with Ana Cornejo, July 5, 2019.

178   **"It's just the two of us"**   Sonya Chavez, funeral director at the time for All Caring, during a funeral on September 18, 2018.

179   **sitcom *30 Rock***   The choking scene is available on YouTube.

179   ***The Great Gatsby***   F. Scott Fitzgerald, *The Great Gatsby* (New York: Charles Scribner's Sons, 1925).

179   **"I want to see my mom"**   Interview with Diana Lynn, August 4, 2021.

180   **public opinion had shifted**   Charles DeBenedetti, *An American Ordeal: The Antiwar Movement of the Vietnam Era* (Syracuse, N.Y.: Syracuse University Press, 1990).

180   **befriended a homeless man**   Interview with Doyle Tolbert, May 23, 2017. Additional details via Michael Goulding, "Homeless Heroes Receive Final Honor," *Orange County Register,* August 1, 2011.

180   **"three hots and a cot"**   Interview with Doyle Tolbert, May 23, 2017.

181   **Doyle examined autopsy photos**   Nicholas Riccardi, "The Fight Against Crime: Notes from the Front: Hot on the Trail of the Next of Kin," *Los Angeles Times,* September 27, 1995.

182   **The rides**   The annual ride is called "Run for the Wall."

183   **reimbursement process**   Interview with John Kades, February 20, 2018.

183   **simple wooden caskets**   Interview with David Smith, February 18, 2018.

183   **said it was disrespectful**   Ibid.

184   **went over his old supervisors' heads**   Interview with Doyle Tolbert, May 23, 2017.

184   **Some greeted the news**   Doyle quoted in Mark Muckenfuss, "Honoring 'Unclaimed' Veterans at Riverside National Cemetery," *The Press-Enterprise,* May 23, 2014.

184   **"they want[ed] nothing"**   Doyle Tolbert quoted in Leff, "People Who ID the Does."

184   **background noise**   He made an exception for Christopher Dorner. Dorner was a disgruntled former navy reserve officer and LAPD trainee who in 2013 went on a shooting spree against law enforcement. (Facebook posting February 12, 2013.) By targeting police, Doyle believed the man forfeited the rights he had earned in his younger years.

185   **live with the choices**   Interview with Doyle Tolbert, May 23, 2017.

185   **received a call**   This and the next paragraphs based on an interview with Elissa Davey, September 4, 2021. In San Diego County, the public administrator worked with Elissa. Their setup for unclaimed differed from Los Angeles County, which refused to grant Elissa permission to bury unclaimed infants.

186   *A morgue attendant afraid*   Interview with Elissa Davey, September 4, 2021.

187   **used in medical schools**   Patricia Collin, "A Place for the City's Tiny Victims," *San Francisco Chronicle,* October 4, 2008.

187   **struggled with addiction**   Pam Kragen, "Giving Babies Dignity in Death: Abandoned, Forgotten Babies Get Name, Proper Memorial from Volunteers," *San Diego Union-Tribune,* October 1, 2019.

187   **"piece of the future"**   Shannon M. Bennett et al., "The Scope and Impact of Perinatal Loss: Current Status and Future Directions," *Professional Psychology: Research and Practice* 36 (2005): 180–87.

188   **"I once was here"**   Interview with Elissa Davey, August 7, 2016.

188   **23,500 stillbirths and miscarriages**   Marian F. MacDorman and Elizabeth C. Gregory, "Fetal and Perinatal Mortality: United States, 2013," *National Vital Statistics Report* 64 (July 2015): 1–23.

188   **parents experience profound grief**   Ariella Lang et al., "Perinatal Loss and Parental Grief: The Challenge of Ambiguity and Disenfranchised Grief," *Omega: Journal of Death and Dying* 63 (2011): 183–96. On disenfranchised grief: Kenneth J. Doka, *Disenfranchised Grief: Recognizing Hidden Sorrow* (Lexington, Mass.: Lexington Books, 1989).

188   **may fail to recognize**   Christy Burden et al., "From Grief, Guilt, Pain, and Stigma to Hope and Pride: A Systematic Review and Meta-Analysis of Mixed-Method Re-

search on the Psychosocial Impact of Stillbirth," *BMC Pregnancy and Childbirth* 16 (2016): 1–12; Maja Sawicka, "Searching for a Narrative of Loss: Interactional Ordering of Ambiguous Grief," *Symbolic Interaction* 40 (2017): 229–46; Bernadette Susan McCreight, "A Grief Ignored: Narratives of Pregnancy Loss from a Male Perspective," *Sociology of Health and Illness* 26 (2004): 326–50.

188   **most women give birth**   Patricia M. Hughes, Penelope Turton, and Chris D. Evans, "Stillbirth as Risk Factor for Depression and Anxiety in the Subsequent Pregnancy: Cohort Study," *The BMJ* 318 (1999): 1721–24.

188   **new birth doesn't erase**   Nancy Berns, *Closure: The Rush to End Grief and What It Costs Us* (Philadelphia: Temple University Press, 2011).

189   **Addicted mothers**   Elizabeth M. Armstrong, *Conceiving Risk, Bearing Responsibility: Fetal Alcohol Syndrome and the Diagnosis of Moral Disorder* (Baltimore: Johns Hopkins University Press, 2003).

189   **it can be deadly**   Lab tests can detect the virus, but they cannot predict which developing babies will become infected with the virus. More than half of U.S. adults over forty are infected with CMV by the time they turn forty, often without symptoms or cause for concern. But when passed from a pregnant mother to her infant in utero, CMV can cause birth defects and long-term health consequences.

189   **sister had been stillborn**   Interview with Elissa Davey, *Garden of Innocence*, YouTube, April 19, 2012.

190   **A woodworker in Arkansas**   There are different versions of his story. On the Garden of Innocence website, it was an urn made of hickory harvested in Tennessee. We drew on the sassafras story as told by Elissa at a fundraising event we attended in May 2017.

190   **"a place none of us knows"**   Joan Didion, *The Year of Magical Thinking* (New York: Knopf Doubleday, 2005), 188.

190   **never fully recovered**   The notion that grief is something you recover from has been problematized as a medical-psychiatric perspective; Berns, *Closure;* Darcy Harris, "Political Grief," *Illness, Crisis and Loss* 30 (2022): 572–89; and Lauren J. Breen and Moira O'Connor, "The Fundamental Paradox in the Grief Literature: A Critical Reflection," *Omega: Journal of Death and Dying* 55 (2007): 199–218.

CHAPTER 11. STANDING IN THE GAP

191   **the third of five veterans**   Information from socalpgr.org.

192   **In their defense**   Interview with Clara Hanna, August 18, 2020.

192   **true total**   See cost information at socalcremationsinc.com.

192   **Bobby had called on him**   Interview with Donnell Wells, September 6, 2020. For literature on estrangement and grief: Kylie Agllias, "No Longer on Speaking Terms: The Losses Associated with Family Estrangement at the End of Life," *Families in Society* 92 (2011): 107–13; Kylie Agllias, "Missing Family: The Adult Child's Experience of Parental Estrangement," *Journal of Social Work Practice* 32 (2018): 59–72; and Karl Melvin and John Hickey, "The Changing Impact and Challenges of Familial Estrangement," *The Family Journal* 30 (2022): 348–56.

193   **had a father**   For literature on how objects affect grieving: Corina Sas and Alina Coman, "Designing Personal Grief Rituals: An Analysis of Symbolic Objects and Actions," *Death Studies* 40 (2016): 558–69; Inese Wheeler, "The Role of Linking Objects in Parental Bereavement," *Omega: Journal of Death and Dying* 38 (1999): 289–96; and Margaret Gibson, *Objects of the Dead: Mourning and Memory in Everyday Life* (Melbourne: Melbourne University Press, 2008).

193   **this summer morning**   The ceremony we are describing occurred on June 22, 2016, and is based on both direct observation and our own recording of the event. A publicly accessible video clip is available on YouTube, *Veterans Without Family Honors June 22, 2016.*

194   **"Vietnam is still killing him"**   This line was spoken by an attendee named Mike Grimshaw. The overwhelming impression among the members of Veterans Without

Family was that Doyle served in Vietnam. They stated as much in recorded interviews and repeated conversations. Doyle also wore a patch that identified him as a Vietnam veteran, and his grave marker in Riverside National Cemetery lists Vietnam (Findagrave.com). For further information on his confirmed service see note with "He spoke often" in chapter 9.

195   **cadets fired guns**   For more on the gun volley and military funeral traditions: TC 3–21.5, *Drill and Ceremonies,* Headquarters, Department of the Army, May 2021.

196   **soldier's creed**   "I am an American soldier. I am a warrior and member of a team. I serve the people of the United States, and live the Army, Marine, Navy, Air Force, and Coast Guard values. I will always place the mission first. I will never accept defeat. I will never quit. I will never leave a fallen soldier behind. I am a guardian of freedom and the American way of life. I am an American soldier." Army.mil.

196   **Dionisio Garza**   Eric Ortiz, "Gunman in Houston's Shooting Rampage ID'd as Army Veteran, Fired 212 Rounds: Cops," NBC News, May 31, 2016.

196   **"Just a Common Soldier"**   The poem was originally published in a 1987 Remembrance Day newspaper column by Vaincourt and reprinted by permission of his son on the Society of the Honor Guard's Tomb of the Unknown Soldier website tombguard .org.

197   **away from the chatter**   Observations during interview with Doyle Tolbert, May 2017.

197   **came under fire**   When we interviewed T-Bone (Ray Gould) on August 10, 2016, he played a video made by a TV show that narrated his fall as a door gunner from the UH-1N Huey.

197   **died on impact**   Interview with Ray Gould, August 10, 2016.

198   **just a coffee club**   Interview with Doyle Tolbert, May 23, 2017.

199   **soldier's name**   "Veterans Without Family, Riverside National Cemetery, Riverside, CA, 22 June 2016," socalpgr.org, posted on June 19, 2016.

200   **short tune**   The song is called "In This Special Place."

200   **grown up singing**   Interview with Elissa Davey, August 12, 2016.

201   **knights' pro-life mission**   Connecticut parish priest Michael McGivney founded the Knights of Columbus in the nineteenth century as a mutual benefit organization offering financial support to Catholic migrant widows and orphans. One hundred and forty years later, the knights continued to own one of the world's largest life insurance companies. The current national knights embraced an active pro-life culture, offering sustained prayer for the anti-abortion cause, supporting AIDS orphans in Africa, adopting and supporting pregnancy support centers, and participating publicly in Marches for Life. Even though it was against Elissa's mission to turn the service into an anti-abortion event, from the knights' perspective the Garden of Innocence ceremony could be folded into their broader pro-life agenda. The knights initially wanted to baptize each one of the babies, but Elissa drew a line. "They are not going to be baptized," she said. She did not know the faith of the children or their birth parents, and it seemed inappropriate to her to impose a faith. She added, "They don't need to be baptized. They're purer than anyone." From interview with Elissa Davey, September 4, 2021.

202   **"When that child"**   Interview with Allan Musterer, August 20, 2017.

202   **Paleolithic times**   Dani Nadel et al., "Earliest Floral Grave Lining from 13,700–11,700-Y-Old Natufian Burials at Raqefet Cave, Mt. Carmel, Israel," *Proceedings of the National Academy of Sciences of the United States of America* 110 (July 2013): 11774–78.

202   **Victorian Christians**   Tony Walter, "Funeral Flowers, a Response to Drury," *Folklore* 107 (1996): 106–7.

203   **"We release a dove"**   The other three doves were released to symbolize the Father, the Messenger ("as your religion believes"), and the Spirit.

203   **"$20,000 fine"**   Raptors such as hawks are protected under federal and California law. The first offense is $100,000 (see information at raptorresearchfoundation.org), but we reported what Jerry stated.

203 **anniversary of 9/11**   Lauren McCarthy, "All of the Names of Those Lost in the 9/11 Attacks Were Read Out Loud," *The New York Times,* September 11, 2021.

203 **Every five years**   According to the Vietnam Veterans Memorial Fund, "For 65 hours over a four-day period, each of 58,281 names on The Wall will be read aloud by thousands of volunteers." Volunteers must be present in Washington, D.C., to participate.

203 **perished in slavery**   Ana Lucia Arauuja, "Raising the Dead: Walls of Names as Mnemonic Devices to Commemorate Enslaved People," *Current Anthropology* 61 (2020): S328–39.

203 **single image**   Drew Gilpin Faust, *This Republic of Suffering: Death and the American Civil War* (New York: Vintage, 2009); Robert Pogue Harrison, *The Dominion of the Dead* (Chicago: University of Chicago Press, 2003); and Thomas W. Laqueur, *The Work of the Dead: A Cultural History of Mortal Remains* (Princeton, N.J.: Princeton University Press, 2015).

204 **#sayhername**   The African American Policy Forum, aapf.org.

204 **"He comes to the garden"**   Interview with Jerry Moore, March 14, 2022.

204 **knew all the cemetery workers**   Ibid.

204 **twenty-four years**   Interview with Jerry Moore, March 14, 2022, email August 24, 2022, and LinkedIn profile. After he retired, he joined the Center for Personal and Professional Development as a leadership instructor and equal opportunity counselor.

205 ***We need more of this***   Interview with Jerry Moore, March 14, 2022.

205 **"That's the wrong question"**   Jerry spoke these words during a garden ceremony on April 21, 2018.

205 **impromptu prayer circle**   Field notes and audio recording.

205 **Thomas**   Interview with Jerry Moore, March 14, 2022.

205 **"lasting grief"**   Bernadette Susan McCreight, "A Grief Ignored: Narratives of Pregnancy Loss from a Male Perspective," *Sociology of Health and Illness* 26 (2004): 326–50; Doka, *Disenfranchised Grief.*

205 **eighty-five-year-old**   Elissa told this story multiple times and the age of the woman varies: At a fundraiser on May 20, 2017, Elissa said the woman was eighty-five; in an interview on August 7, 2016, she told us that the woman was eighty years old. On the website the woman is in her late seventies.

CHAPTER 12. *Presente*

208 **county didn't offer this service**   Interviews with Albert Gaskin, Estela Inouye, and Craig Garnette.

208 **Barbara received another chance**   We called Barbara on October 31, 2019, and asked if she was interested in the ashes, explaining that the ashes would be interred in early December of that year. She said no and told us that she thought an indigent burial fit Midge's life.

208 **she refused to believe**   Interview with Nora Spring, January 16, 2021.

209 **flash flood warning**   Hannah Fry, "Powerful Storm Slams Southern California, Snarls Traffic and Raises Mudslide Fears," *Los Angeles Times,* December 4, 2019.

210 **public administrator's office**   The office told us they always send flowers.

212 **The essay**   We received Midge's typewritten essay from Denise Norden on July 25, 2022, via an email attachment. According to the LMU registrar, Midge took the ethics course in 1991.

213 **"loved into being"**   Transcript of the ceremony, recorded by authors, and edited for flow.

214 **learning to love oneself**   Susan M. Pollak, "Who Has Loved You into Being? A Gratitude Meditation," *Psychology Today,* May 19, 2019.

214 **he cried when he was alone**   Daryl Austin, "The Sad Story Behind Mr. Rogers' Hallmark Empathy," *Reader's Digest,* August 11, 2021.

216 **deeply rooted in him**   David Montero, "Remains of 1,489 Unclaimed, Unidentified

People Buried with Respect," *Press Telegram,* December 10, 2014. Fr. Chris Ponnet, "A Personal Reflection on Life and Death," *A Visit Newsletter,* 2021.

217 **Nearly one hundred Tongva villages**   Sean Greene and Thomas Curwen, "Mapping the Tongva Villages of L.A.'s Past," *Los Angeles Times,* May 9, 2019; Kelly Lytle Hernández, *City of Inmates: Conquest, Rebellion, and the Rise of Human Caging in Los Angeles, 1771–1965* (Chapel Hill: University of North Carolina Press, 2017).

217 **Few traces of the Tongva language**   Thomas Curwen, "Tongva, Los Angeles' First Language, Opens the Door to a Forgotten Time and Place," *Los Angeles Times,* May 9, 2019.

217 **in his early twenties**   Diego Frankel, "Becoming Visible: The Resurgence of Tongva Identity in Los Angeles," *Haute Magazine,* Spring 2021.

218 **was an L.A. native**   Interviews with Susan Rorke, December 13, 2018, and July 5, 2019.

221 **written more than one thousand**   Aaron Green, "'Ubi Caritas'" Lyrics and Translation," liveabout.com, February 17, 2018.

221 **piece had first been performed**   Michael Dorgan, "On This Day Handel's Messiah Premiered in Fishable Street, Dublin," irishcentral.com, April 13, 2022.

222 **cusp of winning**   Anousha Sakoui, "L.A. Times Journalist Jon Schleuss Wins NewsGuild Election," *Los Angeles Times,* December 10, 2019.

222 **Wesley had died in 2005**   Jon Schleuss and Maloy Moore, "At a Boyle Heights Cemetery, a Time to Mourn the Unclaimed," *Los Angeles Times,* December 15, 2015.

222 **"Nobody wants me"**   Quoted in Jon Schleuss, Taylor Goldenstein, and Maloy Moore, "Survivors Find Peace as They Claim Remains Once 'Unwanted' in L.A. County," *Los Angeles Times,* December 6, 2014.

223 **"metaphorical table"**   Louise Steinman, "Unclaimed, Unforgotten," *The Crooked Mirror* (blog).

224 **waited ten years**   Wiesel says he wrote the book ten years after the war, then started to shop it to publishers. "We May Use Words to Break the Prison: Elie Wiesel on Writing *Night,*" video, Facing History and Ourselves, last updated April 19, 2022.

224 **bearing witness**   Thich Nhat Hanh, *The Heart of the Buddha's Teaching: Transforming Suffering into Peace, Joy, and Liberation* (New York: Harmony, 1999).

224 **the tenets provide**   Zen Center of Los Angeles, zcla.org.

224 **hundreds of thousands**   International Committee of the Red Cross, "The Missing in Latin America: Families Will Not Stop Searching, Nor Will We Stop Helping," icrc .org.

224 **"eternal instability"**   Gabriel Gatti and Jaume Peris Blanes, "The Deviated Mourning of the Disappeared: Reimagining Disappearance and Transcending Its Tropes," *Bulletin of Latin American Research* 40 (2021): 54–68.

EPILOGUE. THE KINDNESS OF CLAY

227 *They say we die twice*   The origins of this saying are unclear. We found several references online to this as a Jewish saying, also as a quote attributed to Hemingway, Banksy, and many others. It could also be an African proverb. This is also the premise of the animated movie *The Book of Life* and of memorial services across the world. The quote appears in Irvin D. Yalom, *Love's Executioner and Other Tales of Psychotherapy* (New York: Basic Books, 1989). In the 2012 dark comedy *Stand Up Guys,* Al Pacino's character speaks the line while standing over the freshly dug grave of his childhood friend. Isabel Allende wrote similar words into her 1987 novel *Eva Luna* in defense of the power of memory to keep a mother alive in her daughter's heart. Rapper Macklemore worked the notion of dying twice into a verse of his hit "Glorious" to wonder whether he took more than he gave in life.

227 **ephemeral nature of his graffiti**   Adam Hogue, "Banksy Street Art: When Street Art Is in a Museum, What's the Point?," mic.com, May 13, 2013.

228 **eighty-three abandoned and unclaimed victims**   Letitia Stein, "Katrina's Unclaimed Dead Conjure Memories of Her Ravages," Reuters, August 25, 2015; Doug MacCash,

"14 Years After Katrina, Monuments and Mausoleums Are MUTE Testimony to Storm's Devastation," nola.com, August 26, 2019.

228 **Nigerian officials** Ayodele Oni, "Mass Burial for Unidentified Corpses in Kogi," *The Source Magazine*, September 11, 2022.

228 **annual rate of 8.8 percent** Shin Ji-min and Jang Su-kyung, "Report Documents Instances of Lonely Deaths in South Korean Society," *Hankyoreh*, March 4, 2018.

228 **Ukrainian officials** Carlotta Gall, "Ukraine Struggles to Identify Bucha Massacre Victims, Five Months On," *The New York Times*, September 3, 2022.

228 **estimated 32,000 people** Pre-COVID figure on *kodokushi* consistent with several media reports, including Chris Michael and Keiko Tanaka, "Dioramas of Lonely Death: Cleaner Re-creates Rooms Where People Died Alone," *The Guardian*, June 10, 2019; "Japan's Deaths Exceed Births by Half a Million in 2019," Nippon.com, June 11, 2020.

228 **depend on the government** Nils Dahl, "Governing Through *Kodokushi*, Japan's Lonely Deaths and Their Impact on Community Self-Government," *Contemporary Japan* 32 (2019): 83–102.

228 **country in decline** Norimitsu Ohishi, "A Generation in Japan Faces a Lonely Death," *The New York Times*, November 30, 2017.

229 **recent government survey** In one government survey, 42.9 percent of persons aged sixty or over viewed *kodokushi* as a problem "very close" to them. The survey of 3,484 men and women was conducted in 2010 by the Ministry of Health, Labor, and Welfare; Dahl, "Governing Through *Kodokushi*," 88.

229 **neighborhood checks** Dahl, "Governing Through *Kodokushi*," 93.

229 **Economists hypothesize** Eric Platt, "The 32 Sexiest, Tastiest, Creepiest and Craziest Economic Indicators in the World," *Business Insider*, May 27, 2012.

229 **The industry's consolidation** "How the Funeral Industry Has Evolved," Funeralwise .com. On commodification in the funeral industry: Isabelle Szmigin and Louise Canning, "Sociological Ambivalence and Funeral Consumption," *Sociology* 49 (2015): 748–63.

229 **number of unclaimed increases** Heeju Sohn, Stefan Timmermans, and Pamela Prickett, "Loneliness in Life and in Death? Social and Demographic Patterns of Unclaimed Deaths," *PLOS ONE* 15 (2020): 1–17.

229 **14 percent** U.S. Census, American Community Survey, Los Angeles County, Poverty Status in the Past 12 Months, 2021.

229 **did not fluctuate with poverty levels** Sohn, Timmermans, and Prickett, "Loneliness in Life and in Death?"

230 **"for they know"** Tony Walter, *Funerals: And How to Improve Them* (London: Hodder and Stoughton, 1990), 111–12.

230 **budget caskets can be ordered online** Costco, Walmart, and Amazon all advertise caskets at affordable prices.

230 **appear often among the registers** This is based on our qualitative case analysis from reading the files. We did not investigate this statistically.

230 **random week** We picked the date of Wednesday, June 29, 2016.

230 **deaths of despair** Anne Case and Angus Deaton, *Deaths of Despair and the Future of Capitalism* (Princeton, N.J.: Princeton University Press, 2020).

231 **People who died in middle age** Sohn, Timmermans, and Prickett, "Loneliness in Life and in Death?"; Kenna Quinet, Samuel Nunn, and Alfarena Ballew, "Who Are the Unclaimed Dead?" *Forensic Science* 61 (2015): S131–39. Quinet, Nunn, and Ballew find that the unclaimed in Marion County, Indiana, tend to be younger, male, and less likely white than the claimed deceased.

231 **most common among white Americans** U.S. Census Bureau, Current Population Survey, Annual Social and Economic Supplements 1970 and 1980 to 2021.

231 **significantly stronger for white** Sohn, Timmermans, and Prickett, "Loneliness in Life and in Death?" The data about race are approximate. County records show how many decedents are white or Black, but they don't consistently track other ethnic groups—

and ideas about who counts as white have varied over time. The designations *Hispanic* or *Latino* do not appear in the early ledgers and, until 1930, Mexican Americans were classified as white. Other categories like *American* are ambiguous, and many records noted the deceased's presumed national origin (for example, Vietnamese) rather than race.

231   **one of the fastest-growing segments**   Rachel Margolis et al., "The Physical, Mental, and Social Health of Middle-Aged and Older Adults Without Close Kin in Canada," *The Journals of Gerontology, Series B: Psychological Sciences and Social Sciences* 77 (2022): 1350–60.

231   **For much of our history**   Stephanie Coontz, *The Way We Never Were: American Families and the Nostalgia Trap* (New York: Basic Books, 2016).

231   **enslaved people could not form family units**   Orlando Patterson, *Slavery and Social Death: A Comparative Study* (Cambridge, Mass.: Harvard University Press, 2018).

232   **individual autonomy and self-determination**   Vivian Hamilton, "Principles of U.S. Family Law," *Fordham Law Review* 75 (2006): 31–73.

232   **families were expected to absorb life's blows**   Jessica Calarco, "The U.S. Social Safety Net Has Been Ripped to Shreds—And Women Are Paying the Price," CNN, November 18, 2020.

232   **dropped from 44 to 19 percent**   Mark Mather et al., "America's Changing Population: What to Expect in the 2020 Census," *Population Bulletin* 74 (2019): 12.

232   **"going solo"**   Eric Klinenberg, *Going Solo: The Extraordinary Rise and Surprising Appeal of Living Alone* (New York: Penguin, 2012).

232   **adults living alone has almost doubled**   U.S. Census, 2021, census.gov.

232   **Cohabitation is more common**   Deborah Carr and Rebecca L. Utz, "Families in Later Life: A Decade in Review," *Journal of Marriage and the Family* 82 (2020): 346–63; Sharon Sassler and Daniel T. Lichter, "Cohabitation and Marriage: Complexity and Diversity in Union-Formation Patterns," *Journal of Marriage and Family* 82 (2020): 35–61.

232   **one in four boomers**   On divorce: Susan L. Brown and I-Fen Lin, "The Gray Divorce Revolution: Rising Divorce Among Middle-Aged and Older Adults, 1990–2010," *The Journals of Gerontology, Series B* 67 (2012): 731–41. On living alone: Jacob Ausubel, "Older People Are More Likely to Live Alone in the U.S. Than Elsewhere in the World," Pew Research, March 10, 2020.

232   **"kinless seniors"**   Rachel Margolis and Ashton M. Verdery, "Older Adults Without Close Kin in the United States," *The Journals of Gerontology, Series B* 72 (2017): 688–93.

232   **One in four adult Americans**   Karl Pillemer, *Fault Lines: Fractured Families and How to Mend Them* (New York: Penguin, 2020), 24–25. Pillemer conducted a survey among a nationally representative sample of 1,340 Americans age eighteen and older. Respondents were asked if they had any family members from whom they were currently estranged, defined as having no contact. Of those Americans surveyed, 27 percent reported currently being estranged from a relative, which Pillemer extrapolates to around 67 million Americans.

233   **incarceration or the foster care system**   Beth M. Huebner, "The Effect of Incarceration on Marriage and Work Over the Life Course," *Justice Quarterly* 22 (2005): 281–303; Leonard M. Lopoo and Bruce Western, "Incarceration and the Formation and Stability of Marital Unions," *Journal of Marriage and Family* 67 (2005): 721–34; Dorothy Roberts, *Torn Apart* (New York: Basic Books, 2022).

233   **social distancing and lockdowns**   Alex Bierman and Scott Schieman, "Social Estrangement and Psychological Distress Before and During the COVID-19 Pandemic," *Journal of Health and Social Behavior* 61 (2020): 398–417; Richard Weissbourd et al., "Loneliness in America: How the Pandemic Has Deepened an Epidemic of Loneliness and What We Can Do About It," Making Caring Common Project, Harvard University, February 2021.

233   **"When adult children don't contact you"**   Quoted in Lucy Blake et al., "Family Estrangement and the COVID-19 Crisis: A Closer Look at How Broken Family Relationships Have Been Impacted by the COVID-19 Crisis," standalone.org.uk, 2020.

233 **policymakers use life expectancy**   Mark Luy et al., "Life Expectancy: Frequently Used, but Hardly Understood," *Gerontology* 66 (2019): 95–104. The life expectancy rate works well because it is not influenced by one risk factor but reflects a mix of economic development, living conditions, social well-being, diseases, and environmental factors. In the same way, the rise in the unclaimed is not due to one single factor. Instead, it's a broad reflection of what we think we owe one another and how we balance individualism with belonging to a community.

234 **preneed funeral insurance**   Incidentally, this is also a way to spend down money before entering a nursing home. In California, preneed funds are held in a trust, but this isn't the situation in all states.

234 **Americans still refuse**   Anne Wilkinson, Neil Wenger, and Lisa R. Shugarman, *Literature Review on Advance Directives,* U.S. Department of Health and Human Services, June 2007.

Advance directives were not what patients would wish. The advance directive was legally supported in 1990 as part of the Patient Self-Determination Act, which required healthcare facilities to inform patients at the time of admission about their right to make their wishes regarding refusing or accepting healthcare interventions in an advance directive. All U.S. states and the District of Columbia support advance directives, and the measure has widespread public and health professional support.

And yet, in spite of extensive patient and provider educational campaigns, only 18 to 30 percent of Americans have completed an advance directive. Among people with chronic conditions, the completion rate is only slightly higher, at 35 percent. And even when those documents are completed, they often do not affect care because they are narrow and legalistic.

234 **69 percent**   Funeral and Memorial Information Council, 2015.

234 **fight loneliness and**   Office of the Surgeon General, *Our Epidemic of Loneliness and Social Isolation: The U.S. Surgeon General's Advisory on the Healing Effects of Social Connection and Community,* 2023.

234 **paint a different picture**   Courtney G. Joslin, "The Evolution of the American Family," American Bar Association, 2009; Coontz, *Way We Never Were.*

235 **proxy decision-maker**   Kuldeep N. Yadav et al., "Approximately One in Three US Adults Completes Any Type of Advance Directive for End-of-Life Care," *Health Affairs* 36 (2017): 1244–51.

235 **Forty-six U.S. states**   This is as of December 2022, according to Marlene Arias, "Recent Updates to Default Surrogate Statutes," American Bar Association, January 2023. For more on the eight states with additions of partner and common-law spouses: Erin S. DeMartino et al., "Who Decides When a Patient Can't? Statutes on Alternate Decision Makers," *New England Journal of Medicine* 376 (2017): 1478–82.

235 **looking for a consensus**   Sharon R. Kaufman, *And a Time to Die: How American Hospitals Shape the End of Life* (New York: Scribner, 2005); Arianne Brinkman-Stoppelenburg, Judith A. C. Rietjens, and Agnes van der Heide, "The Effects of Advance Care Planning on End-of-Life Care: A Systematic Review," *Palliative Medicine* 28 (2014): 1000–1025.

236 **don the role of benefactor**   Asli Zengin, "The Cemetery for the Kimsesiz: Unclaimed and Anonymous Death in Turkey," *Comparative Studies of South Asia, Africa and the Middle East* 42 (2022): 163–81.

236 **United Kingdom**   Evie King, *Ashes to Admin: The Caseload of a Council Funeral Officer* (London: Mirror Books, 2023).

236 **In Amsterdam**   De Eenzame Uitvaart website, eenzameuitvaart.nl.

236 **South Korea**   Jessie Yeung and Yoonjung Seo, "South Korea's Middle-Aged Men Are Dying 'Lonely Deaths,'" CNN, December 18, 2022.

236 **portrait of the deceased**   Steven Borowiec, "The South Korean Charity That Tries to Give Everyone a Dignified Farewell," *Time,* December 31, 2014.

237   **"powerful, dangerous, preserved, revered, feared"**   Thomas W. Lacqueur, *The Work of the Dead: A Cultural History of Mortal Remains* (Princeton, N.J.: Princeton University Press, 2015), 4.

237   **"If we are all angry"**   Randall Collins, "Interaction Ritual Chains and Collective Effervescence," in C. Von Scheve and M. Salmella, eds., *Collective Emotions* (Oxford: Oxford University Press, 2014), 300. On the difference funeral rituals make: Jan R. Oyebode and R. Glynn Owens, "Bereavement and the Role of Religious and Cultural Factors," *Bereavement Care* 32 (2013): 60–64; Kate Woodthorpe et al., "'My Memories of the Time We Had Together Are More Important': Direct Cremation and the Privatisation of UK Funerals," *Sociology* 56 (June 2022): 556–73; Kate Woodthorpe and Hannah Rumble, "Funerals and Families: Locating Death as a Relational Issue," *The British Journal of Sociology* 67 (2016): 242–59.

238   **rendering people unclaimable**   Jason De León, *The Land of Open Graves: Living and Dying on the Migrant Trail* (Berkeley: University of California Press, 2015). On ambiguous loss: Pauline Boss, *Ambiguous Loss: Living with Unresolved Grief* (Cambridge, Mass.: Harvard University Press, 2000).

238   **Mothers of the Plaza de Mayo**   Marguerite Guzman Bouvard, *Revolutionizing Motherhood: The Mothers of the Plaza de Mayo* (New York: Rowman and Littlefield, 2002).

238   **U.S. military still spends millions**   Leonard Wong, "Leave No Man Behind: Recovering America's Fallen Warriors," *Armed Forces and Society* 31 (2005): 599–622.

239   **remains precarious**   No public was allowed to attend the ceremony during the pandemic, and it continues to be available via Facebook only as of writing May 2023.

239   **most likely to receive**   In our years of news searches and Google alerts, we've seen several groups spring up to bury unclaimed veterans; for example, Emry Dinman, "Unclaimed Remains of 133 Veterans and Relatives Brought to Final Rest in Washington State Veterans Cemetery," *The Spokesman-Review,* November 17, 2022.

239   **Lafayette Parish**   Dione Johnson, "Lafayette Diocese Will Bury 27 Forgotten, Unclaimed Persons on All Souls' Day," KLFY, November 1, 2021.

239   **Covington**   Bob Warren, "56 bodies, 56 stories—All Have a Sad Ending: Unclaimed Bodies Laid to Rest in Covington," nola.com, April 21, 2018.

239   **"Gone But Not Forgotten"**   Vernal Coleman, "Burial of 278 Unclaimed Bodies a Sign of Homeless Crisis," *The Seattle Times,* October 11, 2016.

239   **In Fort Walton Beach**   Kelly Humphrey, "Dignity in Death," *Northwest Florida Daily News,* November 2, 2016.

239   **In Erie County**   Tim Hahn, "Erie County Honors Its Unclaimed Dead in Biennial Ceremony at Old Alms House Cemetery," *Erie Times-News,* September 20, 2021.

239   **"He died alone"**   The Roxbury Latin School's initiative is called Ave Atque Vale; see the school's website, https://www.roxburylatin.org.

240   *viral justice*   Ruha Benjamin, *Viral Justice: How We Grow the World We Want* (Princeton, N.J.: Princeton University Press, 2022), 54.

240   **"a guiding ethos for regenerating life"**   Ibid., 9.

AFTERWORD: *MEMENTO MORI*

243   **used an online search**   Her name had been published in the *Los Angeles Times.*

244   **The following year**   Our first two interviews with Susan were in December 2018, and our follow-up interview was in July 2019.

245   **Emily**   This is a pseudonym.

245   **Cybil**   This is a pseudonym.

247   **born into a web**   Samuel Scheffler, "Relationships and Responsibilities," *Philosophy and Public Affairs* 26 (1997): 189–209.

247   **"to have repudiated"**   Ibid., 204.

247   **worried that I had come in for no reason**   Medical sociologists call this *doctorable.* Pa-

tients worry whether their problem is worthy of medical attention. John Heritage and Jeffrey D. Robinson, "Accounting for the Visit: Patients' Reasons for Seeking Medical Care," in John Heritage and Douglas Maynard, eds., *Communication in Medical Care: Interactions Between Primary Care Physicians and Patients* (Cambridge: Cambridge University Press, 2006), 48–85.

249 **"Memento mori"** Leo Tolstoy, *Path of Life*, trans. Maureen Cote (Huntington, N.Y.: New Science, 2002).

250 **skydiving** Stefan went skydiving in 2018; Pamela is still thinking about it.

ABOUT THIS PROJECT

251 **social autopsy** Stefan Timmermans and Pamela J. Prickett, "The Social Autopsy," *Sociological Methods and Research* (2021).

251 **Sherri** This is a pseudonym.

252 **as I wrote up Sherri's story** Pamela J. Prickett, *Believing in South Central: Everyday Islam in the City of Angels* (Chicago: University of Chicago Press, 2021).

252 **two books on death and dying** Stefan Timmermans, *Sudden Death and the Myth of CPR* (Philadelphia: Temple University Press, 1999); Stefan Timmermans, *Postmortem: How Medical Examiners Explain Suspicious Deaths* (Chicago: University of Chicago Press, 2006).

253 **deemed less "grievable"** Judith Butler, *Precarious Life: The Powers of Mourning and Violence* (New York: Verso Books, 2004); Judith Butler, *Frames of War: When Is Life Grievable?* (New York: Verso Books, 2016).

253 **125 years** When we finally secured county approval to access the cremation ledgers, we photographed fifty-one years of cremation logs, spending hours bent over the wooden pews in the unused chapel. We hired undergraduate research assistants to help us digitize twelve years of these records, between 1976 and 2013, and to create a database that included 16,186 unclaimed persons. This is the data we later worked with a demographer to quantitatively analyze. Gaining access to handwritten ledgers and digitizing them is an administrative- and labor-intensive process. Given the limited access and resources, we opted to select three years ending in 3, 6, and 9 from each decade to cover as wide a time frame as possible. For more on our data collection and analysis of the records: Heeju Sohn, Stefan Timmermans, and Pamela Prickett, "Loneliness in Life and in Death? Social and Demographic Patterns of Unclaimed Deaths," *PLOS ONE* 15 (2020): 1–17.

254 **we would verify later** As we explain in the note on p. 283, under "office organized about sixty," our best estimate based on the CPRA information and court records was that the public administrator organized between fifty-eight and eighty-one funerals in 2016 for decedents whose assets met the minimum financial amount to authorize a funeral.

258 **official records** We also gathered civil grand jury reports, copies of government contracts with funeral homes and the mortuary science program at Cypress College, training manuals, and form letters used by the different agencies. Some of these records were available online, but the vast majority came from our reporting inside the three agencies and through additional PRA requests, which we continued to file through late 2022.

260 **"Clearly the man had not died"** N. R. Kleinfield, "The Lonely Death of George Bell," *The New York Times*, October 17, 2015.

260 **"I wonder what he would"** Vivian Yee and Amy Zerba, "Readers Respond to Article on the Death of George Bell," *The New York Times*, October 18, 2015.

INDEX

..

PAMELA PRICKETT is an associate professor of sociology at the University of Amsterdam and an acclaimed writer and former broadcaster.

STEFAN TIMMERMANS is a professor of sociology at UCLA. He is the author of an award-winning scholarly book on forensic death investigations.

This book was set in Caslon, a typeface first designed
in 1722 by William Caslon (1692–1766). Its widespread
use by most English printers in the early eighteenth
century soon supplanted the Dutch typefaces that
had formerly prevailed. The roman is considered
a "workhorse" typeface due to its pleasant,
open appearance, while the italic is
exceedingly decorative.